Being a Mother in a Strange Land

Being a Mother in a Strange Land:

Motherhood Experiences of Chinese Migrant Women in the Netherlands

By

Shu-Yi Huang

Cambridge
Scholars
Publishing

Being a Mother in a Strange Land:
Motherhood Experiences of Chinese Migrant Women in the Netherlands

By Shu-Yi Huang

This book first published 2019

Cambridge Scholars Publishing

Lady Stephenson Library, Newcastle upon Tyne, NE6 2PA, UK

British Library Cataloguing in Publication Data
A catalogue record for this book is available from the British Library

ISBN (10): 1-5275-3204-6
ISBN (13): 978-1-5275-3204-5

To my mother, Mrs. Li-Jen Chen and my significant other Shu-Wen Cheng, for making me a better person with strength and freedom.

TABLE OF CONTENTS

CHAPTER ONE

INTRODUCTION

1.1 The Significance of the Rise of Chinese Migration to the Netherlands

It was a coincidence that 2011, being the first year and the first time of my arrival (January 3rd) in the Netherlands, marked the anniversary of one century of migration for the Dutch Chinese immigrants. One hundred years ago, a group of Chinese seamen were brought to a Rotterdam dock to fill the labour shortage because of a union strike (van Heek, 1936). During that year, several celebratory activities were held,[1] with the peak of the celebration being the One Hundred Lions Dance Festival in Dam Square in Amsterdam on July 9th, 2011. It was a beautiful sunny day; I was really excited while standing with people from all over the globe. With the drums and gongs exploding into sound, the city was bustling with life. Following the Lions' parade to China Town, I was surrounded by various languages, such as Mandarin, Dutch, Cantonese, and English. The variety of languages represents the various origins of Chinese migrants in the Netherlands.

My research motivation was a spinoff from this Lions' Dance and March, as if it came to me all by itself. I was following the march and taking several photos when I saw a lion resting on the sidewalk. After taking off the lion costume, to my surprise, it was a woman and a teenage boy (See figure 1-1). This woman then passed a bottle to the boy: I presumed that they were mother and son. This scene immediately drew my attention and intrigued my curiosity. Observing the parade closely until the

---

[1] The celebration activities included a special exhibition in the Amsterdam History Museum, the 100 Lions' Dance and Parade in Amsterdam and some public speeches. A website built by The Foundation 100 Years Chinese People in the Netherlands, http://www.100jaarchinezen.nl/, introduced the rich cultural values and business success of Chinese people who have successfully integrated into Dutch society. Unfortunately, when I rechecked this website in 2013, it had already gone offline.

end, I discovered couples of mothers and children, or fathers and their daughters, dressed in pairs as lions. I had watched lion and dragon-dancing during festivals several times a year in Taiwan; however, this was the first time I had seen women performing the lion dance. Traditional Chinese folk dancing, such as the lion and dragon dance in Hong Kong and Taiwan, is considered a very masculine activity. The scene I witnessed was a breakthrough of a gendered social custom. The more exciting discovery was that it occurred in Western Europe. These migrant Chinese women participating that day were not only writing a whole new chapter of history by passing down the culture but also deconstructing the male-dominant custom at the same time. From that moment, I started to think about migrant Chinese motherhood practice in the Netherlands. I am curious about their real life experiences as migrant Chinese women in a non-English speaking Western European country where the size of the Chinese community is smaller than that in North America.[2]

During these four years of my doctorate study, the bilateral relationship between the Netherlands and the People's Republic of China (PRC) has become closer. For instance, in November 2013, Mandarin was officially made one of the optional second foreign-language topics in Dutch secondary schools. In March 2014, Jinping Xi, President of the PRC, had an intensive eight-day state visit to four European countries – the Netherlands, France, Germany, and Belgium, and Xi also visited the headquarters of UNESCO and the European Union. During his visit, Xi signed bilateral trade contracts worth nearly €1.5 billion.[3] It is noteworthy that the Dutch government is eager to develop and secure more cultural and economic reciprocity with China, which indicates the significance of the PRC as a rising global power. It suffices to say that Chinese migration research in the Netherlands has more contemporary importance than before.

Chinese migration study has become an important aspect of global migration trends. With the increasing numbers of Chinese migrants

---

[2] According to the Netherlands' Centraal Bureau voor de Statistiek (CBS), until 2011 the total number of Chinese in the Netherlands was 76860; see later in this chapter for more information. As for the number of Chinese immigrants in the USA, according to the annual report of Migration Policy Institute (MPI), the number of Chinese immigrants in the United States had reached an estimated 1.8 million in 2010. See http://migrationpolicy.org/article/chinese-immigrants-united-states (access date July 28, 2011).

[3] News resource: Dutch News.nl, Monday March 24, 2014. See: http://www.dutchnews.nl/news/archives/2014/03/dutch_and_chinese_firms_sign_1.php (access date March 25, 2014).

crossing borders to settle down or sojourn in major European cities whilst building up their own communities, several researchers have studied Chinese immigration and emigration in Western Europe under various perspectives, e.g. Chinese migration chains (Pieke, 1998), Chinese identities (Flemming, 1998),[4] Chinese labour (Griffin, 1973), Chinese emigrant ties (Watsons, 1977) and Mandarin learning among Chinese migrants in Western Europe (Liber, 2013).[5] Chinese migration to the Netherlands, according to Pieke, has a unique pattern. "The Netherlands is at the crossroads of at least five migration waves: its Chinese community includes Cantonese, Zhejiangese,[6] Southeast Asians (from Indonesia and Vietnam), and a rapidly growing group of Fujianese[7]" (1998: 8).

Throughout this book, I use the phrase Chinese migrants or immigrant Chinese instead of the term "ethnic Chinese" to indicate Chinese people in the Netherlands, unless scholars use "ethnic Chinese" in their work. I find the definition of "ethnic Chinese" to be controversial and very Dutch, for two reasons. First, most Chinese migration studies in English-speaking countries use the country's name in front of Chinese, such as "American Chinese"; "Canadian Chinese" or "Australian Chinese" instead of "ethnic Chinese". Second, there is an inconsistent definition of "ethnic Chinese" between Dutch academic usage and Dutch official usage which lacks a thorough elaboration. For instance, in the recent doctorate dissertation by Cha-Hsuan Liu, ethnic Chinese in the Netherlands is defined as "all people of Chinese origin born in Chinese-speaking regions (China, Hong Kong, Taiwan, and Macau) or coming from other countries (such as Indonesia, Malaysia, Singapore, Vietnam, and Surinam), as well as the later generations of ethnic Chinese born in the Netherlands" (2014: 17). Liu explains later that her definition of ethnic Chinese follows Pieke & Benton's 1995 work. Yet Liu also indicates that this definition is different to the Dutch official usage in which only people originating from Chinese-

[4] Christiansen, Flemming. 1998. "Chinese Identity in Europe." Pp. 42–63.

[5] Liber, Marylène. 2013. ""“When You Look Chinese, You Have to Speak Chinese": Highly Skilled Chinese Migrants in Switzerland and the Promotion of a Shared Language." Pp. 134–159.

[6] Zhejiang is an eastern coastal province of the PRC and it is a rather wealthy province with 18 economic and technology development zones. Because of its coastal position and economic advantages, most upper and middle-class families take the opportunity to emigrate abroad for a better life or education. It is also a famous *qiaoxiang,* the home county of Chinese immigrants.

[7] Like Zhejiang, Fujian is a coastal province of the PRC. Because of its geographic position, from the 18th century, increasing numbers of Fujianese emigrated to Taiwan or South Eastern Asian areas to escape from famine and war. Fujiannese are famous for their international trade and pirate business.

speaking regions are taken into account. Thus, I tend to use Chinese migrants or immigrant Chinese interchangeably in this book.

Fig.1-1 Mother and son resting during the lion parade. Field note September 07, 2011 shoot by Shu-Yi, Huang.

This research is located at the crossroads, and the intersection, of three disciplines: gender studies, Chinese migration studies and Dutch migration studies. The very structural intersectionality of first-generation immigrant Chinese women's lives is never elaborated and/or systematically illustrated either in the field of gender studies or in Dutch migration studies. This research aims to 1) rewrite history from a gendered perspective, 2) hear migrant women's voices on motherhood practices, and 3) conceptualise migrant women's experiences through a critical reading.

In the field of gender studies, this research places women and gendered politics in the centre to challenge the methodological foundations of traditional migration studies, which continue to treat women as "additional historical subject matter" (Scott, 1991: 53), [8] marginalising women's voices and experiences in the representation of migration from their

[8] Scott, Joan. 1991. "Women's History." Pp. 42–66.

country of origin as well as in the host country. From the data I gathered, gendered power had immersed itself in migrant women's life cycle before and after emigration. Before emigration, in contrast with others, the working-class women in this study had to give up the opportunity to continue their higher education because of their gender and class. They were expected to enter the labour market at a very young age to contribute financially to their families. Most of them came to the Netherlands through quick match-making marriages because of the shortage of young single Chinese females in the Netherlands, and because of the gendered expectations from their natal families. Moreover, they are not only care-givers and domestic workers in the private domain but also non-paid family business employees. In order to combine their work and motherhood, these Chinese women often managed their restaurants downstairs while raising their children upstairs. They also developed mutual cooperation by either preparing a nursing room at the back of the restaurant or babysitting for each-other in order to fulfil their responsibilities as mothers and as wives.

I argue that my study shows the gendered characteristic of Chinese chain-migration means women outnumber men from the second stage of Chinese migration to the Netherlands, and emigration does not liberate women from their gender roles. From the shared experiences of ten working-class migrant women, I found that one male Chinese would bring two female Chinese to this country, one as his spouse and the other as his mother or mother-in-law, brought here to take care of her grandchildren and share the domestic chores. Although working-class migrant women still took the gendered responsibility for children, as time went by, they often became much more autonomous in decision-making in their conjugal relationship. For example, I found migrant women were more willing to learn Dutch because of the financial benefits to their business; when their Dutch proficiency passes that of their husbands; they become the main information collector in the household. They not only control the household and business management but also make decisions about their children's education. Furthermore, migrant Chinese women indeed have the potential to reverse gendered inequality through Dutch learning and individual hard work.

Meanwhile, the experiences of the middle-class Chinese migrant women were different. These women were treated relatively more gender equal before marriage and emigration, as well as being financially independent and more career-oriented. However, most of them had to face a career-downward situation after emigration. They soon found out that, unlike their working-class counterparts, they were hard pressed to find an ideal job in the Netherlands because of the language barrier and racial discrimination in the labour market. They became financially and emotionally dependent on their husbands, and most of them felt they were losing even more bargaining power in their conjugal relationship. Hence, most of them focused on their motherhood practices and paid close attention to their children's education. Because of their perception of Dutch society, middle-class Chinese migrant women took their children's academic performance and language education very seriously and they had the time and financial resources to be able to do so. They hoped that their children would change their cultural capital of bilingualism into material capital in the future; thus, they valued the children's English and Mandarin proficiency more than Dutch. They expected that their children would be able to benefit from both Western and Chinese cultural capital through learning English and Mandarin, which would lead to promising possibilities for them. As one middle-class woman said about her small daughter, "She can be anyone, the world is her stage". Also, on the basis of women's retirement plans, I found that the *quanxi* (personal network), instead of country of origin, is the decisive factor for Chinese migrant women. They plan for their retirement according to their care-giving roles in the family. This dissertation shows that attention to gender allows researchers to point to such patterns in both experiences and expectations.

In the field of Dutch migration studies, this research aims to bring women's voices and gender in women's daily experiences into the centre. Early Dutch studies of Chinese migration focused on fact-finding, which mainly concentrated on its estimated numbers, areas of origin, residential distribution, and occupations. In contrast, this research aims to offer an alternative example for Dutch migration studies by making sense of migrant people's reception by the host country by conducting interviews and participant observation. Two Dutch scholars, Philomena Essed and Kwame Nimako (2006), remind us that Dutch minority/migration studies are intensely lacking in independence from governmental policy and are slanted towards dominant interests without critical reflection and intersectional thinking. Hence, Dutch migration studies become majority-interest oriented; as Essed and Nimako call it, a "minority research industry". Unlike the projects of the mainstream Dutch migration studies, the subject of this research is Chinese migrant women. I put their post-emigration life experience and narratives in the front and centre. In short, this research is part of an ongoing Chinese migration history in the Netherlands on the one hand; and on the other hand, it breaks with that tradition to present Dutch Chinese migration studies from a gendered, transnational, grassroots, Critical Chineseness perspective. In sum, this research speaks from the margin to the centre, from minority to majority, with feminist and intersectional perspectives.

Here I want to give a brief review on the mainstream Dutch Chinese migration studies. The first Dutch study on Chinese migration was published in 1936 by van Heek, who roughly described the Chinese neighbourhoods and occupations mainly in Rotterdam. Benton & Vermeulen (1987) analysed the diverse geographical origins of Chinese migration. Pieke & Benton (1998) described the general demography and migration patterns of Dutch Chinese overseas. Besides, as minority ethnic groups, comparative studies were being conducted between Dutch Chinese and South African Chinese to evaluate the differences and degrees of their social integration or segregation (Pieke & Harris, 1998).[9]

Within the past two decades, scholars have started to pay attention to the internal dynamics and power relations within Dutch Chinese communities; however, this kind of research required Mandarin or Cantonese linguistic skills to acquire insider information. For instance, Minghuan Li, a native Mandarin-speaking government-sponsored researcher from southern China, who is capable of speaking in English, Mandarin and Cantonese,[10] studied the isolated *peranakan*[11] Chinese in the Netherlands; she argued that because of the language and cultural loss of Peranakan Chinese, in general, they have little interaction with other Chinese who come from Hong Kong, Taiwan and China. Later, Li investigated the development of voluntary Chinese associations (1999) and the number of Chinese students and scholars in academic fields in the Dutch higher education system (2002 in Nyiri & Saveliev).[12] Meeuwse (2010) reviewed Chinese migration history from 1911 and described daily life in Chinatowns in Amsterdam and Rotterdam. However, due to her Mandarin linguistic limitations, Meeuwse was only able to conduct interviews with second or third-generation Dutch Chinese. Recently, the issue of senior Chinese health care (Liu et al., 2008) and mental health (Liu et al., 2011) were investigated. Nonetheless, the number of Dutch Chinese migration studies is still rare. I have noted only one publication that studies the beliefs on mental illness of the Chinese in the West (Liu et al., 2013)

---

[9] Pieke, Frank N. & Harris, Karen L. 1998. "Integration or Segregation: The Dutch and South African Chinese Compared." Pp. 115–138.

[10] Li, Minghuan. 1998. "Living Among Three Walls? The Peranakan Chinese in the Netherlands." Pp.167–183.

[11] The so-called *peranakan* refers to those Chinese descendants born in Indonesia and Malaysia who later emigrated to Western countries.

[12] Li, Minghuan. 2002. "A Group in Transition: Chinese Students and Scholars in the Netherlands." Pp. 173–188.

within the last three years.[13] In spite of social, historical and economic research, there are two missing pieces in Dutch Chinese migration studies: one is the contested concept and definition of Chinese minorities, which has long been ignored or considered a natural, primordial and homogenous category. Another is the daily life analysis from a gendered perspective. I will elaborate on the definition of contested Chineseness discourses in respect of the field of Chinese migration studies. The themes emerging from interview texts will be presented and analysed accordingly in every chapter of this book.

In the field of Chinese migration studies, this research aims to break through the mainstream socio-political-oriented tradition by making migrant women visible. The blind spot of mainstream Chinese migration studies points to a political minefield: the words an author chooses can strengthen or contest political ideological economic discourse without including gender perspectives. In this respect, there is a similarity with Dutch migration studies: very often the questions and answers of researchers become part of policymaking and ideological support for migration policies. In addition, this research also seeks to initiate a dialogue with Chinese migration studies in English-speaking countries from a Western-European context. Moreover, considering the strong cultural embodiment, metaphors and political connotations in the use of Chinese characters and spoken language (Link, 2013), this research also pays a lot of attention to linguistic analysis of gendered politics and relationships in Chinese culture and narrative analysis. My study opens an innovative perspective for researchers to combine Chinese migration studies and linguistic analysis.

Within Chinese migration studies, different ways of describing Chineseness can be found. Until recently, most studies partook either in the Greater China discourse or in the Cultural China discourse. I am aware that the subject of the particular jargons and terms defining Chinese migration is politically highly sensitive. Somehow, I feel the words sticking in my throat: every step could be a trigger for a landmine. Nonetheless, I found that no previous Dutch Chinese migration studies mentioned the complexities of Chinese migration, thus it is necessary to clarify some terms and concepts that circulate concerning this topic before further analysis can be done.[14] It is also helpful to deconstruct the long-term myth or taken-for-granted assumption that sees Chinese minorities in

[13] See: http://www.ercomer.eu/publications-2/, accessed date 2 April, 2015.

[14] I thank Professor Dr. Yuk Wah Chan for her remarks and feedback on my initial conference paper presented at the Asian Migration and the Global Asian Diasporas Conference on 6 and 7 September 2013 at City University in Hong Kong.

the Netherlands as a homogenous and persistent group, especially in political orientation, which is dominantly the case in Chinese migration studies. Schematically speaking, Chinese migration theory nowadays can be divided into three discourses, namely the Greater China, the Cultural China, and the Critical Chineseness discourse. They are highly contested in ideology as well as infused with political and historical intricacies. Among them, the Greater China and the Cultural China are the two mainstream discourses when speaking of Chineseness. I will talk about the Critical Chineseness discourse later in this chapter. Given their paradoxes, the various terms referring to Chinese immigrants also have different connotations.

The Greater China Discourse

In general, as Kao (1993) and Lin (1994)[15] argue, the so-called Greater China discourse is a hegemonic political discourse that has been emerging with rising Chinese nationalism in the PRC since 1978, calling for the solidarity of global Chinese migrants and awareness of Chineseness to fight against the Japanese imperial invasion, on the one hand. On the other, by reconstructing the very Chineseness ideology, the real purpose behind this Greater China discourse is to attract capital from global Chinese migrants, especially from Hong Kong, Taiwan, Macau, and Singapore, to invest in the aftermath of the Open and Reform Policy in the economic zones along the coastal provinces (Hoe, 2013). Furthermore, the handover of Hong Kong and Macau to the sovereignty of China in 1997 and 1999, respectively, reinforced the intensity of the construction of a political Greater China, which imposed that the designation by the Republic of China that Taiwan become "a sacred and inseparable part of China" regardless of Taiwan's de facto autonomy (Mangelson, 1992; Pegg, 1998; Fan, 2007; Sun, 2010) for over one century. With these three comparatively more modernised and advanced districts (Hong Kong, Taiwan, and Macau), a wealthier and stronger Greater China is envisioned. To view overseas Chinese as an important national resource is not new,

[15] Some Taiwanese scholars divide The Greater China discourse into two concepts, one is economic China; the other is political China. The former emphasises economic integration through the cooperation of overseas Chinese while the later manifests the PRC's One China Policy on Cross Strait issue. However, both economic China and political China adherents all agree that the One China principle will be the ultimate solution.

according to Gungwu Wang (1998),[16] who argues that from the end of the nineteenth century, the Chinese government in Beijing began to be aware that the Chinese living abroad could be a significant source of investment, a commercial and intellectual asset, and a useful bridge to import new knowledge from the more advanced industrial countries. Thus, the government created several categories to include and upgrade the social status of overseas Chinese and reverse the negative and inferior images regarding Chinese emigrants as malcontents[17] or desperately poor coolies during the Qing Dynasty (p.18).

From this perspective, several terms were being used literally to create an imaginary of China and thereby the imaginary extension of family kinship. The most ambitious and controversial one is the use of *qiao* (僑). From Wang's viewpoint, the concept of *qiao* means sojourning. The combination word *huaqiao* (華僑) originally referred to Chinese nationals (including those of the PRC, Taiwan and Hong Kong residents) who have temporarily left to live abroad. However, with the rise of Chinese nationalism, *huaqiao* and *huaren* (華人; Chinese people), which China insists on using as a kind of continuum, extend the meaning to refer to all overseas Chinese and their descendants, no matter whether they are Chinese nationals or not (ibid: 23-24). Under the Greater China discourse, those living in Hong Kong, Macau and Taiwan are neither *huaqiao* nor *huaren*; they are named as *tongbao* (同胞; compatriots).

The term *tongbao* refers to brothers and sisters coming from the same parents, which indicates that people from Hong Kong, Macau and Taiwan share the same bloodline with people in China and are siblings. Wang criticises the Greater China discourse as an expansionist and imperialist term (ibid.: 28). Moreover, as pointed out by Hongkong sociologist Yuk Wah Chan (2014), despite the fact that the Beijing government does not accept that Chinese in Hong Kong and Taiwan are described as being "overseas", judging by the migration regulations and relations, "these three places are definitely three separate territorial entities" (p.10). As

---

[16] Wang, Gungwu. 1998. "Upgrading the Migrant: Neither Huaqiao nor Huaren." Pp. 15-33.

[17] In order to prevent anti-Qing rebel forces entering into China from coastal provinces, from 1662, Emperor Kangxi started to implement the so-called "Sea Ban" policy, which not only forbade people's freedom to sail, fish and trade but also forbade emigrants to return to China and treated them as traitors to the Qing Dynasty. Not until 1684 did Emperor Kangxi reopen a few ports for international trading. To know more about Chinese monetary policy, see Von Glahn, R. 1996. *Fountain of Fortune: Money and Monetary Policy in China, 1000–1700*. Berkeley: University of California Press.

China transforms to a more pluralised society, this discourse needs to be polished over time with the leadership alteration. Take for instance the intensity of the nationalist propaganda that began to extend to the commercial mass media from the 1990s onwards. The state-run mass media transform patriotism and nationalism as a commodity to the rising middle-class. Its discourse is anti-American imperialism and corrupted Western capitalism (Huang & Li, 2003). Recently, one of the main assertions of President Xi's propaganda *zhongguo meng* (中國夢), "Chinese Dream", campaign is through cooperation among all global Chinese to restore the nation's glory, to bring grace to "our" *zuguo* (祖國; motherland).[18] It is of course a continuum of the Greater China discourse to call for ethnocultural integrity domestically and internationally. In my reading, the Greater China discourse has at least two purposes. Firstly, it functions as a collective Chinese identity formation which makes China a magnet, an authentic symbol for all worldwide overseas Chinese to attract and build their collective identity through historical, cultural, economic, and imaginary nostalgic glory. Secondly, its political ambition is to impose a single and hegemonic Chineseness on its target groups, which also affects the general perception of Chinese immigrant-receiving countries *per se*; namely, that the majority in the receiving countries will treat Chinese immigrants as forever outsiders and temporary sojourners who will never be loyal to their countries of immigration. Moreover, in respect of the debate of being a Chinese, those who have a second opinion about that are seen as a menace and a barrier against the ongoing modernisation project of Greater China (Sorman, 2008; Link, 2011; Gutmann, 2014). Women are considered the indispensable "educators of the next generation", "mothers of the nation" or "symbols and virtue of Chinese people" in China's modernisation and nationalisation project. The definition of patriotic Chinese women is constructed and defined by male elites; although the Chinese Communist Party (CCP) keeps saying that women support the other half of the sky, they are still excluded from the political decision-making mechanisms.[19]

The Cultural China Discourse

To respond to and resist the hegemonic Greater China discourse, Chinese scholars from Taiwan, Hong Kong, Singapore, and the USA propose the Cultural China discourse; among them, the most important scholar is Wei-

---

[18] About the construction of *zuguo* ideology, see chapter seven.

[19] For further discussion, see chapter three.

Ming Tu. His article, "The Meaning of Being a Chinese Today" in *Daedalus* (1991) provoked a heated debate about the Cultural China discourse, and the term Cultural China soon became a catchphrase in mass media and in academia.

Broadly speaking, the Cultural China discourse has two arguments. First, it argues that the term *zhongguo* (中國) be equalised as the country's representation; the sovereign unit known as China nowadays is constructed, not primordial (Tu, 1994; Wang in Sinn, 1998; Ning, 2009). One must understand that there is a difference in how foreigners name China and how Chinese name themselves. Chinese do not call their country China; foreigners named this nation thus because of its fine porcelain and pottery. Ancient Chinese called themselves *zhongguo.* Originally, *Zhongguo* meant Middle Kingdom or Central Country; it was to distinguish the Han ethnic groups from the non-Han nomadic ethnic groups. It is a dynamic, constantly changing landscape rather than a static structure (Tu, 1994: 4). It was only until the late Qing Dynasty that *zhongguo* as an incarnation of the nation was established. In this view, *zhongguo* should be understood as a cultural area, a cultural unity where people follow and practice Confucianism and Taoism, rather than as a political term. Secondly, this discourse resists imposing a nationalist label on Chinese people, who are then equated with China, in particular for Chinese outside China. In other words, Chinese people should be seen as a cultural entity not a political entity. For instance, in reviewing the historical trajectory of Chinese identities in Southeast Asia, Gungwu Wang (1988) argued that Chinese in Southeast Asia were more inclined to individual dialect communities than to a homogenous Chinese nation before the 20th century. There is no single term that can represent all Chinese in Southeast Asia, not even *huaqiao* or *huaren.* These constructed and imposing nametags are foreign and dangerous to them since they became a political excuse for local governments to oppress and suppress Chinese communities, such as the 1998 Chinese massacre in Indonesia, and anti-Chinese riots in Vietnam during May 2014. In sum, scholars of the Cultural China discourse think that only through referring to and reinterpreting classic Chinese philosophy can the Taiwan-China issue be solved. Hence, the single and hegemonic Greater China can be transformed into a plural but united Cultural China (Lin, 1994).

As a feminist, I think that unfortunately both the Cultural China and the Greater China discourses are male-defined speech. They are elite, politically inspired and androcentric. In respect of the Cultural China discourse, it lacks reflection on gender inequality and prejudice, which has long existed in Chinese culture and society. Besides, the Cultural China discourse is still an imposing ideology which denies the individual free will of all Chinese people who do not want to be "Chinese" either politically or culturally. In short, although it promotes a democratic and plural political discourse in interpreting the concept of a still-single *zhongguo* and a homogeneous Chineseness, the Cultural China discourse remains a top-down, patriarchal and gender-blind ideology. A similar ideology is revealed in Dutch Chinese migration studies; I will review it from a historical trajectory and demographic background in the following section.

1.2 Historical Trajectory & Demographic Background

Firstly, let me briefly describe the historical trajectory and demographic background of Chinese immigrants in the Netherlands. To appreciate the variety of origins of overseas Chinese in the Netherlands, one has to draw a picture of East Asia going back to the golden history of the Ming Dynasty[20] (1368–1644).[21] According to *The History of Ming*,[22] between 1405 and 1433, the Ming government sponsored a series of seven naval expeditions. Ho Cheng was assigned by the Ming emperor as a commander and he successfully completed these hazardous missions. During these seven naval expeditions, the Ming government not only developed transnational trade as far away as India but also established systematic mass emigration for Chinese to build trading colonies in Southeast Asia. Roughly 108,000 Chinese emigrated. They settled in the areas known today as Malaysia, Indonesia, Vietnam, Philippines, Burma, and Cambodia.

In 1602, the Vereenigde Oost-Indische Compagnie (United Dutch East Indies Company) was formed, through which the Dutch empire began to broaden its impact in Asia. In 1604, the first Dutch fleet, led by Wijbrant van Waarwick, arrived in Penghu but failed to successfully obtain the right to trade. In 1619, the Dutch took Indonesia then in 1624 southern Taiwan and built het Kasteel Zeelandia (The Zeelandia Castle). Indonesia officially

---

[20] For the difference in Mandarin spelling systems between China and Taiwan, I put Chinese traditional characters for specific words that Mandarin speakers can understand well.

[21] On the exact time of Chinese migrations to Southeast Asia, Chinese historians have diverse perspectives. The origins of Chinese migrations to Southeast Asia should be traced back to the South Son Dynasty (1208-1224); however, at that time, the emperors of the South Son Dynasty did not pay much attention to the situation in Southeast Asia.

[22] *The History of Ming,* Chapter 325.

became one of the Dutch colonies and remained so until 1949.[23] From the 17th century onwards, according to Li-Jen Kao (2010), Chinese migrants in Indonesia played an important role as mediators for the Dutch East Indies to develop international commerce with Asian countries. However, the business relationship between Chinese Indonesians and the Dutch was not an equal partnership; it was military dominance through which the Dutch could control and suppress locals and force cooperation with them.

Although the Dutch had political and economic interaction with the Chinese from the 17th century, it was not until 1911 that the first group of Chinese were brought to the Netherlands by Dutch shipping companies because of the strike in the Rotterdam port. Most were poor seamen from Guangdong. They were very different from the Chinese migrants who came later in the 20th century. According to Minghuan Li (1999), Chinese seamen came mainly from Guangdong and settled earlier than the Chinese entrepreneurs who came from Wenzhou and Qjngtian and had more financial resources. These two groups were sometimes in an intensive situation because of mutual competition in business (p.45). In the next section, I will briefly illustrate the historical background of overseas Chinese immigration to the Netherlands.

There were several ways that Chinese immigrated to the Netherlands. Li (1999) summarised the pattern of Chinese immigration as having occurred in three phases:

a. The first Europe-oriented migration: before 1949.
b. The second Chinese emigration from outside China: 1950–1975.
c. A sudden rise of emigration from China: after 1976.

a. The inception of the first Europe-oriented migration (before 1949)

There were two groups of Chinese immigrants in the first phases: one was a re-emigrant group, which came from the former Netherlands East Indies; the other group came directly from China.

The re-emigrant group was basically comprised of students who were known as Peranakan Chinese. In 1908, the so-called Holland-Chinese school, a primary education, was established in the Netherlands East Indies. Since early 1905, with the increase of local-born Chinese descendants who grew up in the Netherlands' East Indies and received a Dutch education, entry into the Netherlands for secondary and tertiary

[23] However, Indonesia declared independence in 1945. One should notice that there is a different historic interpretation between the two nations.

education became an overriding ambition for some literate Chinese, even though it was a very expensive and difficult undertaking.[24] In sum, according to the statistical data offered by *Chung Hwa Hui* (中華會),[25] there were about 900 Peranakan Chinese who studied in the Netherlands between 1911 and 1940.[26]

The first Chinese group that came directly from China to the Netherlands was the Guangdong or He On group. Most of them had worked for Dutch shipping companies in Hong Kong. The history of Chinese employees hired by Dutch shipping companies can be traced back to the 19th century; ocean-shipping enterprises were already a well-entrenched economic sector of Britain, the Netherlands and some other Western European countries. From the middle of the 19th century, after the cession of Hong Kong to Europe, in a bid to seek higher profits, British shipping companies, followed by the Dutch and other Western companies, began to hire cheap Chinese labour on ships leaving from Hong Kong. If we take this historical background from the Dutch perspective, the hiring of cheap Chinese labour on ships not only allowed circumventing the labour regulations but also lowered personnel expenses. An investigation by the Dutch seamen's trade union in 1930 showed that the wage accepted by Chinese seamen was only about two-thirds of the pay that was offered to their Dutch counterparts.[27]

Life in the Netherlands was arduous for these Guangdong seamen. Besides the low pay, these workers endured segregation in prejudicial living environments; Dutch seamen saw them as rivals and scabs. The Rotterdam seamen's union, De Volharding, ran an inflammatory campaign against the "yellow peril",[28] a degrading term derived from the supposed skin colour of those Chinese seamen. Until the Second World War, this racist "yellow peril" rhetoric remained a trump-card in the hands of the shipping companies.[29]

---

[24] Minghuan Li, 1999, pp.28–29.

[25] According to Li, "Chung Hwa Hui was an association organised by the Peranakan Chinese youth who studied in the Netherlands. It was set up in 1911" (ibid: 261). It was the first officially recognised Chinese voluntary association in the Netherlands and it was considered an extension of the Chinese nationalist movement (Pp. 53–54), which was named after the Mandarin pronunciation of the ROChina (Chung Hwa Min Kuo).

[26] Tan, 1986, p.2, cited from Minghuan Li, 1999, p29.

[27] Ibid, p. 30.

[28] Pieke & Benton, 1998, p.127.

[29] Heek, 1936; Pieke & Benton, 1998, p.127.

The situation became much worse during the economic depression in the 1930s. The majority of the Chinese seamen had no work, they gradually became desperately poor and ill, and the Dutch government forbade them from working on shore. In order to survive, these Chinese men sold peanut-cake, *pindakoekjes*[30], illegal cigarettes and sometimes condoms in nearby neighbourhoods. At that time, the Dutch police considered them a potential threat to public security and hygiene.[31] In a nutshell, the situation for the first Chinese seamen who came directly from China to the Netherlands was difficult. Dutch society treated them as rivals or inferior, dirty outsiders. They survived on their own and through group solidarity during the Second World War period. In short, the early history of Chinese presence in the Netherlands is a gendered one, which mainly consisted of men.

b. Chinese emigration from outside of China (1950–1975)

There were two groups of Chinese immigrants in the first phases: one was a re-emigrant group, which came from the former Netherlands East Indies; the other group came directly from China.

As the Chinese adage "*ku jin gan lai* (苦盡甘來)" goes,[32] post-war reconstruction activities brought new opportunities for Chinese residents in the Netherlands. The Chinese catering business came to the fore with perfect timing. In 1947, there were only 23 Chinese restaurants in the Netherlands. Towards the end of the 1970s, the total number had reached about 2000.[33] The rapid growth of Chinese restaurants created a large number of jobs; however, the chaos of the civil war[34]between the ROC, Taiwan and the PRC severely restricted emigration abroad for citizens. People were monitored on both sides of the Cross-Strait political confrontation. People could not go abroad freely let alone emigrate. Those who had families or relatives outside the country were tightly monitored and their daily communications (letters, telephone calls) censored. They were labelled traitors of the motherland or suspected of espionage by the ROC or the PRC. At that time, the best show of loyalty for both governments was to stay in China and Taiwan and work hard to construct the future new "China". Thus, Hongkongers became the largest Chinese

---

[30] Pieke & Benton, 1998, p.128.
[31] For more information, see chapter six.
[32] It means that when things are at the worst, they will mend.
[33] Minghuan Li, 1999, p.34.
[34] Especially from 1945 to 1950, the second Chinese Civil War.

emigrant group during the second phase of Chinese emigration. Part of this migrant group also found their niche doing catering and restaurant business in the Netherlands.

c. A sudden rise of emigration from China (after 1976)

After the end of the Cultural Revolution (1966–1976), and the more open political attitude towards overseas Chinese in the last quarter of the 20th century, the flow of emigration to Europe was far greater than anything experienced during the first three-quarters of the century.[35] The new PRC leader, Xiaoping Deng, regarded overseas Chinese as the bridge between China and developed Western counties. He welcomed foreign investment to the coastal provinces[36] in China and intellectual cultivation and overseas business competition between Taiwan and China motivated him.[37] The prosperity of democratic Western countries became the dream of middle-class Chinese, willing to spend every penny on emigration, legal or illegal. According to an unofficial statistic, more than 70,000 Wenzhou people emigrated between 1984 and 1995, most of whom went to Europe.[38]

Given the diversity and origins of Chinese immigrants, the actual number of Chinese in the Netherlands is difficult to estimate accurately. According to the UN Economic Commission for Europe (2001), there were roughly 80,000 overseas Chinese in the Netherlands in 2001. According to Li (1998), Chinese association leaders and diplomatic officials of the Chinese Embassy in the Netherlands usually say that there are 100,000 Chinese living there.[39] As of 2011, figures from the Netherlands' Centraal Bureau voor de Statistiek (CBS) show[40] the total number of Chinese is 76,860, as follows,

---

[35] Minghuan Li, 1999, p.37.

[36] These comprise the so-called "experimental zones" such as Wenzhou and Fujian.

[37] Due to the political confrontation, it is very hard to find open information online about Taiwan's emigration history. I wrote a letter to the embassy, hoping they could tell me where I might find detailed information, but I never got a reply. Moreover, there is statistical inaccuracy of the official number of immigrants. For example, Guochu Zhang (2003: 76) found a statistical issue while reviewing the trends on highly skilled Chinese migration to Europe. He pointed out that the exact number of Chinese emigration is impossible to get because of "the recent dramatic increase in self-supported students who are not controlled by the Ministry of Education."

[38] Minghuan Li, 1999, p.37.

[39] Ibid.: 42.

[40] Internet Resource, accessed on 27 July 2011:

First Generation:
38,988 China-born persons (18,173 men, 20,815 women)
9,763 Hong Kong-born persons (4,876 men, 4,887 women)
85 Macau-born persons (31 men, 54 women)
2,213 Taiwan-born persons (808 men, 1,405 women)

Second generation:
16,892 persons with at least one parent born in China (8,651 men, 8,241 women)
8,398 persons with at least one parent born in Hong Kong (4,290 men, 4,108 women)
36 persons with at least one parent born in Macau (18 men, 18 women)
485 persons with at least one parent born in Taiwan (253 men, 232 women)

As one can see from the CBS data, the first-generation Chinese female migrants outnumber the males, especially from China and Taiwan. However, until now I have not seen any Dutch Chinese migration studies discuss this matter or pay attention to these women's real experiences while adaptating to post-emigration life. This scholarly gap is the missing piece that I aim to find,[41] to bring women to the centre and contribute further to the rewriting of Dutch Chinese migration history through a critical intersectional lens with regard to gender, class, race/ethnicity, age, and nation of origin.

The Dutch government defines ethnic Chinese as a "person who has an actual relationship with China, because the parents were or the person was born in China"[42]; the geographical areas of China include China, Hong Kong, Macau, and Taiwan. Other Southeast Asian Chinese who re-emigrated to the Netherlands are not included in the CBS data. It suffices to say that the Chinese groups in the Netherlands are heterogeneous and

---

http://statline.cbs.nl/StatWeb/publication/?VW=T&DM=SLNL&PA=37325&D1=1-2&D2=1-2&D3=0&D4=0&D5=46,90,129,218&D6=0,5,14-15&HD=110428-0914&HDR=G2,G3,T,G5&STB; however, the figures did not contain the overseas Chinese originating from Southeast Asian countries.

[41] I have discussed this phenomenon with my interviewees. Most of them felt very surprised at the fact that female migrants outnumber the males. Some of them considered it is because of the difficulty for single male Chinese to find female spouses in the Netherlands. Thus, male Chinese must go back to China to look for wives and bring their mothers to the Netherlands later to look after their children.

[42] The definition in Dutch is "Persoon die een feitelijke verwantschap heeft met China, omdat de ouders of de persoon zelf in China zijn geboren." The definition of Chinese comes from *Sociaal-economische kenmerken Chinezen in Nederland* (2008) by Marleen Geerdinck & Nicol Sluiter.

miscellaneous based on the Greater China and the Cultural China ideology. It is impossible for any researcher to overgeneralise all the Chinese groups with a single argument. Thus, it is necessary to clearly define the research scope and key terms in the beginning.

1.3 Target Group and Research Questions

In this research, I adopt the Critical Chineseness discourse as my standpoint in dealing with interviewees' Chineseness. I found that they felt sometimes culturally Chinese, sometimes politically or economically connected. For example, in regard to Mandarin learning, all women see it as a way to turn cultural capital into economic capital for children. However, when I asked them if they could introduce me to their Chinese friends from different regions, for instance, women from Taiwan said they always have trouble making friends with women from China; they do not see eye to eye on the territorial and political issues. Or, women from China revealed their resentment towards women from Hong Kong as they complained that Hongkongers in the Netherlands consider themselves superior to people from China because they are often the owners of catering businesses and they treat people from China as their employees. Although these power dynamics are not directly related to motherhood practices, the complexities show the differences and inconsistencies of women's perceptions about their own Chineseness.

The Critical Chineseness discourse emerged contemporaneously with the Cultural China discourse from the 1990s. Most of its advocates are second- or third-generation Chinese descendants living outside China, and their works are seldom translated into Mandarin given their political sensitivity.[43] To put it briefly, Critical Chineseness discourse rejects both Greater China and Cultural China discourses and criticises them on three dimensions. First and foremost is the theoretical fault of using the terms *zhongguoren* or *huaren* to define Chinese people. Eugene Kheng-Boon Tan condemns the development of Chineseness as "a convenient conflation of the concepts of race and ethnicity" (2013: 2). Since the former is based on biological appurtenances and the latter refers to its social and cultural practice, the terms *zhongguoren* and *huaren* attempt to invent a "pure Chinese" identity to establish and naturalise the hierarchy

[43] Readers can find some of the Critical Chineseness discourses in Mandarin from an academic database in Taiwan, for example, Hyread Journal Database: http://www.hyread.com.tw/. Unfortunately, it is not a free open resource; one must apply for membership first and pay the annual fee to gain access.

of cultural superiority among various Chinese communities (ibid.: 5). For Tan, *zhongguoren* implies a single identity that is a Chinese national, a subject loyal to and belonging to the PRC, while *huaren* implies broader and plural identities linked to Chinese culture and global Chinese diasporas. Second, Critical Chineseness discourse criticises the essentialism within Greater China and Cultural China discourses, namely the Han-centralism. According to the criteria of these discourses, an authentic Chinese is one who can speak *Hanyu* (漢語; the Mandarin dialect), write *Hanzi* (漢字; Chinese characters), is able to read *Hanwen* (漢文; the Han language) and follows and practices Confucianism in daily life. However, these criteria are ahistorical and anachronistic in three ways. Firstly, they ignore the other ethnic minority groups living inside and outside China, those who are included in definitions of *zhongguoren* or *huaren.* Only the majority Han ethnic group and its culture is selected to represent so-called authentic Chineseness (Chun, 1996 & 1999; Wang, 1998 in Sinn; Ang, 2001; Chow, 2000; Ben, 2004; Tan, 2013), which is exclusive of other minorities and is taken for granted. Second, it lacks historical insight and knowledge of Chinese history. There are an estimated 129 dialects in China alone[44] and 55 officially recognised ethnic minorities with their own languages. Mandarin is only one of 129 dialects and it is very different to the original *Hanyu,* which is more similar to the southern dialect spoken during the Tang Dynasty. Paradoxically, now the so-called *Hanyu* is mistaken as Mandarin or Chinese, which is actually a northern dialect in China. Furthermore, it does not take into account the social transformations among Chinese emigrants who have integrated into local societies and gradually developed localised and unique cultures. For instance, the mixed language (mostly Fujianese and indigenous language) spoken and used by *peranakan* from Indonesia and Malaysia (Wang in Sinn, 1998; Ang, 2001), or the ancient pronunciations spoken during the Tang Dynasty, preserved in Cantonese and Taiwanese. Ien Ang (2001) argues that this imposed Chinese identity and its criteria are a practice of discrimination to those "unqualified" Chinese, and it also denies its own cultural diversities.

Take my family history, for instance: According to my grandmother's narrative, my ancestors were from Fujian; they moved to Taiwan because of their unwillingness to be ruled by the Manzu regime (Qing Dynasty). Within our family, there were people who were Mongolians. That could explain why I was born with a birthmark, which is considered to be

[44] Generally speaking, they are divided into seven linguistic groups: *Guan*, *Wu*, *Yue*, *Min*, *Xiang*, *Kejia, and Gan.*

evidence of having Mongolian ancestors. Also, after they moved to Taiwan, my ancestors married indigenous Taiwanese from Pingpu (Plains aborigines). The Pingpu tribe was a matrilineal society belonging to the Austronesian linguistic group. The generation of my grandparents (both my mother's and father's sides) were raised as Japanese; they once had Japanese names and spoke both Japanese and Taiwanese as their mother tongues. Thus, who am I? Calling me a Chinese under either the Greater China or the Cultural China discourses is far too simple. From this perspective, one should have the right to claim, using Ang's words (2001: 36), "if I am inescapably Chinese by *descent*, I am only sometimes Chinese by *consent*." [45] Thirdly, the last argument of the Critical Chineseness discourse is against the sexism and totalitarianism within both the Greater China and the Cultural China discourses. Sexism, on the one hand, refers to the male-defined and male-dominant speech, as if women were absent and insignificant within China's 5000 years of historical trajectory (Ang, 2001). Moreover, it considers that neither the Greater China nor the Cultural China discourses reflect critically on the sexism and gender inequality within classic Chinese philosophy and Chinese patriarchal society (Yang, 2005). Besides sexism, the Critical Chineseness discourse also points out the totalitarianism in both the Greater China and the Cultural China discourses for their top-down and elite-dominant characteristics. As I mentioned earlier, the Han ethnic group is merely one of the 55 ethnic groups inside China; without any democratic method and process, their (male Chinese elites and political leaders) legitimacy of defining what is China, who is Chinese, and how to be a Chinese is questionable. For example, in the famous article, "Fuck Chineseness: On the Ambiguities of Ethnicity as Culture as Identity", Allen Chun (1996, 1999[46]) questioned who could speak on behalf of all "Chinese"? For what purpose and in whose interest? Rey Chow (2000) later echoes Chun by pointing out that the construction of Chineseness or "standard Chinese" is a kind of monopoly; the definition of what Chinese means and what it is considered Chineseness are regulated and controlled by political elites who dominantly belong to the Han ethnicity. This kind of speech, thinking control and autocracy have hindered the facility of self-expression of other subgroups. They also diminish the agency, creativity and achievements of Chinese emigrants who have been struggling to integrate into, or assimilate into, local societies and cultures over generations. Yet, the

[45] Italics emphasised by Ien Ang.

[46] In 1999, this article was translated into Mandarin and published in Taiwan. However, the word "fuck" was translated into *jiegou* (deconstruct). After closely examining the two versions, I think that the Mandarin translation was softened.

Critical Chineseness discourse is still very immature. It needs to be a more theorised argument to sustain its concept. Until now, we know too little about ordinary peoples' viewpoints on what Chinese is or what China means to them. It lacks a safe public forum to let everyone self-express freely without fear. Furthermore, we need to be aware that in academia we pay little attention to the intersectionality theory on China or the Chineseness discussion. Simply stated, more empirical data needs to be collected; more dialogues between academia and society need to be created. Unless scholars start to take intersectionality (gender, sexuality, ethnicity, age, class, region, dialect, religion) into account while dealing with Chineseness research, the speech authority will always stay in certain male elite groups.

In this research, I focus on the first generation of migrant women from Taiwan, Hong Kong and China. I call them neither *huaren* nor *huayi* but overseas Chinese, Chinese emigrants or migrant/immigrant women. Given the complexity and diversity of Chinese groups, I only chose migrant women from Taiwan, Hong Kong and China for their cultural and ethnic proximity, since they grew up in milieus where Confucianism and Taoism are dominant social norms, and where the Han ethnic group is in the majority. However, women from these three regions came to the Netherlands in various periods because of their class and social-historical backgrounds. By paying intersectional attention to these three groups, this study can deepen the academic understanding of Chinese migrants in a non-English speaking country, and it is also an innovative work that aims to deconstruct the homogenous myth of Chinese minorities.

Now I shall state my research questions of this book. Being a mother is not easy but being a mother in a foreign country far away from home, surrounded by alien languages, environment, religion, food, social customs, ethnic people and groups, is much more difficult. From the pilot interviews with two Taiwanese women who have been married to Dutch men for several years, I concluded that motherhood practices do not begin after giving birth; it is a process that begins the moment a woman decides to be the wife of her chosen one, regardless of whether the husband is Chinese or not. Importantly, the Chinese migrant women in my study are embedded in a Confucian cultural background and faith about the meaning of marriage and mothering, which has a deep impact on their daily lives. In addition, the interaction with and discipline from their natal families and their in-laws also greatly influence the mothering environment. To date, the lived experiences of motherhood among Chinese migrant women in the Netherlands – which I will call the Chinese motherhood diaspora –

are largely unknown. In this research I want to explore the following questions:

1. How do Chinese migrant women make sense of their motherhood in the Netherlands?
2. What difficulties do they encounter in everyday life? And how do those difficulties affect their practice of motherhood?
3. How do Chinese migrant women negotiate the cultural differences between their Asian and Western contexts?
4. How do they see their relationship with their countries of origin?

My overarching research aim is, with the help of the central research questions, to begin to reconstruct a gendered picture of Chinese migratory history in the Netherlands from the post-war to the present. It is thus my aim to make the subaltern's voice be heard, and to make Chinese migratory motherhood visible.

1.4 Structure

In order to represent the real-life experiences that migrant Chinese women deal with in their everyday lives, I decided to make each chapter an independent themed essay. In this introductory chapter, I firstly reviewed the historical background and demographic summary of Chinese ethnic groups in the Netherlands. Then I gave a brief literature review on Dutch Chinese migration studies. In the second part, I illustrated the contested and paradoxical three main branches of Chinese discourses: the Greater China, the Cultural China, and the Critical Chineseness discourses. By analysing these three discourses, I aim to break the myth and the taken-for-granted assumption of Dutch Chinese migration studies, which generally regard "ethnic Chinese" as a homogenous group, which corresponds to the Greater China discourse and pays little attention to the complexities between the three Chinese discourses.

Chapter Two, Methodology, deals with research methodology, which is divided into two sections. In the first section, I explain why the feminist standpoint theory and intersectionality theory are significant epistemologies in this research methodology. In the second section, I show the process of my empirical research method, the backgrounds of the interviewees, and how I came to understand the different themes from the interviewees' narratives and participatory observation.

Chapter Three, Motherhood Discourse in Western Feminisms and Chinese Confucianism, discusses motherhood from both Western and

Chinese perspectives. In the first part, I provide a literature review of motherhood debates by well-known Western feminists. In the second part, I focus on how motherhood is defined and constructed from Confucian thinking and Chinese social norms, and I subsequently take the "tiger mother" phenomenon as an example to reflect how an elite Chinese woman carries out her motherhood practices in a Western world. After that, I cite some media discussion about the "tiger mother" phenomenon in the United States.

Chapter Four, Running a Restaurant Downstairs and Raising Children Upstairs: Working-class Chinese Mothers in the Netherlands, explores the real-life situations of working-class Chinese migrant women and their motherhood practice strategies. This chapter is divided into three sections. It draws attention to the migrant trajectory and the real-life motherhood practice of working-class Chinese women. In the historical background of this chapter, I explain why the early Chinese immigrants before the 1970s were mainly from Hong Kong and the Guangdong area by reviewing the Chinese household system and immigration policy. The second section deals with the life arrangements among working-class migrant Chinese women. I describe how working-class Chinese mothers combine their work and motherhood by geographical arrangement and mutual cooperation. In the last section, I illustrate the motherhood strategy of how working-class women carry out their discipline from Confucian thinking, and how they adjust their parenting by combining the comparatively freer Western style and the authoritative Chinese style.

Chapter Five, Language Issues for Chinese Migrant Women, addresses the most troubling issue for migrant women: language. One aspect is learning Dutch by the migrant women themselves; the other is their children's language education issue. In the first part, I focus on how language barriers affect women's daily lives and how they overcome them. What difficulties have they encountered in learning Dutch? In the second part, I draw attention to the impact of raising children in a foreign environment, and the tensions and obstacles they face from both inside and outside their family. I also point out the language education decision, which is made according to intersectional considerations among generations, classes and regions within transnational or Chinese families.

Chapter Six, "Too much Rice, no Potatoes?" Dealing with Everyday Racism and Discrimination, touches on the Dutch taboos, racism and social discrimination against Chinese migrant women, externally and internally within the private domain. The knowledge and conceptions about Dutch racism towards Chinese in this study are novel epistemological contributions by bottom-up voices, which are seldom heard or studied in the

Netherlands. The first part deals with the discrimination from Dutch society. I show various kinds of daily discriminations that Chinese migrant women often encounter and how these rude and hate-speech acts affect them. I then explain from women's narratives why most Chinese would rather not talk back or fight against these discriminative behaviours. The second part discusses the internal gender inequality, sexism and discrimination inside both transnational and Chinese migration families. Not only do I pay attention to the tensions and confrontations between husband and wife but also women's relationship with their in-laws. I illustrate how these cultural crossings affect migrant women's motherhood practice and how they negotiate and claim their rights.

Chapter Seven: First-Generation Chinese Immigrant Women's Experiences of Using Kraamzorg (Maternity Care Service) in the Netherlands. The Dutch believe that parenthood is not nature; it needs to be learned and guidance needs to be given, and the post-natal care service is a people-centred health care policy designed to meet this concept. The Dutch government introduced the Kraamzorg (post-natal care services) policy for many benefits: 1. to reduce postpartum depression in women; 2. to help novice parents successfully take care of new-borns; 3. to separate reproduction and care medical service to reduce the waste of medical and social resources; and 4. to enhance the labour force participation rate. This chapter explores the experience of 38 first-generation Chinese (Hong Kong, Taiwan, Mainland China) migrant women in the Netherlands. For most Chinese women, delivering a child in the Netherlands is quite an experience. After their interaction with post-natal care nurses, many Chinese women, who have never experienced childbearing abroad, give positive feedback on the post-natal care service. The Kraamzorg policy allows women living in the Netherlands to enjoy this service regardless of nationality and citizenship.

Chapter Eight, Drifting Lilies without Roots: Diasporic Subjects and Reflection on Motherhood, deals with the relationship between personal belonging and motherhood. "I won't call here my home." This sentence is repeated by most of the interviewees. It is a lifetime reflection of post-emigration life: I would like to go further to address the relationship between diaspora, nostalgia and motherhood practice. For most first-generation migrant women, the Netherlands is a place for living, for raising children, but is not considered their home. One has to realise the context and concept of "home" from a Chinese perspective to understand their inner voice. It is the concept of *kun* (根; root), which is deeply embedded in the reflection of Chinese migrant women.

In the concluding chapter, I first summarise the main findings of each theme and then provide my reading of Chinese migration studies from a critical and intersectional perspective. I also show how this study deepens and broadens the Critical Chineseness discourse from a gendered perspective.

CHAPTER TWO

METHODOLOGY

身穿花紅長洋裝，風吹金髮思情郎，想郎船何往，音信全無通,, …
只有金十字，給阮母親做遺記，放阮私生兒… 愈想不幸愈哀悲，到
底現在生亦死，啊～伊是荷蘭的船醫。

I wear a red dress standing here while the wind blows; I miss my golden-haired lover. Where will he be? No messages, no letters…only a golden cross to me as a farewell gift. He left me and our child of shame… the more I miss him, the more miserable I will become. Is he still alive or dead? Ah ~ he is a ship doctor from the Netherlands.

1951 安平追想曲 1951, *An-ping tui-siong-khik*, Anping Memory Song (translated by Huang, 2014)

2.1 Voice from the Margins

This book is grounded in the real-life experiences of the first-generation immigrant Chinese women in the Netherlands. I start with its methodology and how this relates to feminist epistemology in the first section. In the second section, I show the research methods I used in material collection.

When I started to conduct my interviews, I tried to share my research ideas with other Chinese PhD students and friends. One of them commented, "Of what significance will your research be? The Chinese population is less than one percent of the total Dutch population."[47] For a long time, the majority of Chinese migration studies focused on the Asia Pacific region, the United States and the United Kingdom. Most of these studies are gender-blind, regarding Chinese as a homogeneous unity and excluding women's voices. In chapter one, I elaborated three discourses of Chineseness (the Greater China discourses; the Cultural China discourse and the Critical Chineseness discourse) and their relationship. I also gave a brief overview of the Dutch Chinese migration studies that were either

[47] Fieldwork note, December 27, 2011.

mainly socially-economically-politically oriented or paid little or almost no attention to gender issues. Traditional Chinese migration studies are male-centred and male-elitist (Yang, 2005; Cheng et al., 1984; Croll, 1978). The concepts of the research are top-down, male-gazed, and distant to the research groups. Lucie Cheng (1984), a pioneer Taiwanese feminist scholar who has devoted her life to studying Chinese migrant women, argues that Traditional Chinese migration studies take men's experience as the whole picture of Chinese overseas and objectifies Chinese as Others. Women's experiences are generally excluded from the scholarly discussion of the Dutch Chinese migration studies. Where are they? The scholarly position of female Dutch Chinese migrants is just like Dorothy Smith (2004: 22 in Harding) stated: "There are two worlds and the two bases of knowledge and experience don't stand in an equal relation. The world as it is constituted by men stands in authority over that of women."[48] Will it be different if we see the history of Chinese migrants in the Netherlands from the perspective of women?

The extract of the *Anping Memory Song* in the beginning of this chapter is a popular folk song in Taiwan, and relates a real story that happened in the late 19th century. A young woman from a prestigious family fell in love with a Dutch doctor, but this golden-haired lover never came back to carry out his promise to marry her. She was left heart-broken and shamed. Maybe a sad love story means nothing in the traditional sociology and history studies; however, this folk song reveals that besides taking military action and trading in the Far East, the Dutch also had relationships with Taiwanese women; or at least one Dutch man did. If she had been brought to the Netherlands at a later time, maybe the immigration history of the Chinese would be longer than one century. Could it not be? We know too little about the real-life experiences of Chinese migrants in the Netherlands even though the Dutch and Chinese people have had mutual interactions in culture, economic, and the military for a long time. As a feminist, and as a Chinese, I believe that women tell better stories than only recalling the past. As Patricia Hill Collins (2000), reminds us: "If we will not listen to one another, then who will? (p.24)", I try to build women-centred knowledge from the margin. As a subordinate group which has been long ignored and hidden from Chinese migration studies, the narratives of women can reverse the object position to the subject in epistemology for "women's perspective can discredit sociology's claim to

---

[48] Smith, Dorothy. 2004. "Women's Perspective as a Radical Critique of Sociology" Pp. 21–34.

produce objective knowledge that is independent of the sociologists' situation" (Harding, 2004: 17).

The epistemology of this research is rooted in the feminist standpoint theory offered by Dorothy Smith (1987) as a way of building knowledge from oppressed subjects whose presence and voices have long been excluded by the privileged, male-dominant knowers. "Its methods of thinking and its analytic procedures must preserve the presence of the active and experienced subject" (p. 105). As well as the feminist standpoint theory, I also apply the intersectionality theory and linguistic analysis as another two methodologies. Firstly, I see the feminist standpoint epistemology as a tool for knowledge development in this research in two ways: 1) to see and understand the real life situation through the eyes and experiences of Chinese women; and 2) to theorise and bring the narrations from subordinated Chinese women to the centre of Chinese migration studies, as the feminist standpoint epistemology requires the fusion of knowledge and practice. As Abigail Brooks, and Sharlene Nagy Hesse-Biber (2007), argue, it is both a theory of knowledge building and a method of doing research – "an approach to knowledge construction and a call to political action" (p. 55).[49] As an international student, I had neither relatives nor many other connections here, nor did I speak or read Dutch in the beginning. My situation is in some ways similar to those first-generation Chinese migrant women who came to the Netherlands as expats, leaving most of their kinship and social connections behind. Like them, I have tried to settle down and pursue a new life here. This becomes a very good starting point for me. As an outsider free from care work and a migrant woman myself, I observed and felt the environment and society from the start, like most Chinese migrant women in the Netherlands. However, that I am a single woman with no family and without financial pressure makes me different to them. In this respect, I pay attention to the intersectional differences between Chinese migrant women, and try to make sense of their diverse experiences, which resulted from their backgrounds. Lastly, I use linguistic analysis as my third methodology in this research because I found migrant women's perception about motherhood and womanhood to be highly gendered and culturally embedded. By analysing the particular character, jargon and idioms they use, I consider linguistic analysis as a suitable methodology to make sense of Chinese migrant women's gendered ideology and how they perceive themselves as mothers.

[49] Brooks, Abigail & Hesse-Biber, Sharlene Nagy. 2007. "An Invitation to Feminist Research." Pp.1–24.

There has been at least 100 years of Chinese migration to the Netherlands; however, the presence of Chinese women was hitherto ignored and neglected by both the academic and social world. They seem to live invisibly and quietly behind the windows in grocery shops, restaurants or massage parlours. The general images of Chinese are that they are diligent, polite and hard-working. In 2011, the Institute for Multicultural Affairs Report described how well Chinese children perform in school (p.5), but throughout that report, unfortunately, there is not a single word about how overseas Chinese women teach their children or how their lives are in the Netherlands.[50] Chinese women play a significant role in educating children but their effort and significance have seldom been taken into consideration in Dutch society. As Gloria Wekker mentioned, "It is important to look at the gendered processes of insertion and mobilization of women into migration" (2009: 68),[51] and that is where the research begins. As a Chinese feminist studying in the Netherlands, this is a "women-centred" research through which I seek to break down the gender-blind and male-oriented Chinese migration studies and Dutch migration studies.

Emigration is a significant decision for all migrant women in this research. They see emigration as a stepping-stone to happiness and a better future. Early post-emigrant life is difficult for them and it takes time to adjust to a new environment in the Netherlands. When a seed drops on the ground during a snowy winter, the cold freezes it. While waiting for the spring and the warm sunshine to come back, this seed hears the howling of the wind and feels the frost on its skin. With long patience and diligence, it finally gets sufficient water, air and warmness to sprout, similar to my interviewees, standing in a humble and marginal position. I, as an interpreter and mediator, who devotes herself to recording and writing their real life experiences, to leave footsteps and open spaces in the Chinese migration study and gender study fields. I am eager to urge that it is time for the scholars of migration studies to listen to women's experiences from the margin. I am trying to rewrite the history of Chinese migration in the Netherlands into her-story, make Chinese women's inner voice be heard, make their experiences be seen, and make their narratives be recognised intellectually, just as Smith (1987) argues: "For actual subjects situated in the actualities of their everyday worlds, a sociology for

---

[50] See Forum factsheet June 2011 by Institute for Multicultural Affairs, access date August 01, 2011, http://www.forum.nl/Portals/International/English-pdf/Factsheet-Chinese-in-the-Netherlands.pdf.

[51] Wekker, Gloria. 2009. "Into the Promised Land? The Feminization and Ethnicization of Poverty in the Netherlands." Pp.65–77.

women offers an understanding of how those worlds are organised and determined by social relations immanent in and extending beyond them" (p.106). I hope this research can establish feminist epistemology in Chinese migration studies. Let the presences and voices of Dutch Chinese migrant women become the subjects of knowledge.

I apply intersectionality as a second methodology because I found the classic feminist standpoint epistemology cannot fully represent "women" in my research; although it emphasises the importance of women's subjectivity in the process of knowledge building, women's experiences between white and non-white in the West are totally different stories. Chinese women were entirely absent in the 1970s and 1980s while Western feminists were fighting for women's rights and gender equality. Inspired by Patricia Hill Collins' "Black feminist thought and matrix of domination" (2000), I found that the social position of Chinese women in the USA shares a similar fate and situation with African-American women in the USA, who "simultaneously experience and resist oppression on three levels: the level of personal biography; the group or community level of the cultural context created by race, class, gender; and the systemic level of social institutions" (p.227). Chinese and African-Americans are both victims under Western imperialism. Many Chinese labourers were exported to the USA from the second half of the 19th century as disposable coolies to dig for gold, build the railways or work as cargo workers. Although they were not literally slaves like the African-Americans, as Gungwu Wang (1994), argues, their lives and their treatment by the host society were de facto slavery. They lived segregated from whites. They were seen as inferior, like animals.[52] The research concerning the early experiences and lives of Chinese migrant women in the Netherlands is not valued, like their counterparts in the United States.[53]

---

[52] For instance, in Shanghai 1903, the French government declared the controversial Hongkew Park Regulations when Shanghai was a foreign-leased-territory ruled under French Empire. Article 1 said: "No dogs and bicycles are admitted," and Article 5 said: "No Chinese are admitted, except servants in attendance upon foreigners." Since then, Chinese are seen as dogs in the white Western eyes. This cultural icon was largely used in the Chinese Kong Fu movies as a symbol to show how Chinese are regarded as inferior by the Western world (i.e. Bruce Lee's movie, Fists of Fury). See the argument from Ishigawa, Yoshihiro. 1999c "Inu to Chukokujin ha hairubekarazy" (Review the issue of Chinese and Dogs are Forbidden) Pp.75–94. 「犬と中国人は入るべからず」問題再考.

[53] About the lives of Chinese labourers and the ethnic cleaning of Chinese in the United States from the late 19th century, see Pelzer, Jean. 2007. In chapter five, the

Chinese women are a shadow, hidden in the flow of Chinese diaspora. They have no face, no voice, even no space and record in academic literature. Even the most prestigious overseas Chinese historian Gungwu Wang (1994), who summarised the history of Chinese diaspora from the 18th century, remained nonchalant about the contribution of Chinese women. His only mention of his mother was that she taught him Chinese characters at the age of three, when his family settled in British Malaya to escape WWII (interviewed by Liu 2004[54]). The same situation applies in mainstream Dutch society, where the existence of Chinese women has long been ignored and dismissed. When it comes to Chinese women, either they are eroticised as Orientalist (Said, 1979) or they are seen as potential "gold diggers". Moreover, because of my own personal unpleasant experience at the IND (Immigration and Naturalization Service, Ministry of Security and Justice[55]), which I will explain in more detail in chapter six, I felt obligated to bring Chinese women's experiences forward in academia. Western society simply treats Chinese migrant women differently from class and ethnicity and pays little attention to the power dynamics between their social relationships and intra-connection. Thus, I applied the concepts of intersectionality (Crenshaw, 1994;[56] Davis, 2008; Wekker, 2009) as another methodological approach in this research. With the different geographic regions in which they grew up, the different generations, the different educational levels, and the husbands with different nationalities, my respondents present various narratives on motherhood, womanhood and identities. To be more precise, I found that Chinese migrant women in the Netherlands, especially amongst the first generation, face a variety of discriminations at the same time, such as race, gender, class, and language. In chapter six, I show how Chinese migrant women deal with discrimination, and how oppressions and the product of their intersections impact their daily lives and their motherhood practices.

---

author describes the lives of Chinese women at that time. About the true stories of modern Chinese slavery labour and human trafficking in the United Kingdom, see Pai, Hsiao-Hong. 2008. There are also some famous literature works that reveal the family history on Chinese diaspora and their post-emigration life in America. See, for example, Amy Tan (1995) *The Hundred Secret Senses*; Amy Tan (1989) *The Joy Luck Club;* Amy Tan (1991) *The Kitchen God's Wife;* Fae Myenne Ng (1993) *Bone*; Gish Jen (1996) *Mona in the Promised Land*; and Jung Chang (1991) *Wild Swans: Three Daughters of China.*

[54] Liu, Hong. 2004. "Looking Forward, Looking Back: An Interview with Wang Gung Wu" Pp. 13–21.

[55] To read a complete story, see later in this book.

[56] Crenshaw, Williams Kimberlé. 1994. "Mapping the Margins: Intersectionality, Identity Politics, and Violence against Women of Color." Pp. 93–118.

In respect to the third methodology, linguistic analysis, I was inspired by American sinologist Perry Link's work on analysing political slogans or propaganda from the 1930s to 1960s in China. By the time Link worked in Beijing, he sensed that nearly all the political slogans "carried an aura of correctness but were usually abstract enough" (2013: 14). Link collected these political slogans and propaganda sentences and anatomised their syllabic patterns between phrases and particular grammatical constructions to interpret the political meaning behind them. Ambiguity is one of the characteristics of Chinese languages. I found Link's methodology interesting but I am more aware of the gendered meaning embedded in every character and grammatical construction in special idioms. Inspired by French feminist Luce Irigaray's "interpretive reading,"[57] I try to combine reading migrant women's utterances with a gendered lens and Chinese linguistic analysis. Hence, from chapter three to chapter seven, I interpret Chinese migrant women's narratives with linguistic analysis, which helps me realise the ambiguity of the Chinese language and gendered politics hidden in those narratives.

In the next section, I first illustrate the research methods, the fieldwork and the backgrounds of my interviewees. Then, I describe my interpretive process on how I transform colloquial conversation into texts and how I make these texts into meaning.

2.2 Methods

I used in-depth interviews and participatory observation (Liamputtong, 2010) to collect research materials. As I mentioned earlier in chapter one, my initial research idea was motivated by an accidental encounter in the One Hundred Lions Dance Festival (2011, Amsterdam). Back in Utrecht, I started to contact some of my acquaintances who are Chinese migrants in the Netherlands. I promptly contacted Apple, who has a six-month old baby and lives in Maastricht. I explained my intention to do the research and I volunteered to babysit for half a month. Apple showed great interest in my research idea and she accepted my interview and babysitting proposal. Apple became my first respondent in this research and with her assistance I was able to enter her social network in southern Netherlands. There, I began three pilot interviews and fieldwork. I joined women's family activities, such as a BBQ and tea party. I observed how mothers interact with children, the interactivities between wives and husbands,

[57] See Luce Irigaray (1977), translated by Carolyn Burke (1985), page 75.

daughters-in-law with their in-laws, and the use of mixed languages (Dutch, Mandarin, Cantonese, and Wenzhou dialects) for daily conversation.

I met Apple in a Dutch beginners' class in the School of Professional and Continuing Education, Fu-Jen Catholic University, Taipei, Nehu branch, which is the only place that teaches Dutch in Northern Taiwan. I went to the class twice a week, three hours per session. At that time, Apple[58] was three-months pregnant, and would emigrate in two months' time. While waiting for a visa to the Netherlands, she learned basic Dutch daily conversation after work in order to adjust to Dutch society sooner. Three of our class were married to Dutch men, three were involved with Dutch men, two of us were about to pursue higher education, and the other two were present for career requirements. Back then, I did not realise this short encounter would be significant for my doctorate research.

In the second interview with Betty, I found she was reluctant to talk more with her Chinese husband present.[59] I asked her the same questions while helping her cook in the kitchen and taking a walk with her grandchild. Only in those moments did I hear her real opinion about the questions. After that, I politely asked the interviewees to have a one-to-one, face-to-face, absolutely confidential conversation while conducting interviews.

In order to know how first-generation immigrant Chinese mothers carry out their motherhood in the Netherlands, I chose the in-depth interview as my main research method for it seeks to understand the "lived experiences" of the individual.[60] I am interested in getting at the "subjective" understanding an individual brings to a given situation or set of circumstances. As American feminist scholar Sharlene Nagy Hesse-Biber argues: "The in-depth interview method is issue-oriented, thus a researcher might use this method to explore a particular topic and to gain focused information on the issue from the respondents." (2007: 118). From September 2011, I issued interviewee-wanted information by email to different Chinese organisations[61] in the Netherlands. Thanks to the

---

[58] In order to protect the privacy of the interviewees, I use pseudonyms throughout this book.

[59] Although this phenomenon seldom happened among women with Dutch husbands, three middle-class Chinese women told me that their Dutch husbands asked them "not to share too much family business" with me before the interview.

[60] See Scott, Joan W. and Mohanty, Chandra. 1991. "Under Western Eyes: Feminist Scholarship and Colonial Discourses" Pp. 333–358.

[61] The organisations are The Foundation 100 Years Chinese People in the Netherlands, TaiwanShianChin Association, Voor Welzijn Den Haag, the Chinese women's association in Den Haag, and the Overseas Chinese women's

TaiwanShianChin Association, who were the first to distribute the information through their newsletter and Facebook page, I got several invitations to join the Dragon Boat Festival, Mid-Autumn Festival,[62] and sports matches. I was also invited to family dinners and children's outdoor activities. I even got a few chances to do interviews in the restaurants or coffee shops run by the interviewees. In October 2012, I engaged in participant observation at the Mandarin class in the Chinese supplement weekend school in Utrecht and The Hague. At every event and interview, I observed some humorous interactions, conversations and the interior decorations. For example, nearly every interviewee had decorated their house with some Chinese elements, i.e., Buddha's head, a laughing Buddha, Chinese knots, Chinese calligraphy, fengshui rock, eight trigrams, fortune waving toad statue with a coin in its mouth, a map of Taiwan and China. Some of them proudly showed me their Chinese teapot collection; some shared their current favourite Taiwanese or Hong Kong soap opera on satellite TV channels. The materials were collected by field notes, digital camera and digital recorder. Besides field work and interviews, I also searched for useful data from Chinese newspapers, Dutch magazines and newspapers.[63] I spent one year studying Dutch in both Taiwan and in the Netherlands thus I could have a basic daily conversation with the interviewees and their families.

The interviewees

By the end of February 2013, I had conducted 38 interviews; all were face-to-face semi-structured questionnaires with digital recording[64] lasting between one to six hours. The interviewees have at least one child and the mean age is 48.80. The oldest is 70 and the youngest is 30. The mean number of children is 1.9. Eighteen of them come from Taiwan; 14 come from China and 7 come from Hong Kong. Their mother tongues include Taiwanese, Cantonese and Wenzhounese to Shanghainese. Mandarin is the

---

organizations in the Netherlands. I didn't get any response from The Foundation 100 Years Chinese People in the Netherlands.

[62] The Dragon Boat Festival and Mid-Autumn Festival are the other two important traditional festivals, after Chinese New Year, for Chinese people. People get together to eat and dance and maintain personal connections.

[63] Thanks to my supervisor, Gloria Wekker. She often gave me some interesting articles from Dutch magazines and newspapers otherwise, I wouldn't have even noticed these materials.

[64] All of them read and signed the letter of consent and I made sure they all recognised the purpose of the interview.

official language in China, Taiwan and Hong Kong; thus it can be seen as the heritage or official language of the interviewees. Most of them can speak Mandarin,[65] English and Dutch. The mean living length in the Netherlands is 17.50 – the shortest duration is two years and the longest 40 years. Among the 38 interviewees, two are widows, two are divorced, one is separated, and two are remarried. Sixteen women married white Dutch men, two women married Dutch Chinese.[66] Seven women married Taiwanese men, seven married Hongkonger men, and six women married Chinese men.

The highest educational level of interviewees is PhD and the lowest is elementary level. Three of them received their highest education in the Netherlands.[67] The other 35 received their education from the countries of origin (See table 2-1). Due to the different education systems between Taiwan and China, ten women who received vocational school diplomas are Taiwanese. Six of them majored in international trade, one majored in accountancy, one majored in interior design, and the other two majored in IT technology. Before migration, 37 interviewees had worked full-time for at least five years. The educational level of my interviewees is consistent with the research of Mérove Gijsberts et al. (2011), in which it appears that "Chinese migrants in the Netherlands are relatively well educated....The education level of Chinese women in the Netherlands is higher than that of men…it is caused mainly by the fact that there are more women among study migrants: two-thirds of recent first-generation migrants with a high education level are women." (pp. 183–184). Some are full-time mothers while others work part time and/or full time. Except for one interview which was conducted in a village near the Dutch and German border, 38 interviews were conducted around cities: Amsterdam, Utrecht, Den Haag, Eindhoven, Rotterdam, Leiden, and Leeuwarden.

---

[65] Due to the separate regimes of two Chinas: the PRC and the ROC (Taiwan), the official language has various names. In Taiwan it called *Guoyu,* 國語 (national language); in China it is called *Putonghua,* 普通話 (common language or common speech). In Hong Kong, both terms are local vernaculars.

[66] About these two migrant Chinese men: one came to the Netherlands at the age of three and the other one was born in the Netherlands.

[67] Two were PhD students back then and one got her master's degree in the Netherlands.

Table 2-1 Interviewee's Educational Level

Education level	Number of people
Primary school (up to 12 years age)	5
II level secondary school Senior high school in Taiwan (up to 18 years of age)	7
Vocational school (The old education system in Taiwan study from 16 to 20 years of age)	10
University	9
Master	5
PhD	2

I was constantly aware that my educational level has symbolic power over the interviewees; some of them, being socially isolated from the outside world for years, were very shy and were not confident in what they said in the first place. I would reduce their nervousness and build confidence by saying "There is no correct answer when it comes to mothering. Every woman's feelings and experiences are unique. Besides, speaking of mothering, you are an expert, that's why I am here humbly to learn from you." I tried to build a rapport, which brought trust and connection with my interviewees. Most of them felt relieved and empowered after the interview and we have been friends since then. They told me how happy they were that their life experiences contributed to my dissertation. They had never revealed some words and feelings to anyone because they could not find the opportunity, and they did not think their husbands and children would understand. I keep in touch with some of my interviewees, sharing opinions and daily life on Facebook or on their personal blog. I am constantly being invited to their weekend gatherings and have become very close to some of them. Somehow, I can feel they are longing to look after me as their younger sister in the country of origin, or as their daughter. Furthermore, I am like a living role model for their children to look up to and my presence is a very good opportunity for their children to practice their Mandarin.

The interpretive process

My first three pilot interviews were exploratory. I had no idea about how they raise their children and how they earn a living. I was also curious about why they were willing to leave everything behind to move all the way to the Netherlands. From the first three interviews and field notes, I began to find interesting topics or meaningful sentences, which I started to code. I divided my semi-structured questionnaire into six basic topics, namely, personal background, how they become acquainted with their husbands, marriage decision, delivery experience, motherhood practices experiences, feelings about Dutch society, and migration. There was no absolute order during the interview. Most of the time, I followed the emotion and preference of the interviewees throughout the interview. I made sure they answered all the six topics. Sometimes it took longer than I expected so the interview could not be completed in one session. I visited my interviewees twice or three times to finish all the questions.

To transform digital sound to transcription is a time and energy-consuming process. In order to perceive the feelings and details of the interviewees, I first keyed the interview almost word by word in Chinese characters. I did not simply translate the transcription into English in the first place in order to avoid making the common mistake that Chinese researchers make to shorten data analysis time. As a researcher who chooses to conduct women-centred in-depth interviews, one must understand the sensitivities of and have a high competence in Chinese vocabulary. Meaning can easily be lost in translation and the validity of the data may be compromised in this process. Chinese is a language in which one pronunciation can have several functions and meanings in different sentences and expressions, and with the intonation the meaning can vary quite considerably. Take one simple example; there are 34 characters all pronounced as *jia*. It can mean home, good, furniture, add, wound, or marry out, etc. The researcher must pay attention to the tones very carefully in order to distinguish which *jia* and in what context the interviewees use it. Especially when people express sad or angry feelings, some words will be replaced by others, which are either pronounced exactly the same or the positive sentence can actually mean sarcasm. For example, when being asked about how they feel about Dutch society in general, most people will begin with "Yes, Dutch people are in general very nice and friendly la." *La* 啦 is a very common ending expression for something opposite to the previous meaning. It is just a sound often used at the end of the sentence but it carries significant irony and negative emotion. If the researcher misses this sound, one can possibly misunderstand the whole meaning of the sentence. In fact, the interviewee expressed that Dutch people are nice and friendly in general, but she has some different opinions against this assumption. If the researcher misses this subtle, implicit and very feminine ending expression, one will never realise the meaning behind this sound. I proceeded with initial coding on the original transcription and circled and underlined the phrases and sentences that I thought significant. I used the Find function of Microsoft Word and Excel software to calculate the times of the chosen vocabularies or phrases appearing in one transcription. Along with the six topics, I began to collect the related themes and divided them into different categories.

In conclusion, the knowledge in this book is built on the basis of 38 interviewees' narratives with regard to their post-emigration lives and their motherhood practice experiences in the Netherlands. By conceptualising first-generation migrant Chinese women's narratives, this knowledge building is an outcome of collaboration between the researcher and the interviewees. It has uncovered a long-term neglected hidden voice and allowed it to be heard.

CHAPTER THREE

MOTHERHOOD DISCOURSE IN WESTERN FEMINISM AND CHINESE CONFUCIANISM

3.1 Prologue

Migrant Chinese women constantly deal with cultural conflicts between Chinese and Dutch motherhood. An old Chinese motto goes *chimu chu baier* (a soft mother raises a failed son; 慈母出敗兒) and many Chinese women take this aphorism to heart. They firmly believe that it is their responsibility to educate "successful" children through strict discipline. However, one man's meat is another man's poison. At least five mothers in this study expressed their discontent with the inconsistent childrearing ideas between them and their family members. For instance, Quentin, a 45-year-old, middle-class Taiwanese woman, told me that her husband often complains that she controls and disciplines her two teenage children too much. Sometimes, their (Dutch) husbands or their children even call them "tiger mothers" or "Asian Moms", which makes them feel very upset, frustrated and isolated. They feel that no one understands their efforts to educate their children and their hard work. To address the causes of this cultural contradiction on motherhood, I think it is necessary to look at the trajectories in which motherhood is defined and constructed in Western and Chinese societies.

In this chapter, the concept of and debate on motherhood and maternity in various Western feminisms and Chinese Confucianism are discussed. The content is divided into four main sections: The Western feminist motherhood debate; social norms and motherhood in Chinese society; social norms and motherhood in the Dutch social context; a short review of some Chinese migrant studies in different countries and the discussion on the "Tiger Mother" phenomenon in Western media.

To understand the dynamics of motherhood practice experiences of first-generational Chinese immigrant women in a Western society, it is first necessary to review the development of the motherhood debate in Western feminist theories. Indeed, from a social constructionist perspective, people are brought up gendered and culturally embedded to a significant extent. When women become mothers, their gendered and culturally embedded points of view can be passed on to their children through their everyday-life motherhood practice. The women I interviewed in this research, for example, all grew up in societies that mainly practice Confucian ideology; however, as a feminist scholar, I was aware that gender relations and motherhood in Chinese society have been changing dramatically and rapidly under the influence of second-wave feminism in the West (Lu, 1981; Lee, 1989; Deng, 1994; Su, 1996). Some affirmative actions were implemented to promote gender equity in contemporary Chinese society. For instance, married women can preserve their surname heritage from their natal families. From 1919, a married woman not having to change her surname into her husband's originated from the May Fourth Movement in China. Taiwanese women were forced to change their surname into their husbands' during the colonisation period under the Japanese Empire (1895–1945). After 1945, the new law permits women the choice to freely decide whether they want to change their surname into their husband's or not. Basically, the act of changing your surname into your husband's is considered extremely old-fashioned, conservative and backward in both Taiwan and China nowadays. Or, take another instance, in Taiwan from 2007, children can use their mother's surname without any preconditions.[68] This change is considered a big victory for the feminist movement in Taiwan for it breaks through the Confucian patriarchy.

Thus, one should not essentialise and Orientalise Chinese migrant women's motherhood into simply a "tiger mother" stereotype, but understand it from a subtler approach and take into account different intersections such as class, educational level and age in a host society. Furthermore, I think that the very social context that situates migrant women daily in a host society is also a significant factor that one should pay attention to. In this respect, the dominant motherhood ideology in mainstream Dutch society should be taken into account as well. It will help us realise more about the social interaction and power dynamics of Chinese migrant women's motherhood practice in the Netherlands.

3.2 Western Feminist Debates on Motherhood

The rhetoric of motherhood has always been at the centre of feminist discourses. Feminists have challenged the taken-for-granted dichotomous

---

[68] Before 2007, only if a woman had no other male brothers could her children use her heritage surname with her husband's permission.

assumption in which women are doomed to be a mother and a domestic caregiver because of their biological sexual difference to men. From the emergence of the first-wave feminist movement in the late nineteenth century until now, feminists have undertaken not only to criticise the imposed biological reproduction responsibility of women but have also theorised it to a broader socio-structural gendered inequality. The issue is whether women, as mothers, are the victims of an unequal gendered labour division or are empowered through motherhood practices, and it is still non-conclusive. Their theories break through the private/public dichotomies and call for broader attention to women's differences on the intersections (i.e. class, race, education, age, and sexual orientation). Later in the 1990s, the motherhood debate moved forward to analyse the gendered relationships between women's reproduction and nations; the real-life situation of immigrant women and their transnational motherhood practice in a host country. In this section, I will give a brief review of various representative feminist theories regarding motherhood debates in the Western context from the first wave to now.

3.2.1 The first and the second wave feminist movement

Liberal Feminism

It is generally agreed that Mary Wollstonecraft is one of the forerunners of Western feminist philosophers. Her innovative and bold work, *Vindication of the Rights of Women* (1792), is the origin of modern feminist philosophies. As a white, middle-class British intellectual in the late eighteenth century, Wollstonecraft set out her view that the social systems such as education and suffrage deprived women of equal rights, rationality and participation in public and political affairs. She argues that women can become full persons with intact rationality, equal to men, as soon as they are given the right to education. However, under the then British social restrictions, she urges that women can gain their agency through raising dutiful citizens, and their male children will thus mediate women's political representation. In this respect, she recognises that the significance of women as mothers is a core of self-identification. Moreover, her viewpoint on bringing up male children as a medium for a mother herself to take part in the public domain is quite similar to Confucian ideology in which a woman would be honoured if she educated a great son who makes an abundant contribution to the emperor and to the society. Although her feminist thoughts on motherhood tends to be contradictory to her gender egalitarian thinking (Tomaselli, 1995; Ford, 2009), Wollstonecraft's liberal feminist thinking has greatly influenced the second-wave feminist movement.

Contrary to Wollstonecraft's positive recognition of motherhood, in the mid-1950s, French existentialist philosopher Simone de Beauvoir states that women's oppression comes exactly from motherhood for women are not destined to be a mother just because of their in-born biological reproduction capability. The reason women are regarded as "the Second Sex" (1949) is a myth from patriarchy. Hence, to achieve personal emancipation, women should abandon motherhood which makes them oppressed and discriminated against. Another well-known representative of liberal feminism in the United States is Betty Friedan. In her work, *The Feminine Mystique* (1963), she argues that for middle-class women, motherhood is a myth that is created by patriarchy to imprison women in the private sector. While it may seem a happy life on the surface, from her empirical studies on suburban housewives, it becomes clear that white, middle-class women usually suffer from "the problem that has no name". Friedan argues that the gendered mystique constructed by male-defined patriarchy, which encourages women to devote themselves to their "natural" mission as housewives and mothers, is the ultimate cause for women to lose their autonomy. In short, liberal feminists have challenged the private/public domains in the legal system and have asked for equal rights with men in suffrage and education. Nevertheless, in the motherhood debate, liberal feminism remained very white, bourgeois and heterosexist. Liberal feminists have either treated motherhood as a method for alternative political participation by their male children or have blamed motherhood as the cause for women's oppression.

Radical Feminism

The emergence of radical feminism during the 1970s again stirred up the heated debate on motherhood. On the one hand, it denounced the biopolitics of patriarchy, which subordinates women's position because of their "natural biological difference". On the other, it claimed the corollary of women's role as mothers is a fallacy resulting from the social construction of patriarchy, which is a breakthrough of scholarly thinking on the bio-determination of sex and gender. Consequently, some radical feminists sought for material-based possibilities for women to emancipate from their reproductive nightmare; some claimed that the sex/gender system is a historical product of Western Christianity; others urged that women should distinguish the maternal system from maternal experience, and embrace the value of the uniqueness of individual motherhood practice.

Let us start with Shulamith Firestone, a central icon in the initial development of radical feminism during the second-wave feminist movement in the USA. Firestone seems to be a true believer of modern reproduction science technology as she pointed out in 1970 that if women's oppression originates from their reproductive fertility function in biology, then to dispose of this root, one can fully rely on modern scientific technology. She illustrates the origin of women's oppression from a Marxist materialist perspective and argues that the labour of child producing is the root of women's inequality. Thus, she considers that the only way to achieve women's emancipation is to abandon biological mothering. In her view, women should take advantage of artificial reproduction technology to avoid the biological function of child delivery. Nevertheless, Firestone ignores the power dynamics of class, culture and the historical context of how sex is constructed into gender. She also fails to remark upon the realm in which modern reproduction technology, i.e., IVF, is defined, controlled and carried out by white male elites in a much-gendered medical system.

Apart from Firestone, Gayle Rubin (1975 in Reiter[69]) claims that Western society sees sex as a sin under the large influence of Christianity and Victorian morality. The sex/gender system is a large structural system composed of sexual hierarchy. Inside this sexual value system, an "ideal" women's sexuality is connected to heterosexual, marital, monogamous, reproductive, and non-commercial sex. In her words, the gender order in Western society defines "a set of arrangements by which the biological raw materials of human sex and procreation is shaped by human, social intervention and satisfied in a conventional manner" (p. 165). Her insight indicates that the connection between women and mothering is a historical product rather than a natural outcome. This very sex-gender system pre-dates the industrial revolution and it has been long taken for granted. In a nutshell, motherhood is the artificial outcome of male-dominant socialisation and patriarchy.

Another radical feminist worth mentioning is Adrienne Rich. Rich (1976) argues that one should separate motherhood into the mothering experience and the motherhood institution. The former is positive and valuable and is a source of women's creativity and joyfulness. It is the latter that manipulates and degrades women's value through patriarchy. According to Andrea O'Reily's interpretation of Rich, she indicates that "The term *motherhood*[70] refers to the patriarchal institution of motherhood

---

[69] Rubin, Gayle. 1975. "The Traffic in Women: Notes on the 'Political Economy' of Sex," Pp. 157–210.

[70] Emphasis in original.

that is male-defined and controlled and is deeply oppressive to women, while the word *mothering*[71] refers to women's experiences of mothering which are female-defined and centred and potentially empowering to women" (2008: 3). Hence, what really oppressed women does not originate in motherhood itself. She urges that women in different social positions speak out about their mothering experiences and construct sisterhood bonding. However, O'Reily failed to point out the double oppression (sexism and racism) on black women, such as Rich's black nannies, who not only practiced as surrogate mothers for white women but also worked as domestic labourers in Rich's family during her childhood. The intersectionality of women's motherhood and its value is discussed later in this chapter.

Psychoanalytic Feminism

Psychoanalytic feminist schools focus on the inner meaning of motherhood and the mental development of both sexes by analysing the power dynamics of childrearing. In the Anglo-American context,[72] psychoanalytical feminists such as Dorothy Dinnerstein (1977) and Nancy Chodorow (1978) criticised the phallocentric argument in Freud's theory, which imputes women's inferiority to the lack of male genitals. They are against this male-defined, sexist biological determinist psychoanalysis but address the significance of social and domestic power relations affecting the mental development of both sexes during childhood.

For instance, Chodorow (1978) proposed the concept of "The Reproduction of Mothering", which indicates that motherhood is less of a biological imperative than an interactive production influenced by complex social, cultural, economic, and mental power dynamics. Part of her theory follows Freud's psychoanalytical tradition; for example, she considers that women's desire to become a mother rises from their subconscious. She argues that the cause of men's desire to suppress women is mother-dominant childrearing. This is because during the development of boys' pre-adult lifespan, women are their main caregivers, which triggers the terror to take control back after they grow up. Boys

---

[71] Emphasis in original.

[72] About the same period in Western Europe, especially in France, another psychoanalytical school appeared. They are called Lacanian feminists (Luce Irigarary, Helene Cixous and Catherine Clement). Their approach is to illustrate the relationship between language and sex-gender. In this part, I only focus on the theory of American Freudian psychoanalytical feminists since their arguments are more related to the social construction of motherhood.

learn to separate from their mother for emotional independence while girls tend to acknowledge their mother's femininity and gender role at home. What is important is that boys and girls go through a different asymmetrical trajectory to adulthood. While for boys the love object can remain the same, girls need to switch identification from mother to father in order to make a love object. In this respect, Chodorow urges more balanced and egalitarian dual parenting in childrearing, which she believes will eliminate the male children's anxiety about mothers generated by an extremely gendered parenting style. Psychoanalytical scholars also interpret sexual differences in mentality from women's development. For instance, Carol Gilligan (1982) describes women as relational and men as instrumental and rational. She then concludes further that women's identity is rooted in personal network relationships and connections.

Anne McClintock's work, *Imperial Leather: Race, Gender and Sexuality in the Colonial Contest* (1995), which discusses the nineteenth-century gendered power relationship in domesticity, is significant because she introduces an intersectional perspective, taking class into account. It centres on the relationship between a maid, Hannah Cullwick, and her secret upper-class husband, Arthur Mundy, a barrister. By analysing their photos and Mundy's manuscript, McClintock deconstructs Freud's theory and rearticulates working-class female domestic labourer's agency. Her surrogate caregiver practice takes place in a bourgeois private domain, and it is in her power to be the initiator of a younger man's sexuality. McClintock shows how working-class women have been written out of the domestic bourgeois triangle of the child and its parents.

In short, psychoanalytical feminists challenge the long-term male-centred psychoanalytical study: on the one hand, they keep reinforcing the bio-determinist dichotomy with regard to the gendered division of labour. On the other, their theories remain in a white, middle-class, heterosexual orientation. During the second wave, a different voice from marginal social positions challenges the ideals of white and middle-class-centred motherhood feminism, which is the emergence of black feminism, discussed in the following part.

Black Feminism

One of the most significant contributions of black feminism to feminist epistemology is that it challenges the normative position of middle-class, white patriarchal motherhood and womanhood. According to Collins

(1994),[73] the emergence of black feminism came not from the scholarly debate but from the narrative writings of African American women's autobiographical and fictional works.[74] Their writing stirred up the later scholarly black feminist theory after the 1990s. Through their personal narratives and real-life observations, African American women's work challenged mothering, which is framed as devalued, isolated and private, and which makes women secondary to men (Collins, 1990). Shirley A. Hill (2008)[75] examines the transformation of socially constructed images of African American women's motherhood in the United States from the late 1800s to post-World War II, and she points out that African American women's motherhood is seen as an Otherness in society. She argues that it is a racialised construction of motherhood (p. 109) and it has been given multiple meanings and social images during different periods. For instance, before the abolition of slavery, the notion of the enslaved woman's motherhood was embedded in West African culture, which praises women's fertility and cherishes the procreation ethic. Women's fertility and motherhood are a source of power and esteem for women (p.108). She mentions "some enslaved black women used their childbearing ability as an instrument of personal fulfilment and as leverage in their relations with slave owners" (p. 109). From this perspective, enslaved black women's sexuality, fertility and motherhood are sources for them to fight against heavy labour and slavery. However, Hill's arguments on black women's sexuality and motherhood practices during slavery ignore the impact of the oppression of sexism and racism on them.

As American feminist scholar bell hooks (1982) criticises, "The black female was exploited as a labourer in the fields, a worker in the domestic household, a breeder, and as an object of white male sexual assault" (p. 22). In the African context, women's pregnancy and motherhood were highly treasured and appreciated in various cultures while during slavery, black women's sexuality was treated inhumanely. Most black women were raped; they constantly suffered unwanted pregnancies without proper rest

---

[73] Collins, Patricia Hill. 1994. "Shifting the Center: Race, Class, and Feminist Theorizing about Motherhood," Pp. 371–389.

[74] Collins gives some examples of African American women's autobiographical works such as Ann Moody (1968) *Coming of Age in Mississippi*, Maya Angelou (1969) *I Know Why the Caged Birds Sings* and Marita Golden (1983) *Migration of the Heart*. As for fictional works, Collins mentions, for example, Alice Walker (1976) *Meridian* and Toni Morrison (1974) *Sula* and (1987) *Beloved*.

[75] See: Hill, Shirley A. 2008. "African American Mothers: Victimized, Vilified, and Valorized," Pp.107–121.

and enough nutrition.[76] Black women were treated as the property of the white slavers, and as a result, their sexuality became a machine, reproducing more workers bound to the white masters. As hooks argues: "Breeding was another socially legitimized method of sexually exploiting black women… that white men in colonial America defined the primary function of all women to be that of breeding workers" (1982: 39). hooks further claims that white feminists tended to ignore the dark history of enslaved women and its fundamental double oppression on the black female experience. Some even romanticise its seriousness (ibid: 1). Furthermore, after the abolition of slavery, African American women's motherhood was victimised, vilified and stigmatised. White feminists reinterpret black women's motherhood during the history of slavery as ultimate victims because of racism, sexism and capitalism. Moreover, their sexuality is seen as promiscuous, e.g., sees black women as "reckless breeders" and they are portrayed as poor "welfare queens" (p. 109). Thus, the positive image of African American women's motherhood in the past has been denied. It is stigmatised as a new "social problem" which should be monitored and corrected to "normal" (p. 116). Hill argues that most research on black women is overgeneralised and oversimplified. Only the intersectionality theory and its approach can show the diverse experiences of black women regarding their social class, age, marital status, educational level, sexual orientation, and so on. In sum, black feminism plays an important role among feminist theories to voice from the margin, to shift the centre, and to provide non-white women's values and experiences.

As is clear from this discussion, feminists' scholarly contributions to debates on motherhood before the 1990s have stimulated broader and more diverse discussions and research. In the next part, I mention some important feminists' works relating to gender and motherhood after the 90s.

3.2.2 Motherhood debate: 1990 to the present

Though there is no precise definition of third wave feminism in academia, from the temporal point of view, Gronold et al. (2009) argue that "Third Wave feminism sees itself as a form of inclusiveness, opening up a space for young feminists who enjoy and celebrate the possibility of taking up multiple identities" . O'Reilly, for instance, emphasises in the introduction

---

[76] See also Toni Morrison's novel, *Beloved* (1987), which tells the life story of an African-American slave Margaret Garne.

of *Feminist Mothering* that "the intersectionality of various 'isms,' such as racism, classism, heterosexism with sexism, work against the notion of hierarchy itself, many feminists view this broadened emphasis in feminism as a Third Wave of feminism" (2008: 15). However, I am not convinced that there is a clear line between second and third wave feminism based on the focus on intersectionality. During the 80s, black feminists such as bell hooks (1982; 1984; 1989), Kimberlé Crenshaw (1989), Patricia Hill Collins (1986; 1987), Alice Walker (1982), and Audre Lorde (1984) all spoke out from the margins and called for social attention to the long-running racism, sexism and social inequality towards black women and the different values and meanings of motherhood practices of black women. Among them, Crenshaw is the first feminist scholar who proposed the term "intersectionality" be applied to feminist works. Through this approach, the discussion on differences (e.g. class, sexual orientation, age, and race) between women or social groups would be revealed and could be compared in detail.

Besides, historical research indicates that it was wrongly alleged that only a few black women had participated in the second wave movement. For instance, American feminists Rosalyn Baxandall and Linda Gordon (2000) argue that during the end of the 60s to the mid-70s, there were many small black women's organisations in the United States, but their objectives were different from the mainstream white women's organisations; later, their efforts were ignored by the middle-class white feminist scholars. They also mention that many black feminists were rejected and their voices excluded by the mainstream white women's organisations. In other words, it was the classism and racism inside the women's movement that segregated one group from another rather than that second wave feminists were indifferent to intersectionality. Dutch feminist scholar Iris van der Tuin questions the fairness and justice in defining feminist movements by labelling different "waves" from a Eurocentric, middle-class, heteronormative and even racist point of view (2009: 11). As she argues, "It is a mistake to believe that one wave's strategy is better than the other, because equality did not disappear from the scene when the first wave came to an end... (thus) the idea of generational dialects is founded on generalizations that ignore the complexities of history" (ibid: 12). In this respect, I do not think it makes sense for some feminists to claim that paying attention to "intersectionality" and the "new generation" are the characteristics and new era of the third wave.

Back to the motherhood research after the 90s, how do feminists perceive the scholarly direction of this field? Samira Kawash (2011) considers that new directions of motherhood studies by feminists should pay more attention to the individual's experience, agency, subjectivity, and power, especially in the process of motherhood practice and interaction with power dynamics (p. 979). In this respect, motherhood research after the 1990s should take intersectionality into account and not just stay in the realm of the ideas of white, middle-class-centred patriarchy and deterministic bio-dichotomy. To make a scholarly connection with my research of migrant Chinese women's motherhood in the Netherlands, in this part I focus on the motherhood debate offered by feminist scholars after the 90s, especially on the relationship of motherhood and nation. It is from this research that I found a macro political perspective: there are two main mechanisms which deeply involve migrant women's motherhood per se – one is how the relationship between women's motherhood and nation is valorised by mainstream discourses in their countries of origin; another is how women's transnational motherhood is reconstructed after emigration by their host countries.

Women, Motherhood and Nation

Women have been ignored and excluded from the discourse of state and nation for a long time. The dichotomous social construction of gender roles between civilisation/nature, public/private and superior/inferior are the key elements through which women have been eliminated from nationalism. Many feminist scholars have criticised gender-blind nationalism theories and have tried to rewrite "her-story" from feminist perspectives (Enloe, 1989; Jayawardena, 1986; Kandiyoti, 1991; Parker et al., 1992; Pateman, 1988; Yuval-Davis, 1980; Yuval-Davis, 1997).

Ironically, only on reproduction and educational issues do women become the main stakeholders in their countries of origin. Women are constructed as mothers of the nation, titans of the national struggle, or even held responsible for supporting half the nation (Mao, 1943). Women's biological reproduction ability thus becomes the tool of the nation. Yuval-Davis (1997) points out three main discourses through which authorities put pressure on women to have, or not to have, children. The three discourses are: the "people as power" discourse, which sees maintaining and enlarging the population of the national collectivity as vital for the national interest; the Malthusian discourse, which, in contrast to the first discourse, sees the reduction of the number of children as the way to prevent future national disaster; and the eugenicist discourse, which aims at improving the "'quality' of the national stock" by encouraging those who are "suitable" in terms of origin and class to have more children and discouraging the others from doing so. Under the manipulation of national purposes, women are considered not as independent human beings but as members of specific historical collectives. In short, reproduction decisions become a social act, one that could be regulated legitimately. Take the Netherlands as an example: recently, I read an article titled "Vrouwen: baar meer baby's" (Women: bear more babies) in a mainstream Dutch tabloid,[77] *De Telegraaf*. Robin Fransman, a Dutch economist, was urging the government to make a birth-promotion policy for women because the population replacement rate of the Netherlands will drop to 1.7. He considers that every Dutch woman should have an average of 2.1 children to make sure there will be enough tax to support the aging Dutch society in the near future. The main target population of Fransman's birth-promotion policy is Dutch women, but he didn't indicate specifically white Dutch females. He urges that the government should put pressure on women, give them more incentives to make them breed. According to Yuval-Davis's theory, Fransman firmly believes the "people as power" discourse. When there seems to be fewer taxpayers for a nation, it is women's responsibility to reproduce.

After reviewing the historical development in American society, Sharon Hays (1996) found that by the second half of the 19th century, child rearing was synonymous with mothering. The image of the mother was imbued with purity, piety and patriotism. The state constructed for urban middle-class women, in particular, an important role as "republican mothers," educating and socialising the republic's future citizens (p. 29). This again corresponds to Yuval-Davis's the "people as power" discourse. Women not only give birth but also fulfil the task of being the cultural and moral mediators of the next generation. The state acted as a manipulator to promote the greatness of white, well-educated, middle-class women on the one hand, while it depreciated non-white, alien, low-class women as cultural invaders or potential "social problem-makers" on the other. In this respect, Yuval-Davis's three discourses are not mutually exclusive; women, according to their race/ethnicity and class, are categorised into different discourses. White middle-class women are desired by the patriarchal state and their fertility is demanded based on the "people as power" discourse; while non-white, alien, low-class women are devalued and their fertility is discouraged based on the eugenicist discourse.

What about the situation of migrant women's motherhood in host countries? The research undertaken on women's post-migrant experiences has been scarce. Prior to the mid-1970s, women were not a research topic for international migration studies in the European context (Kofman,

---

[77] As for the relationship between Chinese women's motherhood and their countries of origin, I will come back to that in the next section.

1999). Emigration to Western countries is certainly a new opportunity in a woman's lifetime, but that does not guarantee that a migrant woman will be free from the nation-state's patriarchal control of her fertility and motherhood practice, especially for those from the so-called Third World. On the contrary, it is simply because of her migrant status that she becomes a policy target, which her receiving country is eager to manage and control; as Gloria Wekker claims, the "exotic and barbaric Other" (Wekker 2009 in Hine et al.[78]). This strong dichotomy between native nationals as unproblematic and foreign outsiders as problematic is explicitly shown in the Dutch context, namely, the separation of the autochthonous (natives) as "us" from the allochthonous (foreign) as "them". This dichotomous political rhetoric is gendered and racialised as well. As Dutch social scientists Conny Roggeband and Mieke Verloo (2007) argue, the development of the Dutch gender equality policy between 1995–2005 has a strong indication to construct the populist images that Dutch women are liberated and migrant women are suppressed, especially Muslim migrant women.

Furthermore, the control of migrant women's motherhood is a product resulting from the combination of what Yuval-Davis calls the "people as power" discourse and nationalism. For instance, European demographic studies scholars and politicians warn against future economic development decline because of the low fertility rates in most of the EU countries. Simply stated, they view that recruiting young migrants is one way to increase the population. Nevertheless, they are highly concerned about the large number of migrants with non-Western cultural backgrounds who will sabotage the current European social cohesion. Famous European social demographic researchers Wolfgang Lutz et al. urge European governments to make selection criteria part of their immigration policies for they consider that "to be called a European, there should be some sense of European identity in addition to a strictly national identity" (2006: 5). Unfortunately, they fail to define or offer their definition of "European identity". Austrian scholar Brend Baumgartl (1995) argues that this kind of neoliberal xenophobic nationalism (p. 2) has been carried into the immigration policies in most Western European countries. It resulted from the alleged "cultural fundamentalism" and fear of change. Its objective is to slow down the speed of European integration (p. 5). However, as another author Ernest Gellner in the same book[79] points out, it is harmful

[78] See: Wekker, Gloria. 2009. "Another Dream of Common Language: Imaging Black Europe…." Pp. 277-289.

[79] See: Gellner, Ernest. 1995. "Introduction: Nationalism and Xenophobia." Pp. 6–9.

for future European social development to stress xenophobic discourse and make it into public policy because "by linking dislike of the Other to citizenship rights, nationalism turns xenophobia from what may, in favourable circumstances, be a mere human foible, into a destructive, dangerous force" (1995: 7).

Here I want to provide two empirical studies on non-white migration women's situations in their host countries as examples to show that non-white migrant women are not desired immigrants in European countries because of their alien culture, lifestyle, beliefs, and lack of "some sense of European identity" in mainstream eyes. For instance, Ronit Lentin's research (2004) on migrant mothers' representation in mass media in Ireland is an example of how mainstream discourses reshape non-white migrant women as conniving to subvert Ireland's citizenship and nationality norms. Thus, the white majority can maintain their superior socio-economic position and exclude non-white immigrants from the public realm. Furthermore, their children are also portrayed as "black", "Nigerian" or "Romanian", regardless of their origin. The purpose of mainstream media is to create Ireland as a "racial state"[80] and to deter so-called "third world" female immigrants.

Stereotypical thinking about non-white migrant women by mainstream society may cause serious consequences. To take another example, when Ruth DeSouza (2004) conducted interviews on midwifery in the British medical system for migrant women from India, she found that most of the medical staff express racist discourse towards non-white migrant women, especially towards those of the first generation who speak English poorly. They view them generally as backward, passive, emotional, oppressed, and pathological (p. 465). The stereotypical thinking of medical staff towards non-white migrant women also prevents them from detecting postnatal depression (PND) in its early stages, which results in a more emotionally and socially isolated situation for migrant women after becoming a mother in a foreign country.

Similar gendered and racialised discourse against migrant women by mainstream society also happens in Northeast Asia. In my own MA research, I studied Taiwan's policy construction of the low fertility phenomenon. Applying Bacchi Lee's (1999) "What's the Problem"

---

[80] Lentin explains how Ireland's dominant mass media use mass media opinion to construct a "racial state". In her words, it is a kind of project which tries to maintain the privilege of the majority "because racial states are never complete, they need to reaffirm themselves through population control technologies, imposed on women's bodies, and through prescribing which women are entitled to give birth to the citizens of 'the nation'" (p. 305).

approach as my research methodology, I concluded that the elite discourse linked the so-called "baby bust issue" with lowered economic growth, lower population quality, and even to imbalanced population composition. Yet, while the authorities construct the disadvantages of baby bust on the one hand, they call on patriotism on the other hand, using class and racially discriminating propaganda to devalue those who are not Taiwanese, specifically immigrant women who come from Southeast Asia (mainly from Vietnam, Indonesia and Thailand) through "commodified transnational marriage (CTM)[81]". Moreover, as I also noted at the time, the authorities do not pay much attention to the decreasing numbers of female babies; the preference to have male babies, and the whole reproduction idea, is still firmly built on compulsory heterosexuality and patriarchal heritage. Finally, the government does not foresee population decrease as an inevitable trend in post-industrial society nor is it making a holistic and timely plan in response.[82] In my current research, six middle-class migrant Chinese women compare their social positions in Dutch eyes as similar to "foreign brides" in Taiwan or Hong Kong. In the Netherlands they are called "allochtonen" (foreigners, outsiders, who are not native, white Dutch people). I will leave the examples and further discussion to the following chapters, but to give a short conclusion now, those hegemonic, gendered and dual discourses with hierarchal connotations, such as we/other; native/foreign; white/non-white; West/East, have a greater impact on migrant women's daily-life motherhood practices in Western society.

Nonetheless, non-white migrant women's non-European or non-Western cultural background, which is seen as backward or a burden and which needs to be abandoned after emigration, functions as a source of empowerment for them in motherhood practice and in negotiation within their conjugal relationship. In her empirical research on 24 Asian-French couples in France, Taiwanese family studies scholar Chyong-Fang Ko (2012) discovered that the French language barrier is a major problem for the foreign spouses in the early stage of emigration, and it makes them emotionally and economically dependent on their French partners. However, when it comes to motherhood or during processes of decision-making, some of the individuals feel empowered by their cultural capital or Asian values. In the next section, I discuss how motherhood has been constructed and practiced in Chinese society.

---

[81] This term is coined by Hsiao-Chuan Hsian, 2000, p. 48.
[82] See Shu-Yi Huang, 2008.

3.3 Gender Norms and Motherhood in Chinese Society

To understand the gender norms and motherhood ideology in Chinese society, one can read them from two dimensions: linguistics and the classic works of Confucianism. I came across *An Anatomy of Chinese: Rhythm, Metaphor, Politics* by American sinologist Perry Link (2013), and it provided me with a lot of inspiration. In this work, Link analyses the political slogans during Mao's era, and argues, "The way rhythms can *mean*[83] and it is parallel to the sense in which certain grammatical constructions convey implications" (p. 6). His methodology gave me the idea to uncover the gendered politics and metaphors by examining the regulations of Chinese characters. Let me begin with linguistics. Chinese culture is deeply embedded in its regulations of character creation. The meanings of those characters related to a woman's life cycle show explicitly in them. Every character has its own cultural connotations and all of them begin with its *bushou* (部首; radical or indexing component of a character). Modern Chinese characters share 214 bushou which indicate the category and taxonomy of each character. For instance, the well-known five elements, *jin* (金; gold), *mu* (木; wood), *shui* (水; water), *huo* (火; fire), and *tu* (土; soil), are all *bushou*. These *bushou* can make different characters with various combinations. Take mu as an example. One mu means wood. Two mu makes *lin* (林; bushes or jungle). Three *mu* becomes *sen* (森; forest). No matter how *mu* combines with other characters, even in a complicated form, such as *shu* (樹; tree), One can always find *mu* (木) in it and can guess the character has a connection with wood. This is how *bushou* functions in Chinese characters.

Now let me turn to *nu* (女; a girl or a woman). Every Chinese character that implicates a woman or female has 女 as its *bushou*. Take, for instance, the adjective *hao* (好; good/ positive); if you take a close look, the *bushou* 女 stands on the left and on the right stands *zi* (子; a child, a son). This explicitly tells people that a woman with a son means good. A woman who has a son is a positive deed. Thus, by carefully scrutinising the transformations of characters, one can tell the socialisation process of a Chinese woman embedded in Chinese culture. To realise why motherhood is significant for a Chinese woman, one must understand the *jiaqu* (嫁娶; marriage) system first. Unlike the gender neutral verb of marriage in the

---

[83] Emphasis by Link.

English language,[84] Chinese characters for marriage have quite different meanings when referring to the male or to the female.[85] For a man, to marry a woman is "*qu* (娶)". The word *qu* is composed of two parts. The first upper part "*qu* (取)" means to get or to take; the second lower part "*nu* (女)" means a woman; *nu* is also the *bushou* of this character. Hence, for a man to take a woman constitutes the meaning of the act of marriage. He has the control and power to determine which woman he wants to choose as his wife. It is the opposite for a woman to marry a man, which is "*jia* (嫁)". The word *jia* is also composed of two parts. The right side is a standing *nu*; and the left side is "*jia* (家)", meaning a home. Thus, for women the meaning of a marriage is to walk into a man's home. She has to wait and acquire a husband who is willing to provide her with a home. In the Chinese patriarchy and household system, after a woman registers her marriage in the local household registration office, her family name will be deleted immediately and her name will then be transferred to her husband's household. People think this is the real "home" for a woman.[86] This *jiaqu* not only hides in Chinese characters but is also practiced in Chinese marriage rites. Maurice Freedman observed Chinese marriage rites in his anthropological study of Singapore and Hong Kong . From a Western gaze, he conceptualised Chinese marriage rites as follows: "The main body of rites constituting a wedding segregates the girl from her ordinary life in her natal house, prepares her for the pains and duties of her married life, transfers her in a state of marginality to her new house, and begins the process by which she will be incorporated there".[87] This is the basic concept of *jiaqu* culture in Chinese society: a symbolic heritage with gender inequality expressed both in its characters and in its social customs.

---

[84] In English, the verb "marry", its meaning and concept do not change if the subject is male or female.

[85] This discussion is in the heterosexual social context in Taiwan, Hong Kong, Macau, and China because none of the four areas recognise same sex marriage.

[86] When I discussed *jiaqu* culture and its practice in Taiwan society with my mother, she told me that she burst into tears while watching her name being crossed out by an administrative with a ruler from her natal household column. She had a feeling of being kicked out of her original home that had raised her for almost thirty years. This marriage household registration system still exists in Taiwan, South Korea, Japan, Hong Kong, Macau, and Singapore. Fortunately, from 1998 Taiwanese people can choose to hold their original households or current residence address while having a marital registration.

[87] Freedman, Maurice. 1970, p.183.

After marrying into her new family, to secure a stable position under the husband's roof, a woman must produce a male heir to extend the husband's family line. It is the only way to be truly accepted in this family and her name will either be listed in the ancestors' hall or she will die as nothing and her spirit will suffer endlessly in limbo.[88] Now, let me explain the character of *mu* (母; mother). According to Xu Shen (許慎)'s *Shuowen Jiezi* (說文解字[89]), *mu*'s radical is *nu*, which symbolises a woman holding a baby and breastfeeding it. Those two drops vividly illustrate a woman's post-natal life, breastfeeding her child in her arms. The characters' transformation from nu to mu indicates a women's life cycle from a girl to a mother as well. Then, what are the gender norms imposed on Chinese women during this process? To answer this question, one must turn to how male elites construct and regulate womanhood and motherhood in classic Chinese philosophy.

It is agreed that Confucius's Three Followings is the fundamental principle for all Chinese women to follow to become proper and virtuous. The contents of the Three Followings are "as a daughter one must obey her father; as a wife one must obey her husband; as a mother one must obey her son." Nevertheless, it is said that the appearance of Hongmou Chen's *Jiaonu yigui*[90] (Inherited Guide for Educating Women)[91] during the second half of the eighteenth century set up the ideological foundation of the Maoist discourse on women's roles and responsibilities of the modern China construction[92] (Rowe, 1992; Barlow in Grewal and Kaplan, 1994[93]).

---

[88] This kind of social practice and folk belief is still maintained in some conservative families in Hong Kong, Taiwan and China. See, for example, Freedman, Maurice. 1970. "Ritual Aspects of Chinese Kinship and Marriage". Pp. 163–187.

[89] *Shuowen Jiezi* (說文解字) was the first book in Chinese history that specifically explains and analyses characters and their affiliation radicals; it dates back to the Eastern Han Dynasty (25–220 AD). To check *Shuowen Jiez*i online, please go to Chinese Text Project website: http://ctext.org, where you can read all the Chinese classic works free online.

[90] Chen Hongmou (陳宏謀) (1696–1771) was the prestigious provincial governor and the royal recognized scholar during the mid-Qing Dynasty. Readers can access his *Jiaonu yigui* on the Chinese Text Project website: http://ctext.org/wiki.pl?if=gb&res=636436.

[91] The exact year of the publication is unknown.

[92] As for the Maoist discourse on women's roles and responsibilities of modern China construction, please see chapter four.

[93] Barlow, Tani. 1994. "Theorizing Woman: Funü, Guojia, Jiating (Chinese Women, Chinese State, Chinese Family". Pp. 173–196.

Chen's most critical contribution to modern China is that he promoted women's education in the feudal monarchy of China, when the Han ethnic group was under the reign of the Manchu regime and women's private education was only accessible to the elite class. Chen was of the opinion that educating women could be beneficial to family and knowledge development as he defined a woman's role in the life cycle and her connection to *sangang* (三綱; The Three Bonds); namely, ruler: subject, father: son, and husband: wife under the Three Followings principle:

> As people are living at a *jia* (家; lineage unit/family) they are *nu* (女; female/daughter); by the time they marry out, they become *fu* (婦; wives). When they start to rear their children, they are *mu* (母; mothers). If you start as a *xiannu* (賢女; virtuous unmarried female/daughter) then you will end up as a *xianfu* (賢婦; virtuous wife). If you act as a virtuous wife, you will become *xianmu* (賢母; virtuous mother). A virtuous mother insures (raising) virtuous descendants. A country's civilization begins in the women's quarters. Everyone in a *jia* benefits from women's chastity. This is the reason why women's education is that significant.[94]

Although Chen did challenge the conservative social norms of his time, his views on women's roles still do not surpass Confucian patriarchy. The existence of the well-educated woman serves the family and raises future virtuous descendants for the husband's family. According to Chen, women are not only biological reproducers of the subjects for the monarch but also his cultural reproducers. The primary purpose for letting women be educated is to make sure that they can raise "useful" subjects in the future, and because the children brought up by a virtuous mother are the source of a strong empire which can maintain its authority. Women's personal reputations, achievements and social status depend on her children's academic performance and the political contribution to the emperor.

The social punishment for disobedient women in ancient China was severe. According to Bin Shu & Lin Wei (1993: 6–8), around 200 BC during the Han Dynasty, the so-called *qichu* (七出; seven sins) were legislated in the book *liji* (禮記; Book of Rites). The *Qichu* Articles endowed a man with the power to divorce or exile his women (wife; concubines) based on seven sins. Generally speaking, these seven sins were: unfilial to parents (in-laws); childlessness; adultery; jealousy;[95] a

---

[94] The English translation is mine.

[95] Here it means the wife is jealous of husband's concubines particularly.

woman has a fatal illness; gossip; and theft. Among these seven sins, the most serious one was childlessness. Even now, childless Chinese women are considered useless, sick, dysfunctional, and selfish. Women with only a single daughter have a better and higher social reputation than childless women. The Qichu Articles were strictly implemented from the Tang Dynasty (the 7th century) until the early 20th century (ibid: 9). To deliver an heir and educate the child well are the core values and virtues of Chinese womanhood and motherhood. One must realise that the concept of illegitimate children is a modern product in contemporary Chinese society. It was not until 1941 that the monogamy system was legislated into Marriage Law. Before that, every child, regardless of his/her mother's conjugal relationship with the father, was legitimate by law. Under this revised system, the status of the wife is under constant threat if the concubines' (male) children were better in academia than her children. The most famous example in Chinese history is Empress Dowager Cixi (1835–1908): she was one of the thousands of concubines of Emperor Xianfeng. According to Chinese historian novelist Jung Chang (2013: 3), Empress Dowager Cixi was even nameless on the first day of court registry; at the beginning of her life in the Forbidden City, she was simply written as "the woman of Nala family". Because of her son and her own diligence in learning politics, governance, and her good performance in motherhood, a humble concubine turned out to be the most powerful and influential woman during the second half of the 19th century in China. In other words, I argue, in the game of Chinese patriarchy, that motherhood performance is a competition between women. It is deeply and culturally embedded and it has become a gendered social norm.

Even though later in the upheaval of the Late Qing Hundred Days' Reform (1898) some male nationalists, like Youwei Kang, Chicao Liang and Sitong Tain, urged the emperor to abolish female foot binding and to open public schools for female pupils, Chinese historian Lydia Liu (1994) points out that the ultimate purpose of the Hundred Days' Reform was not women's emancipation but rather "the need to mobilize the nation in the face of imperialist powers which gave rise to the tantalizing notion of women in order to *preserve the nation* and *save the Chinese race*".[96] The objectives of these reformists on women's emancipation through education and the abandonment of foot binding were indeed considered as progress then; nevertheless, women remained as a medium and instruments to serve

[96] Liu, Lydia. 1994. "The Female Body and Nationalist Discourse: The Field of Life and Death Revisited". p. 42. Italics mine.

the interests of the patriarchal state, to ensure they can deliver healthy heirs through their healthy bodies. The Chinese historian Wei-zhi Deng points out that one of the significant arguments for foot-binding abolishment that reformists proposed to the Emperor was *baozhung baoguo* (保種保國; protect seeds in order to strengthen the kingdom) (1993: 31). These reformists considered that foot binding made women ill and unhealthy. An ill mother cannot possibly produce healthy children. Thus, the seeds are the metaphors for children. In their minds, to reconstruct a strong Qing Dynasty, the first priority was to ensure women's healthy bodies. In this respect, the reformists' women emancipation policy corresponds to Yuval-Davis's "people as power" theory. As Lydia Liu argues that the national identity of Chinese from the late 19th century is largely a male prerogative (ibid: 55), the honour and the praise of the tantalising notion of women in China are nothing but through patriarchy and nationalism, men control and manipulate women's sexuality, body, and their free or low-paid physical and emotional labour in both the public and private domain to serve their interests. To be more precise, Chinese women are considered living human-producing objects, a collectivity to perpetuate the patriarchal lineage. Under the control of the Confucian patriarch, women have no freedom of independent thinking and opinion: their individual and national identities are the same as those of the men. A Chinese woman's value is judged by the achievement of her children, in particular epistemological achievement. Educating children well is a way for a Chinese woman to be praised and rewarded with reputation, financial support, and social class upgrading. On the one hand, it is an imposed, compulsory and homogenous identity which has been constructed and strengthened by Confucian patriarchy and nationalism throughout history. Yet, on the other hand, her relationship with her children and her way of disciplining and educating them are her leverage and agency to bargain and overturn Confucian patriarchy and nationalism (Wolf in Freedman, 1970;[97] Wolf, 1985; Xin, 2002; Koh et al., 2009).

As we now understand the cultural background of Chinese woman, in order to know which new social milieu she will encounter while being a mother in the Netherlands, in the next section, I will shift my focus to the gender norms and motherhood in Dutch society.

---

[97] Wolf, Margery. 1970. "Child Training and the Chinese Family". Pp. 37-62.

3.4 Gender Norms and Motherhood in Dutch Society

In Dutch society, images of motherhood and its social norms can be discussed from at least two angles. First, it can be analysed from the representation of images of motherhood. Second, it is valorised by the discourse construction of ideal motherhood from government public policy. The definition of an ideal Dutch motherhood changes chronologically. Let us start from the first domain: representation of images of motherhood. In her research about the contemporary literary representation of Dutch motherhood, Josje Weusten (2011) argues that Dutch literature represents motherhood as an idyllic, rosy-spectacled image (p. 271). It is the result of long-term social construction from the 1970s and it has become dominant since the 1980s. The subject of idyllic Dutch motherhood is a white, middle-class, heterosexual, full-time mother in a nuclear family, content with her choice to be a mother with young children. If a woman does not feel joyful and blissful as a mother, she must seek professional help. Since this idyllic, rosy-spectacled motherhood image is taken for granted in Dutch society, the negativity and mental depression of motherhood have been taboo topics and not mentioned in public. It is only in fictional novels that the dark side of motherhood can be discussed and made visible. Weusten analysed that since the 1980s, Dutch female fiction authors, (e.g. Vonne van der Meer, Saskia Noort, Renate Dorrestein, and Maya Rasker) started to write about the social taboos of unwanted motherhood, depression and the life pressure of traditional Dutch housewives.

Furthermore, after World War II, images of Dutch motherhood have been gradually transforming from the traditional family style into an individualised tendency in the mass media (Knijn, 1994 & 2004). After analysing two popular Dutch women's magazines, *Libelle* and *Margriet* from the 60s to the 80s, Trudie Knijn (1994: 185–191) found that three images of motherhood emerged within these three decades; in the 1960s, the motherhood image was self-sacrifice exclusively in the household and the motherhood style was intuitive. The mother played a pivotal role in the big family with many children. In the 70s, motherhood was constructed as a professional job, which put children's development at the centre and followed the instruction from male intellectuals' childrearing suggestions. In the 80s, motherhood was viewed as a choice, a self-asserted matter, but once a woman chose to have a child, she was still expected to put her child and family first before pursuing her own career. Knijn then conducted a survey among 543 mothers who had at least one child under seven years of age, with the purpose of finding out modern Dutch mothers' attitudes toward motherhood practices. She concluded that modern Dutch women are facing a "social dilemma" to become mothers. The social presupposition about the modern woman's image is in contradiction to the real-life constraints that women must deal with: the fixed gender role distribution in a traditional breadwinner/caregiver model causes women to be stuck in a double bind situation. Another research corresponds to the individualising tendency among women in the Netherlands. Carine T. G. M. Ex and Jan M. A. M. Janssens (2000) conducted a survey of 165 (predominantly white) young women under 22 years of age about their motherhood expectations in the future. The results are that young Dutch women perceived themselves as less traditional and are more inclined to have their own economic independence as well as being a mother.

Let us look at two recent quantitative studies as examples of the social dilemma of women's individualisation. By analysing data from the Netherlands Kinship Panel Study and Tobit regression, de Meester et al. (2007) found that only in strongly urbanised areas do women work more hours than women living elsewhere, while men in strongly urbanised areas work fewer hours than their rural counterparts. According to their research result from table 4 (p. 594), the mean number of working hours for women living in a very strongly urbanised area is 33.2 whereas their counterparts living in a moderately urbanised area is 26.8. In the men's situation, the mean working hours for men living in a very strongly urbanised area is 40.5 whereas their counterparts living in moderately urbanised area is 43.0. They gave two explanations for the result. First, Dutch women in general still bear more household burdens than men because of gender inequality. Second, only women who live in a very strongly urbanised area[98] perform more hours of paid work (p. 598). This research shows that not only do personal life course concerns matter to Dutch women's social dilemma, the gap and opportunities for married women with children to participate in the labour market also relate to her residential context. In other words, the geographical developmental gap between urban locations and country areas is significant to women's employment opportunities.

Another research done by Cecile Wetzels (2005) examines the effect of the Child Care Stimulation Act from 1990 on the price of childcare and its relation to female labour supply. By cross-analysing the 1995 AVO (*Aanvullende Voorzieningen Onderzoek*) data, Wetzels argues first that

---

[98] This research does not indicate the precise name of the so-called "very strongly urbanised area" but it provides the criteria of the measurement. It used the degree of urbanisation which takes the address density of a municipality (p. 591). There are five categories in this system, ranging from "not urbanised" (< 500 addresses/km2) to "very strongly urbanised" (≥ 2500 addresses/km2).

compared to the Swedish government, the Dutch government spends a much smaller social efficiency cost in the child-care subsidised system: the total costs of the formal childcare was 33 percent in 1996 while the Swedish percentage was 85. Second, she found that Dutch parents generally pay 42 percent of childcare costs in parental fees and their employers pay about 22 percent. Third, Dutch mothers are much less likely to participate in the labour force than their Swedish counterparts, and most Dutch women work part-time, with fewer working full-time when compared to Swedish mothers (2005: 199). This research gives a clear indication that although the Dutch government keeps emphasising that childcare costs and responsibilities should be shared by the government, employers and parents, the real cost borne by government and firms is still low, which allows women to only work part-time, and it also leads to the common and famous Dutch one-and-a-half breadwinner model. As Dutch gender scholars Jet Bussemaker and Rian Voet (1998) point out, Dutch women have been stereotypically depicted as being very good housewives (p. 3) because family policy and welfare policy design in the Netherlands has a strong "breadwinner model" tradition (p. 5). This model started to transform from 1976 onwards because of the *emancipatiebeleid* (emancipation policy). This policy aims to promote women's social status by encouraging them into the labour market; however, women still carry most of the domestic care responsibilities, which results in women having mainly part-time, low-wage and short-term jobs. Conny Roggeband and Mieke Verloo (2007) called this phenomenon the "1.5 Dutch model" (p. 285).

Another point I want to discuss here is the contradictory nature of the gender role assumption and contested social policy reforms. For instance, Knijn reads Hobson's idea of female individualisation as "the autonomy of women in all respects, economically, biologically, and socially, is considered to be a condition for social participation, self-esteem, and power, as well as offering an exit option from unhappy intimate relationships" (Hobson, 1990 in Knijn 2004: 57). Nevertheless, Knijn criticises some current Dutch social policy transformations, such as pension reforms, taxation, social assistance, and the "life course redistribution" policy proposal, in three ways. First, Dutch policy reforms lack consistency in dealing with individualisation. Second, with these reforms, it is in fact, hard to achieve "full individualisation", especially for women. Third, the Dutch government on the one hand takes gender equality into account but on the other, to some extent, continues to assume the traditional gender dichotomous distribution of the (male) breadwinner model, which hinders women's career opportunities to become full-time adult workers (ibid: 58–63). The tendency of individualisation and the rights aspects of citizenship can be observed from the policy shift as regards to single mothers. For example, in 1996, single Dutch mothers were required to search for paid work as a condition of social assistance benefit recipients when their youngest child turned five. However, it turned out in Knijn and van Wel's research in 2001 that only a small number of single mothers, one out of ten, actually leaves welfare dependence (cited from Korteweg, 2006: 318). In Anna C. Korteweg's comparative ethnographical research on workshops for helping single mothers with job hunting training in the United States and the Netherlands, she describes the intersectional conflicts and differences on the Dutch side between trainers and participants. She then concludes that in real social policy implementation situations, "the original social policies that try to institute gender-neutral social rights can lead to distinctly gendered form of citizenship" (ibid: 334).

In sum, motherhood in the Netherlands has been changing from nature's course after marriage from women's destiny to women's personal delightful choice. Nevertheless, given the gendered social realm and gendered role assumption of women as mothers, most Dutch women are still the sole caregivers in the domestic sphere and can only participate in low-wage, part-time jobs.

3.5 Motherhood Studies of Chinese Migrant Women

In this section, two parts are presented. First, I will give a short review of some previous studies about motherhood experiences and the practices of Chinese migrant women in order to give a global picture of transnational motherhood. Studies of recent motherhood experiences all show that contemporary Chinese migrant motherhood practices have a strong inclination to acquire Western education and cultural capital for their children. I start from Asia with studies on Hong Kong and Singapore, and then I turn to studies on North America. Although these first two regions are in East Asia, empirical motherhood studies tell different stories. Before 1997, Hong Kong was a colony of the United Kingdom in Pacific Asia. Hong Kong was built as a modern advanced centre and the Asian headquarters for Western transnational business. Thus, new generations of wealthy Chinese entrepreneurs moved to Hong Kong as a stepping stone to the next destination. Aihwa Ong, an American Chinese researcher, studied the so-called "astronaut families" in Hong Kong[99] and discovered that these upper-class Chinese developed unique and flexible understandings

[99] In Taiwan, people call this kind of family a "migrant bird family".

of citizenship.[100] In "astronaut families", the husband uses investment immigration to get a visa for America, Canada or Australia first. Then, he sends his wife and children there and he stays in Hong Kong or travels all over the world to do business. The family work distribution is typical: husband–breadwinner and wife–caregiver. The only difference is that the husband and wife do not live together, and the wife must raise her children on her own in an alien country. The wife acts as a "sacrificial mother" who supports her husband's career and educates her children in a better environment as well. However, Ong mainly focuses on the capital circuits under globalisation and how they affect businessmen in Hong Kong. She did not conduct further anthropological research on the motherhood experiences of "astronaut wives".

The case of Singapore is different. In order to encourage upper-class Chinese people from China to send their underage children to Singapore to receive a better education, the Singapore government issued a special visa called the Long-Term Social Visit Pass (LTSP) in 2000. The original purpose of the Singapore government was to encourage mothers to spend more time with their children, especially when the child is just starting school in Singapore. Those who hold the LTSP visa are called '*peidu-mama* (陪讀媽媽[101])' and in Singapore, this term is a particularly negative label for women from China. Wan-Jung, Chao (2009) argues that in Singapore these *peidu*-mamas were seen as a deviant and promiscuous other. Under the Confucian ideology of motherhood and in the social imagination, a *peidu*-mama should act like the perfect mother, sacrificing all for her children and always being there for her children. The Singapore immigrant policy constructs *peidu*-mamas as non-paid caregivers; however, most *peidu*-mamas have to stay at least five to eight years for their children to get permanent residence. The long time apart from their husbands in China causes the breakdown of the marriage. These women cannot find decent jobs in Singapore; their desperate financial crisis forces them to become underground prostitutes. Singapore society thus blames *peidu*-mamas for damaging the social order and Chinese female virtues. However, Chao only interviewed 12 women and her analysis fails to see the resistance and agency of the *peidu*-mamas to fight the social stigma.

I mention the above-mentioned studies to show readers that even inside the Asian countries where societies follow Confucian ideology in daily-

[100] See Ong, Aihwa. 1999.

[101] The term *peidu* means "accompany child for study." In Singlish they are also called study mamas. But *peidu* mama in Mandarin especially describes a woman who brings her children from China.

life practices, social control and the gender norms about motherhood are still different from each other because of the migrants' individual intersectionality. Now I turn to migrant Chinese women's motherhood practice studies in North America.

Most motherhood studies in North America focus on the middle-class, highly educated Chinese migrant women's educational or discipline strategy to find out how they apply their cultural capital to their motherhood. For example, Yi-Jiuan Huang (2011) wonders how well-educated Taiwanese women practice their motherhood in America, and how they deal with their marginal status in a new environment. She interviewed seven Taiwanese women, all of them followed their Taiwanese husbands to America. Huang found that even though these women are well-educated, in the initial immigration stage the responsibility of their caregiver roles are more stressed. They must comfort the young children and husbands first and help them adjust to the social isolation and integrate into American culture. The attitudes of the husbands are more important than their educational level. If husbands share some housework and childcare, women are relieved from some of the responsibility. However, none of her interviewees can be voluntarily childless. Their American dream is based on providing the next generation with a better life and not on their individual development. Two of Huang's interviewees continued with an MA degree, with the purpose to equip them for a future job. Thus, the family will have extra income expenditure for the children. As the children grow, these women have to deal with the cross-cultural conflict in motherhood practices. How to balance the American and Chinese culture becomes the greatest challenge. Most of them feel empowered by mothering. Their relationship with their children becomes closer if mothers can slightly revise the Chinese authoritarian model. In sum, how these women use their social capital to negotiate with Chinese patriarchy and cultural pressures from their societies to perform a flexible and creative motherhood is significant.

Chinese migrant women's agency in negotiating with Chinese patriarchy and gendered culture in the host country corresponds to Ong's cultural citizenship concept. Ong (1996) pointed out that the new middle-class Asian immigrants in metropolitan countries perform a model of self-made cultural citizenship in relation to nation-state and transnational processes. On the everyday processes people negotiate the boundaries and lines of difference established by state agencies as well as ethnic groups in civil society (Pp. 740–741). From the experiences of Chinese migrant women in the United States, one can say that women as mothers are the cross-cultural mediators who may not be totally emancipated from

Chinese patriarchy, but they have more space and power to bargain with than women in Hong Kong by making their own unique motherhood practices.

Motherhood is a vital role for Chinese women, particularly for them to survive in a new environment. These two recent Chinese transnational motherhood studies undertaken in Singapore (Chao, 2009) and the United States (Huang, 2010) revealed that within migration an incommensurable burden is put upon women to keep the family together, and it is the stressed mothers' Confucian responsibility to educate children well regardless of their social class. The richer middle-class or upper-class Chinese families directly emigrated to English-speaking countries while not-so-well-to-do middle-class or working-class Chinese families seek the nearby Westernised Asian countries as a stepping stone to the West. The migrant Chinese mothers' main task is to assist their children to acquire Western higher education (e.g. English proficiency, Western cultural capital) first, and then the possibility of acquiring foreign citizenship in the future. To achieve this task, migrant Chinese mothers endure the separation from their spouses and family members and raise their children in a new environment by themselves. In the next section, I use the "tiger mother" phenomenon as an example of migrant Chinese mother's motherhood image representation in Western countries.

3.5.1 Migrant Chinese women's representation in Western mass media: "Tiger Mother" phenomenon

Recently, Amy Chua's[102] memoir, *Battle Hymn of The Tiger Mother*, dropped a bomb in motherhood and parenting practices and debates. The term "tiger mother" has rapidly become a buzzword and a symbol to describe the authoritative, top-down Chinese motherhood style. Her essay "Why Chinese Parents are Superior" in the *Wall Street Journal* provoked over 7000 comments. The Chinese mass media are going crazy about interviewing her; "Tiger mother" now represents not only the authoritarian and demanding motherhood practices of Chinese migrant women but also the Chinese ethnic glory, and an answer to why the Chinese can perform as a "model minority" in Western countries.

Here, I collected some negative critiques and positive feedback from some major newspapers and magazines. Christine Carter, author of *Raising Happiness*, mentioned three points in Huffpost Living why Amy

---

[102] Amy Chua is a professor working in the law school at Yale University. She is a second-generation American Chinese who has two daughters.

Chua is wrong about parenting: (1) "Chua defines success narrowly, focusing on achievement and perfection at all costs: Success is getting straight As and being a violin or piano prodigy"; (2) "Chua argues that happiness comes from mastery but she's wrong that forced mastery will lead to happiness" and (3) "Chua is prescribing life motivated by perfectionism" but "Perfectionists are far more likely to be depressed and anxious, and in college they are more likely to commit suicide". Carter values social connections, social skills and children's self-esteem more. She criticised Chua's coercive and insulting motherhood ideal, claiming it will destroy her children's mental health.[103] Psychologist Oliver James stated that the military-like parenting could reduce children's creativity. Lacking creativity is a major problem in Asian schooling.[104] Meanwhile, there is also positive feedback to *Tiger Mother*. Janine Wood says in the *Christian Science Monitor* that although she feels like a loser next to Chua, she admires that Chua struggles against "an unrelenting culture of stupidity".[105] Wood argued that most people missed Chua's main point. Chua pointed out a key idea is that "parents in this country need to give their children more direction." Chua's first daughter Sophia Chua-Rubenfeld was interviewed by *The New York Post* and admitted that "having a tiger mother was not a tea party" but she thanks Chua for teaching her one thing, that "even creativity takes effort".[106]

Some people discuss *Tiger Mother* from socio-economic perspectives. An article from the *Beijing Review* reflects how Chinese education has become a never-ending competition for rare resources. Both teachers and parents only focus on children's academic performance. Children have a heavy load of homework and suffer great mental pressure in competitive national exams. The educational system might be the origin of the tiger parents.[107] Patricia J. Williams, a law professor, analyses the possible reason why Chinese immigrants feel uneasy in America. Williams says it

---

[103] Source from (viewed August 6, 2011): http://www.huffingtonpost.com/christine-carter-phd/chinese-motherssuperior_b_808344.html?view=print&comm_ref=false

[104] Source from (viewed August 6, 2011): http://www.bbc.co.uk/news/magazine-12249215

[105] Source from (viewed August 6, 2011): http://www.csmonitor.com/Commentary/Opinion/2011/0125/I-m-not-a-Tiger-Mother-but-I-secretly-admire-Amy-Chua

[106] Source from (viewed August 6, 2011): http://www.nypost.com/p/entertainment/why_love_my_strict_chinese_mom_uUvfmLcA5eteY0u2KXt7hM

[107] Source from (viewed August 6, 2011): http://www.bjreview.com.cn/print/txt/2011-02/21/content_332637.htm

is the very American prejudices and divisive ethnic generalisations that constructed "the Tiger Mama Syndrome". This anxiety is not Chua's alone; "Her anxieties are no different from a lot of 'buffer' groups whose inroads on the edges of assimilation mark them, and whose successes are watched reproachfully, jealously by the larger society".[108] I could relate with her struggle as a Chinese migrant who insists on bringing up her children in a traditional Chinese way in a Western society. The social context and social expectation of a "qualified" modern, Western mother sometimes clashes with her cultural identity. As she mentions,

> ...Chinese parenting is incredibly lonely—at least if you're trying to do it in the West, where you're on your own. You have to go up against an entire value system—rooted in Enlightenment, individual autonomy, child development theory, and the Universal Declaration of Human Rights—and there's no one you can talk to honestly, not even people you like and deeply respect (p.160).

However, one must read the "tiger mother" phenomenon through a critical lens. As far as I am concerned, it is a cultural continuum and product resulting from the Chinese marriage system and Chinese patriarchy. Second, from a gendered division of the domestic sphere, I do admire how much time and effort Amy Chua has devoted to her children. Nevertheless, I found that even in an upper-class American family, Chua herself, a middle or upper-class career woman, is still stuck in the double-shift dilemma and plays the main caregiver of the family. According to her own description about her tight daily schedule to pick up the girls after school, send them to music class, and accompany them practising, Chua performs typical intensive motherhood in the States, as Hays (1996) describes. However, she seems to take this for granted and fails to see that her husband has an equal responsibility for child rearing. Once again, while Chua emphasises how significant the carrying out of Chinese discipline and motherhood style is, she makes the patriarchal and gender inequality within cross-cultural marriage absent and invisible. Besides, from a social class perspective, Chua's narrative represents the middle-and-upper class second generation of Chinese migrant women. She is a professor at Yale University and she received an American education, holding comparatively more social capital than first-generation Chinese migrant women. The material conditions she and her husband (also a professor) can provide for their daughters are much better than working-

---

[108] Source from (viewed August 6, 2011):
http://www.thenation.com/article/158285/tiger-mama-syndrome

class migrant families can. Third, with her belief about how a qualified mother should act and should be, Chua's actions are a continuum of the standard Confucian patriarchy argued by Hongmou Chen, which makes women the pivot for educating virtuous next generations. In short, the "tiger mother" phenomenon not only relates to Chinese migrant motherhood, it also involves the educational system, the immigration issue, ethnic pride, cultural identity, and cultural contradiction. Amy Chua's memoir is definitely a meaningful case for showing how migrant Chinese women define their subjectivity, and then modifies it with the advantages of Western culture. Being from an ethnic minority, Chua shows great agency and the capacity of what a migrant mother can achieve.

3.6 Conclusion

This chapter deals with motherhood theories and debate on two angles. One is Western feminist theories; another is Chinese Confucianism. I first gave a general review from two sides and then I gave an overview of the social norms and motherhood ideology in the Netherlands and recent Chinese migrant motherhood research. In the final section, I took Amy Chua's "tiger mother" phenomenon as an example of the representation of migrant Chinese motherhood in the West. To conclude, firstly, from the development of the motherhood debate in feminist scholarship, the attention has been shifting from a white, middle-class, single-nation-centred approach into a multicultural, intersectional and transnational discussion. Different motherhood subjects are surfacing in scholarly research because of globalisation and modernisation. Secondly, the social norms and motherhood development trajectory under Chinese Confucianism put the sole responsibility of education on women, to properly educate "successful" children has been considered an ultimate life task for Chinese women. Furthermore, transnational motherhood is seen as positive and is encouraged by Chinese society in Northeast Asia, to push Chinese mothers do their best in their motherhood practice, and assist their children to acquire a Western higher education, and then to ultimately gain foreign nationality in the future. Contemporary Chinese women, regardless of their class and educational level, are expected to perform transnational and migrant motherhood for the sake of the children and the family's future. From a feminist perspective, I argue that this very type of Chinese motherhood social requirement is a continuum of Confucian patriarchy.

In contrast, motherhood in Dutch society is perceived as a self-conscious choice made out of women's free will. Those who decide to become a mother must be content with their social roles. However, because of the individualising transformation of the Dutch welfare state, every Dutch citizen, regardless of their gender, has the obligation to work in order to fulfil their social moral virtue and become a qualified welfare claimant. Nevertheless, this transformation does not value women's non-paid domestic care work as an equal, paid labour force. Dutch women with children, by and large, work part-time in low-wage temporary jobs and they are still expected to be the main caregivers for their family members.

CHAPTER FOUR

RUNNING A RESTAURANT DOWNSTAIRS AND RAISING CHILDREN UPSTAIRS: WORKING-CLASS CHINESE MOTHERS IN THE NETHERLANDS

4.1 Introduction

This chapter aims to provide an understanding of the experiences of motherhood practices among working-class, first-generation, migrant Chinese women. To distinguish these experiences from more recent Chinese migrants in the next chapter, all the interviewees in this chapter had already emigrated to the Netherlands before the 1980s and are mainly from Hong Kong. In the first section, I analyse the gendered characteristics of the Chinese chain migration, particularly from the perspectives of women. I address the empty scholarship on why the first generation of migrant women outnumbered men from the analysis of the gendered characteristics of the chain migration. In the first section, I briefly summarise the historical background of the urbanisation development of Hong Kong. How did Hong Kong become a significant gateway for Chinese immigrants towards their promising future in the West? I aim to conceptualise the phenomenon of working-class migrant Chinese women within the chain migration from China or Hong Kong to Europe, specifically in the Netherlands. In the second section, I provide two case studies to discuss how women resisted and negotiated Communist state patriarchy and sexism by autonomously making themselves illegal, and then regaining their legal status (foreign residence) through autonomous marriage before emigration. In the third section, I elaborate their motherhood practice experiences from a micro-political perspective through analysing how working-class Chinese immigrant mothers combined their work with childrearing, and how they make sense of motherhood on a daily basis. My aim is to link this early Chinese migration pattern and process by using the framework of motherhood and intersectionality to illuminate Chinese migrant women's reproductive and caring experiences from the Dutch context.

Dutch people seem to have a high acceptance of Chinese food; one can easily find various regional-style Chinese cuisines all over the country, especially in the metropolitan cities like Amsterdam, Rotterdam and Den Haag. Spicy Lanzhou ramen, Sichuan hot pot, Taiwanese fried chicken and instant noodles, crispy duck, frozen bapao in the supermarket, wok takeaway restaurants and, the most popular, dim sum, are all successfully integrated into the Dutch society. Chinese immigrants not only substantially add to the Dutch demographic composition but form part of the Dutch horeca (hospitality or catering) industry itself. According to CBS statistics,[109] by the end of 2007, an estimated 42% of Dutch Chinese immigrants, or about 18.5 thousand people of Chinese origin, worked in the horeca industry, most of them self-employed; while less than 4% of the native Dutch make their living in the horeca business. The mainstream tabloid Dutch newspaper, *De Telegraaf* (2004), praised the Chinese as "ideal (outsiders) immigrants" for the Netherlands because "they don't complain, they don't cause trouble and they work hard".[110]

Dutch and Chinese scholars working on Chinese migration studies, such as Pieke 1992; Benton & Pieke, 1998; Li, 1999b; Mak, 2000; and Benton, 2011, see the upsurge of Chinese emigration to Western Europe for the catering business starting from the 1950s, especially from the New Territories and the rural areas of Hong Kong. Before that, only a small number of immigrant Chinese, mainly male, settled in Western European countries. Before World War II, Chinese minorities did not have the positive public image they have today. In her research, Geertje Mak (2000) describes the ethnic image of Chinese men in the 1930s as poor, ill,

---

[109] See: http://www.cbs.nl/NR/rdonlyres/2D28519C-1DD5-4977-ADD4-97E5FD4C7CF7/0/2010sociaalbestek09p26.pdf, accessed on September 23, 2013.

[110] This news was from Dutch national daily *De Telegraaf* (January 24, 2004) with the title "*Chinees Ideale Allochtoon*"; it describes Chinese as "*Ze klagen niet, halen geen narigheid uit en ze werken hard*" (translation, Shu-Yi Huang 2013). I deliberately translated the word *Allochtoon* into outsiders because the origin of this word means people from other countries. I found this word ironical for an ethnic minority who have settled in the Netherlands for almost a century and have fully integrated into the Dutch society; still in mainstream eyes, they remain *Allochtoon,* foreigners and outsiders. This ideology is also deeply rooted in the mindset of Dutch Chinese. I discuss this topic more elaborately in chapter seven and its racial and ethnical notions in chapter six. Source: Marie-Therese Roosendaal, "Chinees Ideale Allochtoon", *De Telegraaf*, 24 January 2004, T13. Available at Utrecht University Library Newspaper Database LexisNexis,
http://bibe.library.uu.nl/zoek/biblio/index_e.html (accessed on October 4, 2013).

possibly dangerous to public health, and harmful to Dutch morality (p. 142). She found that desperate Chinese seamen tried to earn a living in the Overijssel area by clandestinely selling condoms in parks to Dutch teenagers. The authorities tried to prosecute them but in vain. There were several charities to help these abandoned Chinese migrant workers but they still found their niche selling peanut sweets or little trinkets, even condoms when using contraception was still illegal in the Netherlands. The self-supporting and bitterness-enduring character of this Chinese minority group helped them through the difficulties of the inception of migration in the first half of 20th-century Netherlands.

Half a century later, the relatively low social welfare dependency and high labour participation rate of the Dutch Chinese community meant it was excluded from the Dutch ethnic minority policy in 1983 (Minderhedennota, 1983). According to George Muskens (1996: 9), the Dutch Chinese ethnic group was not considered as "backward and special attention needed" by authorities. In addition, according to FORUM's report (2011: 6), this was coupled with the distrust of the Dutch government among Chinese opinion leaders: the latter did not want the Chinese minority to be labelled as an inferior, trouble-making ethnic minority group that needed government financial help. Furthermore, the second generation of Dutch Chinese was praised as a "model minority group" (modelminderheidsgroep) in the 2011 national report (Gijsberts et al., 2011, p. 20). The very image of the diligent, hard-working and self-sufficient Chinese model minority also prevails in neighbouring countries. In his research, Leung (2003) points out that in Germany, the Chinese migrants are seen as "ideal-typical" because "the limited entrance opportunities and prospects in the formal labour markets have made them self-employed" (p. 115). Although they lack higher education, German language proficiency and financial capital, the low criteria for starting a small-scale Chinese restaurant allows them to be self-sufficient and not dependent on state social welfare. This model minority impression is held by most Western European people, but only a few academic literatures address the real life of working-class Chinese migrants in Western Europe, especially from the working-class women's perspectives.[111]

One cannot comprehend post-migration life fully without knowing the past. To understand the turning point of the contemporary Chinese

---

[111] Two books by Pai Hsiao-Hung, a Taiwanese who works as a journalist at *The Guardian*, describe the real life of Chinese migrant workers in the United Kingdom and are considered contemporary gendered-life illustrations of the Chinese working-class in Western Europe after China's Open and Reform Policy. See Pai, 2008 and 2013.

emigration trajectory, we must refer to 1949, which was the year that China split into two political regimes (People of the Republic of China versus Republic of China, Taiwan). It was a year of countless tears and separations and a year of escape. Millions of people flocked to Hong Kong and Macao to escape the civil war and the fear of the coming Chinese Communist regime. The local, poorly educated Hong Kong peasants were pushed out to search for a new living. At the same time, another continent across the ocean, Western Europe, was being reconstructed after World War II and became an ideal destination for Hong Kong villagers to begin their new life. As Commonwealth citizens of the United Kingdom, they were free to settle in Britain until the 1970s (Benton, 2011, p. 63).[112] These ambitious catering entrepreneurs, mainly from Hong Kong and Guangdong, successfully established their Chinese restaurant businesses in the Netherlands and were in need of cheap labour. With personal connections, *guanxi* (關係), they employed desperate Chinese who were willing to separate from their families to work overseas in their restaurants or to start a business in various countries; first the UK, i.e. in London and Liverpool, then across the North Sea to Belgium, the Netherlands and Denmark. According to Benton & Pieke (1998), they are the fifth early stream of Chinese immigration in Europe. In 1947, there were only 23 Chinese restaurants in the Netherlands (Chen, 1991: 29, citied by Li, 1999b: 34); by the end of the 1970s, there were around 2000 Chinese restaurants across the Netherlands (ibid: 34).[113] Pieke (2004) points out that mass Chinese emigration not only provided cheap labour for the restaurants and shops owned by the established Chinese communities in Western Europe but also inserted a dynamism and appetite for expansion that led to the exploration of new economic sectors (p. 3) and frontier areas in Southern, Eastern and Northern Europe (p. 3). Even now, the Chinese catering businesses in major cities like London, Amsterdam, Rotterdam, and Den Haag are still under the control of Hongkongers.

The success and the prominence of the Chinese migrant catering business also drew some attention in academia. Gordon Redding (1993)

---

[112] It was only after 1985, with the introduction of Emigration Law, that people from China started to have the freedom to go abroad without serious restrictions. Even now, in China, peasant migrants' movements into urban labor markets are still under very strict monitoring by authorities. See Cindy Fan (2008) for more information about internal migration and socialist market economy transformation in China after the 1980s.

[113] However, there is no further recent statistics about the exact number of Chinese restaurants in the Netherlands. I reconfirmed this topic with CBS information service on November 13, 2013.

argues that "Confucianism" plays a significant role in Chinese business management. His work inspired later studies discussing the characteristics of Chinese migrant entrepreneurs. For example, Souchuo Yao (2002) elaborates Redding's concept further as "Confucian Capitalism", which is the key element in the success of Chinese migrant business. Denggao Long and Qiming Han (2008) found that a common characteristic of Chinese immigrants in the United States is that they have a stronger desire to be self-employed than other ethnic groups. Their grocery stores, restaurants and laundry shops are always family-run enterprises and they are oriented toward family/ethnic clan utilisation (p. 52).[114] The first step towards ownership was to work for several years in Chinese restaurants or in China-owns doing multiple part-time jobs until they had accumulated enough money to start their own business in a different region (p. 56). In this study, I also found a similar phenomenon in that large proportions of working-class Dutch Chinese are self-employed and their business is family-run. They are reluctant to work under native Dutch people and are highly cohesive,[115] as emphasised by a 61-year-old woman who has retired from running a Chinese restaurant, sharing her opinion on her daughter-in-law's job-hunting activity: "Why does she need to go out making little money by looking at Dutch people's faces?"

However, Long and Han hold an opposite opinion on so-called "Confucian Capitalism". They consider economic considerations are far more important than cultural predispositions for migrant Chinese entrepreneurs, particularly those in Southeast Asia (2008: 63). A family/clan-run business is also one of the characteristics of Chinese restaurants in the Netherlands. Guanxi plays a vital role in the Dutch Chinese chain-migration pattern (Pieke, 1992; Benton & Pieke, 1998; Li, 1999b). Pieke (1992) argues that "the ethnic Chinese minority is very isolated from mainstream Dutch society, thus Chinese restaurants provide an important social function for the Chinese community itself" (p. 31). Restaurant owners prefer to find employees who have guanxi with them from their country of origin. It could be family members, relatives, friends, or children of people in social networks who work for them. These employees can endure long working hours, bad working conditions and

[114] Long, Denggao. & Han, Qiming. 2008. "Beyond Culture: Economic Analysis of the Characteristics of Overseas Chinese Business." Pp: 52–65.

[115] During the field work, my interviewees or the owners of Chinese grocery shops often offered me warm greetings or gave me extra free rice, noodles and some home-made dishes. They told me that if I had any financial problem, I could always have a part-time job in their business. Their hospitality and kindness really comforted me.

low pay. They are also loyal to the boss because, in fact, the whole family's living depends on the success of this restaurant. By reducing the remuneration expenditure, Chinese restaurants can thus serve meals at a lower price than their Dutch counterparts and so attract customers.

Due to the gender blindness of transnational economic theories of Chinese migration, women are a missing piece in the existing literature of Chinese diaspora studies. Women as a migrant subject are invisible not only in Chinese migration studies but also in American migration studies. Pessar and Mahler (2003) point out that "most twentieth century research up through the early 1970s focused almost exclusively on male migrants, while women were presumed to play passive roles as companions" (p. 814). They also remind us that the state has been privileged as a unit in migration studies while gender has been excluded. Lutz (2010: 1659) also argues that should one wield gender as a tool to re-examine existing migration economic theories, "a multiplicity of motives other than purely economic ones" will reveal their complexities. In this study, I found working-class Chinese migrant women not only provide their labour for the family business to save the expenditure of an additional worker but also fulfil the care-giver roles as mothers, wives and daughters-in-law in the domestic domain. From their gendered life experiences, this chapter aims to "bring gender into the study of migration" (Pessar & Mahler, 2003: 838) in the Dutch Chinese context, with attention on intersectionalities and linguistics from the perspectives of first-generation, working-class Chinese migrant women.

The role of women in the global Chinese chain-migration and their contribution to the migrant family and the self-sufficient business have seldom been discussed. They were buried in statistics, in the shadow of "his"tory. People encounter them in small grocery stores, in Chinese restaurants and, more recently, in massage parlours. People see them working but they do not know their real backstories. Only a few historians and gender studies scholars have given them a position in literature and made their presence in the Western world visible. In 1984, Lucie Cheng, the pioneer of Asian American Studies of UCLA, and her colleagues describe early Asian Americans before WWII in the context of globalisation and capitalism. In her work, *Linking Our Lives* (1984), she focuses on the post-migration life experiences of Asian immigrant women in Southern California. Only 1% of the total population of Chinese were women during the Gold Rush era (the 1860s to the 1870s), and most of them were enslaved prostitutes[116] or the wives of Chinese merchants

---

[116] Only a small number of Chinese women were merchants' wives. Most of them were young girls who were kidnapped in south coast rural villages and trafficked to America. See Jean Pfaelzer (2008), chapter 3.

shipped from Hong Kong to San Francisco, living in poor conditions under the constant threat of physical abuse. American historian Jean Pfaelzer (2008) found traces of them in local newspapers, court records and personal memoires. She praised these women as pioneers of the American Chinese community: "They not only formed the first family units of Chinese America, they also helped construct the early Chinatowns" (p.106). I hope this study can make Chinese migrant working-class women in the Netherlands visible and acknowledged epistemologically, like their sisters in North America.

4.1.2 Some reflections from fieldwork

Before analysing my research findings, I need some space to discuss my personal reflections while conducting the interviews with working-class women all around the Netherlands and the choices I made in interpreting their transcriptions. First of all, most of the interviewees in this chapter grew up during the turbulent Maoist period in China and Hong Kong. The Great Leap Forward Movement (1958–1961) came hand in hand with the Great Famine (1958–1961) and then the Cultural Revolution (1966–1969); the endless political chaos and poverty made them suffer in childhood. To live a relatively stable life and escape from the Communist regime, they were pushed out and uprooted by the wheel of history. Their names and sufferings are not mentioned in the history text books I studied during secondary school. The knowledge I was taught about that period is a series of wars, and the male "heroes" in the military, and the political confrontations between different ideologies. After hearing the intimidating past from my interviewees, I could not help wondering which is more important: the experiences of subalterns or the selfish military tyrants launching those wars. Did they realise how many tragedies they caused at least three generations of Chinese people? Recording their stories changed my way of looking at this period of history. "I am not a lucky girl like you." This sentence haunts me in every way. In contrast to the lifeless characters and roughly estimated numbers of the dead written in those textbooks about the Great Famine and the Cultural Revolution, they are real people who struggled and fought bravely against the cruelty. They are the deleted, the abandoned, the useless knowledge that the ROC government presumed I did not have to know about. From these women's narratives, I comprehended that the process of the post-war reconstruction of the knowledge apparatus in Taiwan excluded and erased the collective memory of women, civilians, the displaced, and the forced migrants. The institutionalised knowledge and epistemology of contemporary post-war

Taiwan mythologised warlords, war felons and totalitarians. I was taught by a serious, purposely manipulated knowledge apparatus, which brainwashed me and made me a loyal and docile authority believer. Growing up under this top-down educational institution, I was a model student in class and a patriot until I started to read about feminism and engage much more with feminist theories. I turned my passion towards women and to the social minorities. I was really inspired by the Canadian feminist and sociologist Dorothy Smith's standpoint theory. She uses a metaphor, "the line of fault" (1987: 49), to elaborate on why women's experiences and standpoints are significant in knowledge making. According to Smith, the line of fault exists between two parallel worlds, one is based on women's real experiences and the other is fabricated by deliberate discourses that affect people's ideas and thinking. Smith elaborates further on why the line of fault exists.

> The forms of thought, the means of expression, that we had available to us to formulate our experiences were made or controlled by men. From that centre, women appeared as objects. In relation to men of the ruling class, women's consciousness did not, and most probably generally still does not, appear as an autonomous source of knowledge, experience, relevance, and imagination. Women's experience did not appear as the source of an authoritative general expression of the world (Smith, 1987: 51).

If I learned about Chinese migration only from the standard education I received, I would never have come to understand the real situation of migrant women and their stories. This is exactly why I must include working-class Chinese women's experiences in rewriting the history of Chinese migrant women's motherhood practices in the Netherlands. However, these incredibly brave and diligent women are so humble that they regard their experiences and stories as useless and not worthy of mentioning in front of a young but highly-educated young woman like me. I was even more surprised that two middle-class women had the same attitude towards their lives in the Netherlands: "I'm just being a wife and mother here" or "I've nothing successful to share with you, just an ordinary housewife". Several times, I felt ashamed of myself. I have been a diligent and hard-working student all these years but the culture and the institutions that brought me here do not give basic respect: more specifically, they are pejorative to these people who are striving so hard, especially women.

The common dialect they speak, Cantonese, is difficult for me.[117] I took some time to learn some basic Cantonese from a Cantonese-learning website and several Hong Kong soap operas with Cantonese dubbing. Another issue is that the way they described their own stories is very fragmented. Most of the time they answer questions obliquely. It takes patience and paying close attention to their words, and then reconfirming some key words with them. I found that writing down keywords is a good way to reach mutual understanding when interviewing women who speak a different regional dialect. Besides, in order to make quotes more logical and readable, I had to make some alterations and change the order of part of the sentences. I kept the Cantonese style of some terms, as they may be different from Standard Mandarin, and I will add footnotes to explain that.

4.2 Chinese Women's Role(s) in the Chain-migration

In this section, I want to analyse the characteristics of Chinese chain-migration from three geopolitical aspects. First, its geographical uniqueness, which resulted in the fact that most of early Chinese migrants came from Guangdong Province, and especially Hong Kong; second, the household policy that directly causes the formation of chain-migration; and third, Chinese women's role in chain-migration and how its gendered division could possibly explain the theoretical emptiness I highlighted in chapter one, that female migrants outnumbered their male counterparts among first-generation Chinese immigrants.

4.2.1 Hong Kong: A gateway to the brave new world

Why early Chinese migration to the Netherlands originated by and large from Hong Kong and Guangdong Province has hardly been addressed by Dutch academic studies. To understand that, it is necessary to realise the historical and geographical background first. Hong Kong, which was a part of Guangdong Province, used to be a small island port facing the Pacific Ocean in Southeast China. It played a role as a relay station for south and north trade in Asia Pacific. It was one of the first provinces in China with a special international trading administration for the outside world, since the sixteenth century.[118] In 1841, Hong Kong was occupied

---

[117] Most of them did not have a chance to learn Standard Mandarin at school; for more details, see chapter five.

[118] To know more about the emigrant patterns and features of Guangdong province before 1850, see Hoe, Yow Cheun (2013), chapter two.

by the British army during the Opium War (1839–1842). From 1846 until 1997, Hong Kong officially became a colony of the United Kingdom as part of the reparation of war.[119] Since 1846, Hong Kong functioned as an important entrepôt for the British Empire in East Asia, importing opium into China from India and exporting Chinese porcelain, tea, Indian cotton, and spices to Europe. Hong Kong rapidly developed to become the biggest international port in East Asia since 1849. The gold rush in San Francisco and the need for large numbers of cheap labour (*coolie*, 苦力, literally means bitter, harsh labour) and goods made people in the Guangdong Province eager to embark for America. According to historian Elizabeth Sinn (2012), in the late nineteenth century, the geographic advantages of Hong Kong transformed it to Asia's leading gateway linking to North America. Goods from Hong Kong to San Francisco took only 45 to 50 days, which soon made Hong Kong one of San Francisco's major trading partners, and at that time the Hong Kong–San Francisco route became one of the world's most occupied sea-lanes (p. 3).

The transpacific connections also triggered mass Chinese emigration to North America despite the hard work that was required and the seemingly limitless anti-Chinese violence. The prevailing assumption was that the United States was a gold mine which was full of opportunities for lower-class people, who would become rich and prosperous. This assumption was also deeply rooted in coast people's hearts. Taiwanese historian and feminist Lucie Cheng (1984) claims that it was because both capitalism and imperialism constructed exploitative and hostile conditions pulling Asian migration to the United States before WWII. After 1978, Guangdong lost its influence as an important migrant export area compared to other provinces in China. Since Hong Kong has historically been a Chinese merchants' and cheap labourers' export harbour, it is easy to understand why the first groups of Chinese diasporic migrants, who were brought by British ship companies to replace the striking port labourers in Rotterdam, came mainly from Guangdong Province and Hong Kong. During the upheaval of 1949 and until the political-economic reform in 1978, only people from Hong Kong[120] had more freedom

[119] From December 25, 1941 to August 15, 1945, Hong Kong was occupied by the Japanese Empire.

[120] During this period, many people from Guangdong, Shanghai and other cities in China either spent a large amount of money to move to Hong Kong or they illegally slipped into Hong Kong seeking job opportunities either internally or overseas to make life better, especially during the famine in the Great Leap Forward in the late 1950s and the Cultural Revolution from 1966 to 1976.

(compared to the PRC and the ROC) to travel and cross the borders to fill the post-war labour demand in the Western world.

4.2.2 Hukuo system as a control mechanism

Why were there only a small number of Chinese female migrants before the 1980s to the West, and why was it so difficult for them to emigrate abroad? To answer these questions, and to realise the contemporary Chinese intra- and external- migration, one must know the controlling mechanisms behind the population flow. The origin of the Chinese *hukuo* (戶口; household registration) system can be traced back to as early as 685 BC (Zhuo Dynasty) as "registration records existed that defined segments of the population by occupation" (Yu, 2002: 14). Every household was registered as a unit and the occupation of the male head determined the social status of the family, while women were nameless in the registration system. The design blueprint of this gendered system originated from Confucian thinking of women's virtue as the "Three Followings". Women could not exist independently from the head of the household or by themselves alone. As a daughter, a woman's hukou was under her father. After marriage, her hukou was moved under her husband. After the death of the husband, the widow's hukou was under her son's or the deceased husband's brother. Women were either treated as goods (maids, concubines) with a market value or as wives, the possessions of husbands, and they bore the obligatory responsibilities to reproduce, to educate heirs, and to take care of all the family members under the Chinese patriarchal family system.[121] Women's mobility was severely confined domestically and was seriously limited by this tight surveillance mechanism. The hukuo system has been used until now as a population float monitor mechanism both in Taiwan and China. According to Cheng (2002), before the introduction of the Opening and Reform Policy, only 20% of the Chinese population worked in state-owned enterprises (SOE); the remaining 80% lived and worked in the rural villages. Living conditions and the educational environment were harsh for Chinese peasants; the hukuo system thus functioned as a highly centralised state tool for human mobility control. Only by joining the People's Liberation Army (PLA) or

---

[121] Although, this hukuo system was drastically reformed during the 70s and 80s, it is still a gendered population control mechanism for both China and Taiwan. The most prevailing outcome is to strengthen and deepen the class and urban-rural inequalities because it reduces the opportunities of rural farmers to settle down in the urban cities for pursuing better living and social welfare, see Yu, 2002 and Cheng, 2002.

climbing to a higher position in the Communist Party could one gain the opportunity to convert from agricultural hukuo to non-agricultural hukuo (Fan, 2008: 42), as will be seen, for example, in the case of Cathy in the latter part of this section. It was impossible and illegal for single women to acquire a passport for migrant labour work aboard. The only method was to have one of the male family members (i.e. father, brother, husband, or son) who already had legal residence status in the West apply to the PRC government for family reunion. There was no transparent and standard application procedure for people to follow and the number of successful cases remains unknown (ibid: 40). Fan (2008) points out that before the 1980s, the only legal way to emigrate abroad was to have a non-agricultural hukuo in particular coast cities such as Wenzou, Shanghai and Guangzhou (p. 4). This state of affairs was confirmed by Cathy; she told me it was extremely hard during the 1950s to have Wenzou hukuo. Her family had that privilege only because her big brother served as a youth soldier for 15 years and the Party awarded his family Wenzou City non-peasant hukuo as a reward for his loyalty.

The case shows how the hukuo system functioned not only as a state mechanism to regulate people's position by location and by occupation but also as an institutionalised state power to rigorously manipulate people's lives in every facet, including the possibilities and the freedom of international migration. The decisions of both migration-receiving countries (the West) and the sending country (China) bind people's freedom of movement as well.[122]

4.2.3 A proper socialist woman

From the 1960s Mao started to advocate the significance of women's contribution to society in order to use all human resources regardless of gender and class to construct a new China. It was considered a policy shift from the Five Goods Movement in 1956, part of the first Five Year Program, which frames the definition of a so-called "proper socialist woman". According to Elisabeth Croll (1978: 257), women under the Five Goods Movement should 1) be united with the neighbourhood families for mutual aid, 2) do housework well, 3) educate children well, 4) encourage family production, study, and work, and 5) study well themselves. This policy mainly stresses women's domestic responsibilities of caring for and

[122] For instance, during the 1960s, temporary migrants such as "guest workers" in Germany and the Netherlands were not allowed to bring their family members or to settle permanently (Castles & Miller, 2009: 67).

educating children and themselves intellectually. Croll argues it was because the economy in 1956 was not materially prepared enough to provide full-time employment for women. However, from the 1960s, Mao's statement changed. His famous slogan was "women can hold up half the sky (*banbiantian*, 半邊天)." To liberate women from feudalism, from the subjugated position of the household, and to participate in national construction with men, it was necessary to implement "socialist spiritual civilization" (*shehuizhuyi qingshenwenming*, 社會主義精神文明) (Robinson 1985: 30). "Socialist spiritual civilization" required gender equality, thus raising Chinese women's social status to be equal as men's became necessary. According to Croll (1977), "numerous women study groups have been formed in factories, government institutions, schools, neighbourhoods… it was aimed to educate women that male supremacy was neither an immutable social principle ordained by heaven nor one dating back to time immemorial, but was a principle developed by Confucius in a specific historical period at the time of the transition from the slave to the feudal society" (p. 593). However, she argued that the idea of overthrowing the Confucian fallacy ideology was only restricted to the Department of History at Peking Teachers' University and the Message Station of a women's unit of the PLA because rural female cadres resisted and refused to abandon Confucianism completely (p. 595). This means that women's liberation during Mao's period focused on women's labour participation and its symbolic value, but it did not totally criticise and try to overthrow the core patriarchy in Confucianism.

Women's contribution to economic production was highly praised and emphasised. The political propaganda and spiritual slogans were full of model proper socialist women. From cities to rural villages, women were assigned their job unit according to their hukuo. Mao gave women's jobs symbolic meaning; their work outside the home represented their personal liberation from the oppression of domestic labour, from the oppression of five thousand years of patriarchal feudalism. Wolf (1985) concludes that from the 1960s there is a process of masculine demystification going on, especially in rural China (p.137), and the symbolism of women's labour was both sign and source of the improved status of women in the new China.

I noticed that working-class women in this study valued their paid labour much more than their middle-class counterparts. They came to the Netherlands at a very young age and raised children mainly during the 60s and the 70s when most of the native Dutch women became full-time housewives after marriage. Unlike middle-class Chinese migrant women, most of them continued working full-time or part-time even after selling their restaurants, when retiring is considered a milestone of glory among the Dutch Chinese working-class community. Financially, they refuse to rely on their husbands and children. Whether in domestic matters or business decision-making, their opinion counts. They reported that children tended to obey their orders or accept their suggestions much more than from their fathers. I will provide more examples and analysis in the third section.

Table 4-1 Sex and numbers of Chinese from China, 1931 to 1975*

Year	*Male*	*Female*	*Total*	*Year*	*Male*	*Female*	*Total*
1931			±2,000	1962	1,250	424	1,674
1939			± 900	1963	1,264	443	1,707
1944			±1,487	1964	1,280	434	1,714
1955			±1,766	1965	1,306	377	1,683
1956	1,360	448	1,808	1966	1,383	376	1,759
1957	1,292	462	1,754	1967	1,422	361	1,783
1958	1,265	457	1,722	1968	1,429	351	1,780
1959	1,250	438	1,688	1971	1,590	600	2,190
1960	1,253	435	1,688	1973	2,078	726	2,804
1961	1,249	427	1,676	1974	2,259	844	3,103
				1975	2,403	987	3,390

*Source: *Social Status of Dutch Chinese*, Pieke 1992, translated into Mandarin by Zhuang. The table was translated into English and reproduced by Huang, 2014.

4.2.4 Gendered migration pattern

Why were there fewer Chinese migrant women before the 1980s in the Netherlands? This results from the subordinate socio-economic status of women in Chinese society as well as the strict restriction of emigration policy over the last two centuries by the *hukuo* system.

From table 4-1, we can see clearly the number of Chinese men was almost two times (in 1975), to three times (in 1956), more than that of Chinese women. Early Chinese migration to the Netherlands was sex-selective and it resulted in an imbalance in gender structure.[123] This meant that there were many single Chinese men in the Dutch Chinese community

[123] The same situation also appeared in late 19th century in Eastern Mill towns in the United States; see Mott (1972).

seeking possible marriage candidates. Why did these single Chinese men not marry locally but fly across half the globe to find wives in Hong Kong? The truth is, unfortunately, that it was very difficult for them to find proper spouses in the Netherlands because of the stereotype of Dutch people towards mixed marriage. I think it can be explained in three ways.

First, according to Dutch historian Jet Bussemaker (1998), given the consequences of the Dutch traditional pillarisation society, single Chinese men could hardly marry native Dutch women because of racial/ethnic, class and religious differences and native Dutch women rarely married men from "other" groups; even in post-pillarisation Dutch society, they still tend to marry endogenously. Bussemaker seems to imply that because of the pillarisation tradition, people act according to their group regulations. However, what she did not mention explicitly, and which is also my second argument, is there has been a long history of racial hierarchy in Dutch society (Essed, 1990; Altena 2012), a colonial inheritance of the notion that people with white skin are superior to others (Essed, 1990: 43). Thus, in Dutch eyes, single Chinese men were regarded as a socially, ethnically and economically inferior minority in Dutch society. In addition, along with racial hierarchy from the colonial inheritance and the pillarisation tradition, mainstream society generally regarded ethnicity and race to be an insurmountable biological difference. People judged mixed marriage with a gendered and racist double standard; for white Dutch women to marry coloured (foreign) men was considered an anathema.

In her research on the archives of the famous mixed marriage of a white Dutch woman, Mia Cuypers, and a Chinese businessman, Frederick Tean Err Toung, in the late 19th century, Dutch historian Marga Altena (2012) points out that Mia was described as an irrational, hysterical woman not only in the mass media representations but also in family anecdotes. Her decision to marry a Chinese man brought shame and disgrace to the prominent Catholic family. Meanwhile, the British Chinese man, Frederick, was an opportunistic alien (p. 40) and a "ferocious Mongol" (p. 51). This famous Chinese and Dutch marriage ended in a painful divorce, which was seen as a "terrible disaster" and "the worst that ever happened to the family" because of Mia. Altena concluded that there exists an unequal sexual double standard in Dutch society towards mixed marriage. White Dutch women who marry foreign men are disgraced and even filthy because they challenged social conventions and cast doubt on existing ethnic[124] categories (p. 154).

---

[124] The author chose to use the word "ethnic" rather than "racial" in her comment. As a reader, however, I think that the racial issue was indeed involved in Mia

Given the outcome of gendered Chinese migration to the Netherlands and the double standard of social propriety towards white Dutch women, it is telling that there was a large demand among single Chinese men in the Dutch Chinese community to seek an endogamous marriage. The quickest and easiest way to approach that is through transnational marriage from the countries of origin. While taking a short vacation back to Hong Kong, a man who was searching for a wife would make available the information to his relatives and friends, through his social network, and thereby was able to choose one of the young women willing to uproot with him to the Netherlands. On the other side, according to my interviewees' opinion, for a peasant daughter in Hong Kong to be able to marry and go abroad as the wife of a second-generation son of a Chinese restaurant owner was the best result for a woman back then. In short, quanxi not only plays a vital part in Chinese labour migration but also significantly within the marriage culture in the Chinese chain migration pattern.

Now, let us go back to the unsolved puzzle, why do the CBS statistics in 2011 show that women outnumber men among first-generation migrant Chinese? What changes took place in the migration pattern during the 36 years from 1975 to 2011? My own explanation, resulting from this study, is that one male migrant will bring at least two female family members to the Netherlands in the whole process of chain-migration. The first woman is the wife; the second is his mother or mother-in-law, particularly after the birth of the first child. One can see this pattern from Cathy's family, for instance. Her father came to work in Germany first and his son-in-law came to work in the Netherlands a decade later. Because no one could take care of the children, Cathy's husband soon applied for a family reunion with his mother. Women are the primary caregivers in the household, and this gendered division does not change because of the transnational movement. Especially in a working-class migrant Chinese family, young women must work double shifts: they not only fill the labour shortage in the family business but also manage the household chores. After the first child is born, the grandmother comes to the Netherlands to be another caregiver. She babysits her grandchild so her daughter (or daughter-in-law) can continue working in the family business. To conclude, the so-called "Confucian Capitalism", as Yao (2002) defined it, cannot exist without women's contribution to the gendered division transnationally. I will now turn to the working-class women's experiences in the next section.

Cuypers and Frederick Tean Err Toung's failed marriage. Perhaps it is a Dutch taboo to mention "race" when discussing people's dissimilarities.

4.3 Women on the Move

In the following part, I illustrate the migration pattern of working-class Chinese migrant women who came to the Netherlands before the 1980s. I first describe their backgrounds and lives before migration to capture the social atmosphere and women's daily activities among working-class families in the second half of twentieth century Hong Kong and Guangdong.

There are 10 working-class women who emigrated to the Netherlands before the 1980s in this study. Table 4.2 shows their mean age is 53.1; they were mostly born in the 1960s. The oldest one is 63 and the youngest one is 42. The mean age of marriage is 23.6; however, two of them followed their parents to the Netherlands as teenagers and their mean age of marriage is 31.5. Basically, the first-generation working-class Chinese women in this research married rather young, aged around 21.6. Their mean number of children is three. Six women are from Hong Kong, with the other four from nearby Guangdong areas. One of these four women had been working in Hong Kong for eight years before emigrating. The educational level of women from the PRC is as follows: two are at elementary school level (one followed the Chinese education system, another followed the Dutch education system) and one is at secondary school level (Dutch education system) while for the women from Hong Kong, five of them are at secondary school level (three followed the British education system; two followed the Chinese education system) and two are at elementary school level (British education system). Their mean living length in the Netherlands is 31.5 years. Some information is not included in table 4.2, namely, that only one woman had no working experience before emigration, and the other nine women had at least five years of working experience before marriage. Three of them had started to work full-time to support their family at the age of 14, working in garment factories ten hours a day, six days a week. They all grew up in peasant families with more than five children. It is clear that working-class Chinese women generally marry young and have a basic educational background.

One important characteristic is that seven of the women kept fulfilling economic obligations to their parents in Hong Kong, or in China, after emigration until the delivery of the first baby. This is quite different from the middle-class immigrant Chinese women, who often stop economic obligations to their natal families after marriage. The material advantages that a migrant Chinese working-class man can provide are twofold: first, to improve the living conditions for the bride's natal family in a short period

Table 4.2 Backgrounds of 10 Working-class Chinese Women*

Name	Age	Age of marriage	Numbers of children and their sex**	Educational level	Living length in NL (years)	Occupation	Living region before migration
Betty	42	25	3 M	Secondary school (the Netherlands)	35	Owner of take away sandwich shop	China
Cathy	61	19	2M 2F	Elementary school (China)	35	Retired from Chinese restaurant	China
Wendy	51	21	3 M	Secondary school (China)	31	Owner of Chinese restaurant	China
Daisy	58	29	2M 2F	Secondary school (Hong Kong)	28	Factory operator	Hong Kong
Ella	51	18	2M 1F	Elementary school (Hong Kong)	33	Owner of Chinese restaurant	Hong Kong
Fiona	50	20	1M 1F	Elementary school (Hong Kong)	30	Cleaner	Hong Kong
Ivy	53	18	1M 4F	Secondary school (Hong Kong)	34	Cleaner	Hong Kong
Grace	44	38	2F	Elementary school (the Netherlands)	29	Cleaner	Hong Kong
Jessica	63	23	2F	Secondary school (Hong Kong)	38	Cleaner	Hong Kong
Kitty	58	25	2M	Secondary school (China)	22	Factory operator	Hong Kong

*The field work and all the interviews of this research were conducted between July 2011 and December 2012.
**M refers to male, F refers to female. The biological sex order is according to their age.

(usually one to two years) in the Netherlands compared to the work in garment factories in Hong Kong and second, the possibility to live and to raise children in a Western country like the Netherlands.

4.3.1 I told my mom "I am going to swim"

The political turbulence in China also affected women's marriage and emigration decisions. Here I will discuss two case studies. These two examples show how working-class women resisted the state authority through marriage and moving during the notorious Cultural Revolution (1966–1976) and Educated Youth Movement (1968–1973). Cathy (61) was born in Qinftian, Zhejiang Province: her family has a long history of male members working abroad to support the family in China. Cathy's grandfather worked in France and her father worked in Germany. She told me that her grandfather tried several times to apply for family reunion to the Chinese governments but in vain. When she was four, her grandfather finally came back home but died after three months. Her father left his family behind to work in a Chinese restaurant in Germany when she was seven and the last time she saw him was in a German hospital in 1977.[125] Cathy's case is the typical split-household family[126] in the Guangdong areas, with one or two male family members earning money in Western countries because of the great demand for cheap labour, waiting for the chance to bring their wife and children later. Cathy told me when the Cultural Revolution broke out, all the unmarried teenagers had to become Red Guards and overthrow the backward, old-fashioned and oppressive Chinese tradition by physically criticising and denouncing landlords, merchants and teachers, even their own (grand) parents in public and in inhumane and brutal ways. According to American scholar Frederick Teiwes (1974: 335), the main target of the Cultural Revolution was to break down elitism and feudalism. Given the circumstances, Cathy felt this political movement was not moral or ethical; she decided to get married in order to have a politically correct excuse to stay at home as a responsible socialist mother and a docile wife. Soon after her marriage, her father-in-law, who ran a Chinese restaurant in the Netherlands, became critically ill;

---

[125] Chinese male migrant workers often sacrificed more than their spouses before the 1980s. They were mainly financial providers working abroad and had little emotional connection with their children; to know more. see Pieke (1992), chapter three.

[126] The split-household strategy is also very common in circular domestic peasant migrations in China after the Reform and Opening Policy. See Fan (2008), chapter five and chapter seven.

her husband thus went alone to the Netherlands to take over his father's business in 1973. Four years later, she and her eldest daughter joined her husband. During her absence, her mother-in-law took care of the other two grandchildren at home with the money Cathy transferred once every half-year.

This case shows that it was difficult to keep virtues such as filial piety, trust, kindness, and respect for the elders, which were considered as less important than the class struggle during the Mao era. Women resisted state power by voluntarily changing their social identity through marriage, from single to married. It also reveals women's role in the chain migration pattern before their migration as a wife and caregiver who has to handle the household chores and financial expenditure under the split-household family condition.

The second case comes from Kitty's experience. Kitty (58) is short, thin, and looks ten years younger in appearance. While listening to her story, I could not believe how she made it to Hong Kong. At first, she was reluctant to tell me how she went to Hong Kong alone. She said at least three times, "I am not a lucky girl like you or young people nowadays," along with two long deep sighs. She paused several seconds or filled my mug with more tea and tried to change the subject. I felt her hopelessness whilst reflecting on her life before migration. I told her that I understood her reluctance and fear of thinking back. She faced a state power notorious for human rights violations and countless political prosecutions. Her powerlessness to alter the fate and history that deprived her of her dream, her happiness, her ambition to become a college student and to contribute to her family made a painful impression on me. It was a chaotic period of Chinese history that I learned about from textbooks, films and novels. My ancestors had immigrated to Taiwan in the early Chin Dynasty during the second half of the 17th century but I have no connections in daily life with anyone who escaped to Taiwan during the 1950s. When I finally had a chance to interview a real person who struggled through that chaotic period, I simply had no clue how to deal with my own complex, which is how to see someone's great pain in their eyes and act as a researcher at the same time. I attempted twice to shift the conversation back to her childhood life in China but in vain. Only after sharing my father's tragedy[127] with her did she finally open her mind.

---

[127] My father went missing around the Gulf of Aden in the Arabian Sea when I was 16. He worked as a chief officer for an international cargo ship company called Ever Green. His body was never found, nobody knows what exactly happened and my mother has remained single since then. When I told Kitty that I know of the real pain of not being able to bury your beloved parent and the true sorrow of not

She grew up in Guangzhou City, Guangdong Province. She is the youngest child of five. In 1972, she finished her secondary education. Under the regulation of the Communist Party, as an educated urban youth, she had to join the movement, working in the remote countryside or in the mountain areas to fulfil her patriotic duty. Sending educated youth to the countryside was one of the educational reforms before and after the Cultural Revolution. It has been much more thoroughly implemented since 1968 (Tiewes, 1974: 343). It was designed to destroy the elitism of the educated young people on the one hand, and to link higher education to the needs of society and the party on the other (ibid: 339).[128] Bernstein (1977) estimates that "between 1968 and 1978 about 17 million young people were sent to the countryside after they completed their education in an idealistic attempt to bridge the ever-widening gulf between city and countryside and a realistic attempt to circumvent a massive unemployment problem" (cited from Wolf 1985: 279). For the educated youth back then, working in the countryside did not just mean a Party order but also a patriotic performance to demonstrate their absolute loyalty to the Communist Party. However, Kitty saw so many friends come back with serious injuries and in a poor health that she knew that she would have no chance to come back home and go to university if she obeyed the party order. One month before the order, she told her mother, "Mom, I am going to swim." She left her hometown with a last glance at the dinner table: "I thought that would be the last meal my mother cooked for me." At midnight, she jumped into the bay and swam. "I didn't think too much then. I kept swimming and swimming. I didn't dare to stop. I knew if I gave up, I could be caught or be eaten by sharks."

"What if you got caught?" I asked Kitty.

"If you are lucky you would be alive in prison for several years, if *laotain* (老天; god) wouldn't help you, you died…. That's a serious crime." She finally made it to the shore before dawn. She made a phone call to her sister's friend and the lady helped her settle down in Hong Kong.

I asked Kitty why did she not tell her mother something else and why she used the word "swim"? She told me the term *youshui* (游水) was a

knowing his life and death, Kitty just grabbed my hands firmly and we shed tears and cried together. I was truly touched and really appreciated her heartfelt company and encouragement.

[128] Frederick Teiwes documented in his short visit to China report in 1974 that all university students should spend one-third of their time outside the universities in factories, rural communes or other relevant units (p.339).

vernacular for stowaway from Guangzhou to Hong Kong. Her mother was a plain and simple factory worker, she feared the cadres of the Party. Kitty knew that her mother would panic if the cadres came and she had left without saying goodbye. The consequences would be unimaginable: both her parents, even the whole family, could die in the labour camp in the North East province. Thus, she thought telling her mother the truth would give her hope, a positive thought that maybe ten years later, after Mao died, she would have a chance to take her beloved mother out of this living hell. Until now the exact number of illegal migrants from China to Hong Kong during the 1950s to the 1980s is still unknown but one can have some idea from Yow Cheun Hoe's research. According to Hoe (2013), the registered population in Hong Kong increased sharply from 849,751 in 1931 to 2,360,000 in 1950. The continuous flow refugees and migrants from China during the Great Leap Forward famine in the late 1950s and the Cultural Revolution from 1966 to 1976 led to the British government restricting border crossings in May 1950; however, desperate migrants from China kept finding ways to flock into Hong Kong (p. 23).

For the following ten years, Kitty made her living working in a garment factory for nine to ten hours a day, six days a week. In order to save money to pay for tuition for an English cram school, she only ate two meals a day. "In Hong Kong, if you can speak fluent English, you can work in a fancy hotel or restaurant with many tips… so I went to the night school." However, she did not realise at first that her refugee status blocked her opportunity for college application. Kitty could not connect with her family through normal means like letters or phone calls. Her poor living condition and her refugee status meant that she was constantly mocked and despised by local Hongkongers. At that time, making a pen pal through small advertisements in the last pages of fashion magazines or regional newspapers was very popular. Kitty found a Chinese man working abroad; they started as pen pals. She told me love in that time was very simple and pure without the internet and mobile phones. All their communication was through hand-written letters. She waited every week for that precious letter from across the Atlantic Ocean. With only one photo of the man, their long-distance relationship lasted for two years before he asked her to be with him, away from Hong Kong. "I got the chance to see my parents again after ten years, after my marriage…after *kaifang*[129]…. I chose my own job, my husband, I made all the decisions

[129] *Kaifang* (開放) in Mandarin refers particularly to the Reform and Opening Policy held by Deng Xiaopin from 1979 in China, which made transnational movement easier for ordinary citizens. However, Kitty still had some concerns

since I was 18 (years old) including (the decision) about going to *dakon*[130] (in the Netherlands)." Kitty's agency shows how a young Chinese woman broke through the iron curtain, state patriarchy and sexism by autonomously making herself illegal and regaining her legal status (foreign residence) through autonomous marriage. For the other seven working-class women about the same generation as Kitty, all of their marriages were considered arranged marriages which were approved by their parents. However, Kitty's marriage was through a process of a two-year transnational letter exchange and she married the man she fell in love with. It was quite progressive and modern in Hong Kong then.

Cathy's and Kitty's pre-migration experiences show regional differences within the same generation between women from Hong Kong and those from China. In Dutch Chinese diasporic literature I hardly see the intersectionality of Chinese women from different regions discussed. Although most of them have similar jobs after migration, from Cathy's and Kitty's pre-migration stories we can see how women in China and Hong Kong back then resisted and negotiated with the patriarchal state power through migration and marriage. From a feminist perspective, as Helma Lutz reminded us, their personal experiences show how groups of women who have the same ethnic background and are in the same generation "are positioned differently towards each other and that they face different opportunities as well as structural constraints in performing their agency" (1997: 107).

4.4 Running a Restaurant Downstairs and Raising Children Upstairs

Despite the long history of Chinese emigration to the Netherlands, there has been little discussion of the individual lives of Chinese migrant women. Only Pieke mentioned that working in a Chinese restaurant with their husband is a double-shift for Chinese women (1992: 47). In this section, I illustrate the post-migration lives of Chinese migrant working-class women. I elaborate on their motherhood practice experiences from a micro-political perspective through analysing their working life and their

---

about her escape during the Cultural Revolution so she chose to meet her parents in Hong Kong instead of in China. To know more about daily life of peasant women in pre-Liberation China, see Fielde (1887), Pruitt (1945), Yang (1945), Highbaugh (1948), Shue (1980), Andors (1983), Johnson (1983), and Wolf (1985).

130 *Dakon* (打工) is Hong Kong jargon at that time especially for people making their living by working as a waiter in the catering or hotel sector.

strategy for combining work with childrearing. Not only must they work but they must also manage the house chores and raise children. The life of the working-class Chinese minority is very different from the mainstream Dutch middle-class family (the so-called 1.5 Dutch model[131]), where the husbands are the breadwinners in the public domain while the wives are the caregivers in the private domain and only work part-time. As I mentioned earlier in this chapter, the main purposes of the women who married Chinese restaurant owners or migrant workers is first to make money, and second to open their own business. They kept financially supporting their natal families until the first child was born. Before that, they often worked and lived together with relatives until they took over the restaurants or until they saved enough money to move out and start their own restaurant in a different city or village. Pieke (1992) defines this kind of family as a uterine family, not like a nuclear family in Western society (p.43). He considers that under Chinese patriarchy, a woman's task is to produce (male) heirs to secure her own status in the husband's family, especially for the first-generation Chinese migrant woman. Since she has no family members from her natal family in the Netherlands, to build a good mother-child relationship is a guarantee of her stable authority and power in the husband's family (ibid: 43 & 47).

One element to specify about Pieke's understanding of the Chinese uterine family is that he utilises Margery Wolf's concept from 1985.[132] Based on her fieldwork and interviews in rural farm villages and model cities of China's coast provinces, Wolf argued that in Chinese society the wife is a stranger, an outsider and a (potential) threat to the mother-in-law in her husband's family. "She needs to create her own base of security by creating a family from her own body" (p.9). To secure her position in that family, she must establish a tight connection with her children for "her own uterine family was composed of children who valued her praise, her affection, and her support of them over that of all others, including that of their father" (ibid: 9). The concept of a uterine family is very similar to the jai-qu concept I mentioned in chapter three. A daughter is considered a temporary guest in her natal family until she finds her "true home" through marriage. However, based on my research, since not too many first-

[131] For more information, see chapter three.

[132] However, several feminists and anthropologists later criticised Margery Wolf's research methodology and her conclusion as oversimplified and overly general. The biggest controversial issue is that she used her fieldwork results, which were mainly conducted in Taiwan during the 1960s, to assume that women in China were living in the same situation. For a more complete discussion, see Teng (1996).

generation Chinese working-class migrant women lived with their in-laws after emigration, I am less convinced by Pieke's uterine family arguments for two reasons. First, this theory assumes that all Chinese women are willing to reproduce without sensing the patriarchal oppression in Chinese society. Second, Pieke fails to explain the motherhood practice in the transnational migratory trajectory. In the Dutch context, these women have more autonomy than those in China who live with their in-laws all their lives. Also, after the Cultural Revolution, traditional Chinese patriarchal gender inequality is seen as harmful, feudal and backward. Women who grew up in that socialist period, the series establishing new China movements from the 1950s mentioned earlier in this chapter, value female self-achievement and gender equality within the family. Nearly all these ten interviewees controlled the household's and restaurant's expenditure and made decisions about children's education within a few years after emigration through quick language accumulation (also see chapter five). In fact, they have more bargaining power and financial autonomy than the middle-class Chinese women who married native Dutch men. First, the labour participation rate of working-class Chinese women after marriage is 100% versus 60% labour participation rate of middle-class Chinese women in this study. Second, less than 30% of middle-class Chinese women who married native Dutch men have the full power to manage the household finance. Third, half of the middle-class Chinese women constantly negotiate with their Dutch husbands about their children's education, unlike the working-class Chinese women who took full charge of their children's education.[133] I would argue that the fixed concept of the Chinese uterine family under Western scholarly comprehension does not fully explain the migrant Chinese working-class family in the Dutch context.

In order to save enough money to start their own business or to pay back the loan to relatives and friends,[134] young couples often work at least ten hours a day, six to seven days a week. Three interviewees told me they had only have two days off (Christmas Eve and Christmas Day) a year during the first five business years. Not all women chose to work full-time while their children were small but they had relatively lighter financial pressure than those who had to work full-time. Since they were so busy working, how did women manage their work and childrearing on a daily

[133] See chapter five about the Mandarin education issue of transnational families.

[134] Chinese seldom take their business loan from Dutch banks: most of them borrow money from a previous boss, colleagues or relatives with lower interest. This is business cooperation inside Chinese community based on quanxi and mutual trust.

basis? I found they developed two ways of combining work and childrearing in one site by geographical arrangement; here I give two examples from Cathy's (61) and Ivy's (53) narratives.

> When they were little, we always looked for places where there were houses upstairs. Thus I could take care of (my children) during work. I cooked some dishes for them and bathed them when the time came. I took care (of children) on my own, running the restaurant and taking care of children at the same time. (Cathy)

> I carried the child in a baby buggy to the small back room in the restaurant. I worked in the kitchen and took care of the baby at the same time. When he was older, I brought him toys and books. When there were no customers, I taught him how to write and speak Mandarin. Until he went to elementary school, I was more at ease...I lived very close by (the restaurant), only two blocks. (Ivy)

Apparently working-class Chinese women developed a strategy to be a worker and a mother at the same time by working in restaurants downstairs and raising children upstairs or nearby. Since they are the owners, they can arrange their work time and meet their children's needs. Ivy told me that the small nursing room still functioned years later when she could afford to hire a part-time waiter, who had a child under four years old. She told the woman not to send her baby to the day-care centre, she let her use that nursing room for free. "She helped me and I helped her, she didn't have to worry about the baby while working, that's called win-win, right?" said Ivy. This is an example of the sisterhood between the working-class Chinese women of different generations. Ivy's case is not an exception; when I asked Betty how she could breastfeed all three children for half a year when she was so busy working, she told me that her boss had prepared a small room at the back of the restaurant in which to place the baby. That was how she could combine her work and breastfeed her three children for six months without leaving her work. However, with the rise of rental prices and the intensifying competition between Chinese restaurants, the phenomenon of "working restaurants downstairs and raising children upstairs" is disappearing. Women choose to live nearby the restaurants or hire a Chinese nanny who works eight hours to look after small children at home.

The long strenuous working hours means working-class Chinese women to have little time to discipline their children and pay attention to their academic performance. When children perform badly academically, the mother is always blamed. Betty (42) emigrated to the Netherlands at the age of seven to join her father. Her father was busy working all day long in the restaurant and had no time to take care of her. Her father did not care about her academic performance in school either. When her mother finally joined them, she had already finished her secondary school (MBO) and was working full time in her father's restaurant. Years later, she had a Chinese boyfriend, who is also the son of a Chinese restaurant owner. She got married at the age of 25. Betty has three sons and she told me she really does not know how to be a mother of teenage children because she had no role model to learn from while she was a teenager. Neither of her two older teenage sons like studying; they simply play online games or *daji*[135] all day after school. Her youngest son is four years old. Her husband blamed her for being an unqualified mother who did not educate her children well, and she found that she had no excuses to give. Her in-laws have already retired and have returned to Hong Kong. They were furious after hearing that their oldest grandson has little chance of going to college; they phoned her and criticised the shortcomings of her unqualified motherhood performance:

> Your two older sons are fixed, they (have) already gone wild….your parents didn't have time educating you, that's why your educational level was low. Now, you should bring the small one to us; let him receive education in Hong Kong while he is little, for his own good because you have no time.

Here we see the triple burden of working-class Chinese women: they not only have to work long hours to make money, they also have to take care of all the household chores and decide on financial expenditure, and when it comes to their children's education, it seems they have the full responsibility for that, too. Betty's husband does not consider her long working hours and, according to her, he constantly escapes his fatherhood responsibility with many excuses (i.e. feeling very tired from working long hours or does not know how to communicate with children). In the transnational confrontation between his parents and his wife, he kept silent to his parents but declared his wife to be at fault. In this research, I found that working-class Chinese women have few resources with which to help their children with their education, especially those who followed their parents to the Netherlands as teenagers. Two interviewees who emigrated

---

[135] *Daji* (打機) is Cantonese, particularly to describe children who are obsessed with playing TV games such as Play Station or X-Box. When Betty invited me to join her family BBQ, I saw at least three TV game devices under a wide-LCD TV screen. Game CDs were spread all over the living room. Betty laughed at me and said, "That's the boys' territory." She has another TV in her bedroom.

to the Netherlands as teenagers both reported that they felt neglected and discriminated against in schools, and they found it very difficult to keep up with their studies. Their parents could do nothing to help them academically because they were mostly busy running their restaurant as the business was in its initial stage. Like Betty, her mother did not get her permit to the Netherlands until she was an adult. Thus, they gave up on education early and then started to work in their parents' restaurants at a very young age while most Dutch teenagers were still in education.

4.4.1 Motherhood: "Exercise is better than precept"

In this part, I focus on the motherhood practice of working-class Chinese women. There are four major findings based on their narratives. Firstly, all mothers expressed powerlessness and regret that they could do nothing to help their children academically due to their own different cultural background and low educational level. But they tried to provide every possible financial resource for their children's education; for example, learning Dutch. Wendy told me she was so afraid that her Chinese-Dutch accent would have negative impacts on her son like discrimination from Dutch people in school and in future job seeking. She purposefully hired a white, native, college-graduated Dutch woman to be a half-day nanny when he was two. She asked her nanny to speak more to her son to let him grow accustomed to the correct Dutch pronunciation. Whenever her children have a question regarding Dutch, she said:

> If my son asked me "Mom, what is this?" or "Mom, how do you say this word?", I told him, "Write it down, we will ask teacher tomorrow in school." Then, he can learn the correct pronunciation.

I found there is a complex feeling of working-class women in regard to children's education. On the one hand, they want their children to surpass their own educational level so they do not have to continue with the hardship of the restaurant business and have the chance of finding a white-collar job in the future. They also feel sorry for not being able to help the children with their school work; if their children perform badly academically, they blame themselves more than their children's laziness. I want to quote Ella's opinion about children's education as an example:

> No, we can't help them (study) at all. We know little about Dutch, (my children) they help themselves, they depend on themselves.... (I think) Studying requires some gifted talent; it is useless for parents to yell (their own children) as stupid.

Like Betty, whom I mentioned earlier in this chapter: she was angry at her first son for playing video games all day long and thereby possibly failing to enter college. Her in-laws and her husband dumped the mistakes on her. They questioned her irresponsibility as a mother and she swallowed all the charges. Besides the impotent feelings as to children's academic performance, among the seven women from Hong Kong, six of them expressed that their child-rearing practices are totally different from their husbands'. The cleavages between parenting styles leads to many confrontations in the conjugal relationship. As Daisy illustrates the differences between her and her husband:

> I grew up in Hong Kong, he grew up in China. The culture is different. For example, I want to let children learn music, he objected. He said it is too costly. But I think children are not study machines, (they) need to cultivate various interests. They (people from China) are like that, they only read Mao and they only know Mao. At last, I insisted on my choice….That's what Chinese education is, beat beat beat; he won't listen to you, even if you beat him today, he remains the same tomorrow. He only hates you; if you explain to him, he might listen to you. So, I forbid my husband to beat my children.

Due to the difference of regions of original and educational background, women from Hong Kong received a British education; their perspectives on motherhood are inconsistent with the views of their husbands from China. All of them are against physical punishment, which is a common way of disciplining children in traditional Chinese education and parenting. Like Daisy spending money on extracurricular activities (i.e. piano lessons; chess class; dancing and singing class) to help her children develop their interests even though her husband considered it too expensive. I found that the intersectionality of regional differences in Chinese marriages has a direct influence on motherhood practices. Most women, especially those from Hong Kong, would fight with their husband to support their children's needs.

The third theme I discovered from working-class women's motherhood practice I called "exercise better than precept". This characteristic is an extension from the first one, although all mothers feel a great powerlessness in children's academic performance; the only way they can educate their children is through themselves. Nearly all mothers quote an old Chinese maxim: "*Shenjiao zhong yu yanjiao* (身教重於言教)." Literally it means physical education is more significant than verbal education. This maxim puts more emphasis on parents' own behaviours, meaning one's act is everything to one's children. These hard-working mothers believe that children will understand how hard it is to survive as an ethnic minority in the Dutch society. You need to work 12 hours a day, six days a week, to feed a family. Wendy shared with me how she disciplined her oldest son when he was not diligent enough in his schoolwork:

> (When he was) in middle school, his teacher told me that my elder son could only go to HAVO not VWO. I was really angry back then, but I didn't lose my temper. He became lazier and lazier and thought of playing all the time, his grade dropped, at the end he was distributed to brugklas.[136] So, I asked him to help in the kitchen at weekends for two hours. I want him to know how hard to work in the kitchen. (That is) you need to earn money by sweating all your head thus you will know where money comes from in the future.

Wendy's three sons are all college-graduated; her first son has a master's degree and works in a Dutch bank. She is very proud of her achievement on her children's education. She worked even harder after becoming a mother because she wanted to provide as best as she could for her children. She told me that at the beginning of her marriage her mother-in-law looked down upon her because of her illegal status in the Netherlands, constantly making sarcastic remarks behind her back and referring to her as an opportunist. Her mother-in-law thought she was too poor to be compatible for her son even though Wendy's educational level is higher than that of her husband's. She felt the vivid preference and prejudice from her mother-in-law towards her children compared to the children from her brother-in-law. When I tried to ask her for some examples of the indignant remarks her mother-in-law made about her, she just replied to me with "That is too embarrassing." or "I don't want to discuss that." After the interview, she invited me to a dinner made by her husband and her son. While walking me to the car park, Wendy asked me "Do you think my son is ugly in appearance?" and I was shocked by her question, then she revealed to me that her mother-in-law in the past kept saying how ugly and how silly her son looked; it hurt her feelings for

[136] According to Wendy, the brugklas is for pupils who fall behind the average and for those who are distributed to the brugklas it means they have nearly no chance of going to VWO. The major difference between HAVO and VWO is that VWO is considered pre-university education while HAVO is pre-education for professional school (HBO). HAVO pupils are actually required to start a one-year pre-admission schooling programme if they wish to enter a bachelor degree at a university.

several years. Only after her first son entered VWO did her mother-in-law change the negative attitude towards her and start to praise her efforts for her children's education.

I also want to quote Ivy's narratives as another example. Ivy (53) married at the age of 18 and became a mother within one year. Here is how she thinks of her motherhood by physical demonstration:

> I had my first baby when I was 19; I knew nothing about it but I was going to be a mother (which) was very difficult for me…Our restaurant is small, not big, very few people (She means customers). Business varies every month; we actually have no extra money to hire other people. But this small restaurant let me raise my children, let them receive education. They all understand how hard it is to run a restaurant, (they) study very hard, that is the most delightful thing for me.

The final theme I generated from working-class women's motherhood practice is that they value moral ethics in the motherhood practice more, i.e. courteousness, benevolence and diligence. All mothers mentioned the significance of teaching children as the basic principle of being a human, "*zuoren doali* (做人道理)". They can accept their children falling behind in school performance as long as they tried their best but they cannot tolerate a child's impolite attitude towards elder seniors, friends or guests. For instance, Grace shared her opinion about teaching children the basic principle of being human:

> I do care more about children's courteousness…I couldn't help my daughters' school work while they were seven. I told them that you must depend on yourself, mama studied little and I can't help you….mama won't be angry about your bad grades only if you do your best…it is no use that one is well-educated but doesn't know how to respect others. *Zuoren doali* matters most.

Grace's narrative shows that the most significant value in motherhood practices is to teach children the basic principle of being human. How you treat others shows what kind of a person you are. Studying is important for you as a student; however, without showing respect or courteousness to others, one fails to be a member of the intelligentsia. I am deeply moved and impressed by the philosophy behind the motherhood practice of working-class Chinese women. *Zuoren doali*, which they mentioned several times during the interviews, reminds me of the meaning of human in the Chinese character *ren* (人), which is: standing with two feet on the ground makes you human. Passing on this simple but meaningful belief to their children is much more substantial than children's education; this is the core of the motherhood practices of working-class Chinese migrant women.

4.5 Conclusion

To conclude, the present study is an empirical research on real day-to-day motherhood practice experiences of working-class Chinese migrant women in the Netherlands. Based on in-depth interviews and participatory observation, this book describes the gradually disappearing phenomenon of the real life of first-generation Chinese immigrant women working in the horeca (hospitality) business in the Netherlands. Three of them are from Wenzhou City, Zhejiang, Province China, and seven are from Hong Kong under the governance of the United Kingdom. In order to improve their living conditions, through quick-match marriages, eight of them followed the chain-migration to the Netherlands at a young age (18–20) before 1980 to fill the labour shortage when the Chinese restaurant business was booming. Meanwhile, they are also a gendered ethnic minority who perform the roles of wives and mothers in an alien country with no parents or relatives to support them.

In this chapter, I first filled in the blanks by explaining why the early Chinese migrants mainly came from Hong Kong and the coast provinces of China before the 1980s. With the political background and under the restrictive authoritarian population control management, people in China, especially women, had limited freedom of mobility before the Reform and Open Policy. In the second section, I illustrated how these working-class women combine their roles as restaurant employees and mothers in a particular geographical arrangement in the same space, what I called "running a restaurant downstairs and raising children upstairs". Additionally, I also gave some examples of how working-class women form a sisterhood child-caring system to help each other nurse their young children and work in the same place.

In the third section, I collected and generated four themes on the motherhood practices of working-class Chinese diasporic women: 1) mothers are unable to assist their children with their academic performance given the consequences of their different cultural background and low educational level; 2) women, particularly from Hong Kong, expressed that their child-rearing styles are different from their husbands'. The cleavages of parenting styles lead to many confrontations in the conjugal relationship and most of the time they will stand their ground to provide their children with the best they can; 3) another motherhood characteristic is that "exercise is better than precept". They work very hard year after year to physically demonstrate to their children the significance of diligence; 4) in their motherhood practice, they put more value on moral ethics than children's academic performance, for instance, courteousness, benevolence, honesty, and diligence. Teaching children the basic principles of being human is at the heart of motherhood practice among working-class Chinese migrant women in the Netherlands.

CHAPTER FIVE

LANGUAGE ISSUES FOR CHINESE MIGRANT WOMEN

5.1 Introduction

This chapter deals with the most troubling issue, namely language, which impacts Chinese migrant women in two aspects in their daily lives. One is for women themselves, the Dutch barrier and learning, and the other is for their children: Mandarin education. Language plays a vital part in our daily lives; people use language as a tool to express themselves, communicate with each other and convey their thoughts. Language is not only a bridge enabling human beings to interact with the outside world but also a carrier for heritage as parents pass on their cultures to their children. What happens when you emigrate to another country where people with an alternative culture use a different language? How does emigration affect transnational motherhood practice regarding multi-languages? What will first-generation migrant mothers encounter while trying to teach their children their heritage language? What are the considerations behind their decisions on language education? In this chapter, I show how migrant Chinese women perform their motherhood in language education in the Dutch context. By applying Pierre Bourdieu's notion of capital and field, I argue that Chinese mothers tactically set the priorities in children's language education in order to break through the ethnic ceiling, and to connect with the global Chinese fraternal network and material counterpart. My research shows that for the first-generation immigrant Chinese mothers who moved to the Netherlands where the official language is alien to them, language becomes the primary obstacle. All of them identified that the Dutch language became a barrier for them that they had to break through after emigrating; at the same time, teaching their children Mandarin was not only a critical challenge but also a matter of performing Chinese motherhood and identity construction. Both tasks happen mostly parallel and language issues play a significant part in daily-life motherhood practices. In a nutshell, parents and children must all learn new languages – for mothers it is Dutch, for the children it is Mandarin.

Pierre Bourdieu (1991) argues that language is not only a tool for daily communication in a semantic field[137] but that it also represents symbolic power itself in political representation in a society, a material field. According to Bourdieu, language is one of the compositions of human capital, which has its own economic and market value. The official language, in particular, represents symbolic power as excellence, as it turns language into material capital which supports individuals to establish or expand their positions in a social space structured by power relationships (Bourdieu, 1993). From his point of view, the official language has its legitimacy, thus it is interwoven with symbolic capital. Elites must rely on this power to sustain their superior social position and privileges. Dominated people acquiesce because language imposes schemes of classification that produce a legitimate form of social order that hides the arbitrariness of its foundations (Kelly, 1993: 1200). To put it another way, what if migrants' language from their country of origin has an overwhelming symbolic and social capital, more than the language of the host country? Then how do migrant women decide whether to teach their children their heritage language? In this research, this issue is exactly what all my interviewees constantly struggled with. For them, Dutch and Mandarin represent two symbolic powers that intersect with migration and children's education: one is the official language (Dutch) of the host country; the other one is the heritage language (Mandarin) from the pre-migration country. Each language is valued differently in conformity with where people are situated.

According to Bourdieu, a field is a form of social organisation with two main aspects: (a) a configuration of social roles, agent positions and the structures they fit into, and (b) the historical process in which those positions are actually taken up and occupied by individual or collective actors (Hanks, 2005: 72). Family, educational institutions and government authorities can be regarded as fields, which are relatively bounded. A language is socially valued; through speaking a language one is embedded in a universe of categorisation, selective distinctions and evaluations. Symbolic systems are structuring as well as structured (ibid., p.77). I regard motherhood as a field (Bourdieu, 1991) where several powers operate at the same time to various dimensions especially on language education matters. Like Bourdieu says:

---

[137] A semantic field can refer to a group of words in a specific category. For instance, cars, buses, flights, trains, and boats belong to the field of transportation.

> A field is always the site of struggles in which individuals seek to maintain or alter the distribution of the forms of capital specific to it. The individuals who participate in these struggles will have differing aims, depending on where they are located in the structured space of positions (1991:14).

In this study, Chinese women who marry Dutch men are very much opposite actors on languages. Family thus becomes an arena where Dutch and Mandarin performed by fathers and mothers is endorsed by various symbolic powers. Moreover, intersections of gender, age, class, ethnicity, nationality, and financial inequality all intertwine with languages in migrant families.

5.2 Theories on Post-migration Language Proficiency and Social Integration

Research on relations between post-migration language proficiency and social integration has, in general, been divided into three dimensions: economic benefits, socio-emotional impacts, and family communication. First, the relationship between post-migration language proficiency and economic benefits is of major importance. Some researchers argue that post-immigration language proficiency is an economic resource for immigrants, causing them to have better socioeconomic outcomes than those who have a lower dominant-language proficiency in a host society (VandenHeuvel and Wooden, 1997; Bleakley and Chin, 2004). Age at arrival also matters with regard to language capital. In her research on the effect of premigration language capital among adult immigrants in Canada, Adamuti-Trache (2012) argues that female immigrants from South and East Asian countries aged from 25 to 29 and 30 to 34, with a university education, perform economically well within four years of arrival. Also, their premigration language capital continues to affect immigrant settlement and integration for a long time after arrival (p. 123). Roughly speaking, current Chinese migration studies show that the younger, more educated women adjust better and assimilate quicker with regard to age, education level, premigration language capital, and gender.

Second, post-migration language proficiency can have social-emotional impacts on immigrants especially for adults as learning a new language necessitates time, money and determination. Language differences are reported as the most frequently experienced stressor among Northeast Asian immigrants in the United States (Koh & Bell, 1987; Mui, 1996; Lee, 2007). English language proficiency and communication are essential problems affecting immigrants' well-being (Watkins et al. 2012). Thus, language barriers can also cause low immigration satisfaction (Ying, 1996), and without sufficient social network support, immigrants can often suffer from depression and social isolation, especially the Asian elderly (Hossen, 2012). Contrary to the position of dominant language proficiency as economic capital for immigrants, some researchers argue for the importance of language as a noneconomic resource that can connect social networks and is of benefit to the nature of social capital among immigrants (Nawyn et al. 2012). In the United States, if first-generation immigrant parents achieve a moderate level of English proficiency, their children perform better academically, and it is then more possible for the family to maintain bilingualism (Mouw and Xie, 1999). That is to say, whether the official language of the host country acts as a social-emotional barrier or as a benefit to immigrants depends on age, class and the educational level of immigrants.

The third group of studies focuses mainly on the relationship between postmigration language acquisition and family communication. Previous research was mostly conducted in English-speaking countries. Along with the rapid increase of the Chinese population in English-speaking countries like the United States, the UK, Australia, and New Zealand, the successful academic performance of second-generation Chinese caused this group to be labelled as a "model minority group". However, the quicker they become proficient in English, the faster the heritage language is lost among the second generation. This issue has only been noticed by academics this decade. Wen-Jui Han (2010) criticises past researchers and policymakers for focusing too much on migrant children's academic performance and paying too little attention to their socioemotional well-being. Lily Wong Fillmore (1991) found that 50.6% of Chinese immigrant families reported that children had a language shift from Mandarin to English at home. Laurie Olsen (2000) believes that this phenomenon might result from "language shock" in the early assimilation process of children from minority families. Learning English is not only for academic performance; it is also for being a "real" American and for surviving socially. The political ideology in a monolingual country is implicated in this issue. Some scholars point out that societal pressure and political ideology around monolingualism accelerates the loss of the home language. When speaking English is constructed as a symbolic icon for national loyalty, children will abandon their home language (Fillmore, 2000; Taylor, 2008; Ho, 2010). Desiree Boalian Qin (2006) vividly illustrates in her study how sad and hopeless Chinese migrant parents feel when children become more assimilated into American society, migrant parents become more passive and silent at home. As they grow apart emotionally, the parent-child relationship splits and their connection stops being emotionally intimate. Things become worse under the traditional Chinese style of obedience and discipline. Mandarin is not only a tool for ethnic identity construction and the connection between parents and children, it is also an economic resource and capital in the worldwide Chinese community (Li, 2006). Some researchers claim that in the United Kingdom, second-generation Chinese learn Mandarin both for the instrumental benefits for their career and ethnic identity (Francis et al., 2009). Aihwa Ong (1999) analysed tycoons from Hong Kong, Taiwan, Malaysia, and Indonesia: they hold passports from Western countries, which offer them socially flexible citizenships. Another key point that makes them successful is the Mandarin capital, which she illustrates as an Asian fraternal network. These networks are representative of the modern Asian way of doing business, namely, man to man, usurping the paternalistic role of the government in economic activities. Ong recognises the importance of Mandarin as social capital for Chinese heritage, to stand out in a capitalistic world and compete with the West. It seems that learning Mandarin for Chinese migrants is more instrumentally oriented than identity-oriented. The ability to use Mandarin functions as significant cultural and economic capital, and also as a potential return ticket for second-generation Chinese immigrants, to go back to their "home" country with symbolic Western cultural capital or to join the global Chinese economic unity.

In this chapter, besides language as marketable capital, I focus on a discussion of the cultural and social capital of languages; especially on why teaching children Mandarin is significant in Chinese motherhood. I divide the analysis into two sections. In the first section, I look at the postmigration social adjustment of Chinese migrant women resulting from the acquisition of Dutch and their personal development. I describe the differences in class, generations and intercultural families. How do different Chinese migrant women break through the Dutch language barrier, and how does the language barrier affect their daily lives, both domestically and socially? The second section focuses on Mandarin education. In this study, all the interviewees reported that they tried to teach their children Mandarin themselves from the age of two or by sending them to a weekend Chinese school from five to seven years of age. My finding is different from Ying's (1996) Chinese American research. She identifies the English language difficulty as the most pressing and immediate postmigration issue for Chinese immigrants in San Francisco. Mandarin education is not identified as a problem there. This may be directly related to the fact that San Francisco is a city where immigrants can easily access the large Chinese American community and have ample opportunities to enjoy most of the Chinese cultural activities available in Chinese societies (p. 14). The difference in scale of the Chinese communities in the United States and the Netherlands may explain why Chinese Americans do not consider Mandarin education as the biggest problem for them, while Chinese Dutch do. The same result is also presented in Halleh Ghorashi's comparative research (2002) of Iranian immigrant communities between the States and the Netherlands. Iranian immigrants in Los Angeles can adapt to the new environment and find a paid job more easily than those in the Netherlands. They feel at home in America and often celebrate traditional Iranian festivities. Apparently, the scale of the immigrant community in the host country is an important factor for migrants settling in and adjusting to a new country.

My own reading of this difference is that going to America was the ultimate goal for most Chinese people during the turbulence of WWII. The American Dream for Chinese people represents total emancipation and rebirth (cf. Ghorashi, 2002: 112). When one has settled down in the final destination, surrounded by Chinese people, the most important task is to forget the past and be a "real" American. Compared to English, Mandarin seems weaker in its social symbolic power. This kind of discourse also appears in popular Chinese movies, soap operas [138] and novels. For example, in the preface to Amy Tan's *The Joy Luck Club*, the author describes an old woman's reminiscences before leaving for America: "In America I will have a daughter just like me…Over there nobody will look down on her, because I will make her speak only perfect American English" (p. 17). However, this "English-only" attitude is also changing among Chinese American communities. From September to November 2014, I lived in San Josè and had the opportunity to share my research with local Chinese families, all parents. Some second-generation Chinese (about 11 people) told me that nowadays, they must learn Mandarin to keep their jobs and/or to negotiate for better salaries because China is the second-largest business partner of the USA; employers hire Chinese for their Mandarin abilities. For families with school-age children, parents will send them to private Mandarin study groups or weekend Mandarin schools for the sake of their future career opportunities.

Lieber and Lévy (2013), who recently conducted research on Chinese immigrants in Switzerland, show the same finding as mine. In a country

---

[138] For example, in 1992, *A Chinese Woman in Manhattan* was a hit on CCTV, China.

where the immigrant Chinese population is less than 0.5% of Switzerland's foreign population,[139] Chinese parents regard the Mandarin education for children as compulsory in order to remain "Chinese" for symbolic inclusion within the Chinese nation, and also for career advancement. They discovered that all the first-generation Chinese immigrants, no matter which regional dialects parents speak as mother tongues, made their children learn Mandarin in Switzerland, but most of them failed when the children became teenagers. They called this "as a Chinese you must speak Mandarin" phenomenon "a common racialized vision of language" (p. 158). Although my finding in this study was similar to Lieber and Lévy's, I look at this inference in a different way. I argue that teaching children Mandarin is deeply culturally rooted in Chinese motherhood; I also consider that learning Mandarin is a way to compete with the symbolic mainstream power of the official language in a Dutch context. I argue for this viewpoint in the second part of this section.

In the later section, I discuss why teaching children Mandarin is necessary for first-generation Chinese migrant mothers. I am also curious about the cultural and linguistic connection between Mandarin education and motherhood practice. Two types of families are researched in this study. The first is Chinese family immigrants who came to the Netherlands before the 1980s, who are mostly working-class and involved in the catering and restaurant business.[140] Their native languages are different Chinese dialects rather than Mandarin, which begs the question of how they make children learn Mandarin. Second, how do highly educated, middle-class women married to Dutch men deal with language education in a transnational family? To conclude, I connect the Mandarin education of Chinese migrant families to a global Mandarin fraternal network and material counterpart to understand how the rising "the Greater China" hegemonic discourse directly results in the "Chinese must speak Mandarin" presumption which reconstructs and reshapes the transnational motherhood practices.

---

[139] According to the data Lieber and Lévy (2013) provided, in 2010, there were only 8,606 Chinese officially settled in Switzerland (p. 137). See, Lieber, Marylène and Florence Lévy. 2013. ""When you look Chinese, you have to speak Chinese": Highly Skilled Chinese Migrants in Switzerland and the Promotion of a Shared Language." Pp. 134–162.

[140] For more information about the Chinese migration wave to the Netherlands, please see the Introduction. For information about the Chinese population working in the catering business in the Netherlands, see chapter four.

5.3 Definition of Mandarin as a Heritage Language

Before entering the analysis, I want to clarify why I refer to Mandarin as a heritage language rather than a mother tongue. Given the historical and post-colonial context of official languages in both the PRC and the ROC (Taiwan), I tend to define Mandarin as a heritage language rather than a mother tongue. One must realise that Mandarin, or as it is known today Standard Mandarin, was originally called Bejing Guanhua (Bejing dialect) and only became an official language in 1949, a little over half a century ago, in the year the PRC was founded under the rule of the Chinese Communist Party (CCP). In China, Mandarin has been taught in every educational institution since 1956.[141] People who were born before 1956, and who did not grow up in Beijing, actually cannot speak Standard Mandarin well. There are an estimated 129 dialects (generally divided into seven linguistic groups: Guan, Wu, Yue, Min, Xiang, Kejia, Gan) in China alone, and 55 officially recognised ethnic minorities with their own languages; for instance, people may speak Cantonese, Hakka or Hunanese as their mother tongues. This is also why early Chinese migrants from Hong Kong and China had a difficult time teaching their children Mandarin themselves; nor could they find qualified Mandarin teachers to instruct a Standard Mandarin class. According to Li Minghuan (2002), at the end of the 1990s, there were 41 Chinese weekend schools established by huaqiao (Chinese overseas) in the Netherlands, which all used Cantonese as their language of instruction (p. 181).[142] It is relevant here to consider the history of Hong Kong's official language education: Hong Kong was a British colony in Northeast Asia for 150 years until the handover in 1997. During the colonial period, English was the official language. Until 1974, Mandarin was recognised as the second official language in Hong Kong. According to John Flowerdew (1999), at that time approximately 98% of Hongkongers spoke Cantonese as their mother tongue. This is why the early Chinese migrants from Hong Kong to the Netherlands did not speak Mandarin, and therefore they were unable to teach their children Mandarin themselves.

Take myself as an example; having grown up in Taiwan, my mother tongue is Taiwanese (a dialect belonging to the Min group) not Mandarin, the official language taught in educational institutions, used in the media,

---

[141] Mandarin has been used as the governmental language since 1945, when ROC declared its regime in Taipei, Taiwan by the *Kuomintang* (KMT, the Nationalist Party).

[142] Li, Minghuan. 2002. "A Group in Transition: Chinese Students and Scholars in the Netherlands." Pp: 173–188.

and any interaction with government bureaucracy after 1949.[143] Chinese people are, in fact, very used to diglossia. People grew up in a diglossic society where Mandarin is regarded as the advanced and modernised language whilst local vernaculars, or Mandarin with heavy regional accents, are considered backward and uncivilised.[144] Although Chinese people from different regions may speak various vernaculars as mother tongues, the writing of Chinese characters is the same, while some non-Han ethnicities have their own characters, i.e. Tibetans and Manchurians. In general, there are two styles of Chinese characters: the traditional style and the simplified style. The traditional style is officially used in Taiwan, Hong Kong, Macao, and Singapore whereas the simplified style was officially used in China after 1956. Nowadays, both traditional and simplified Chinese are used worldwide though simplified Chinese is the mainstream.

5.4 Analysis and Discussion

5.4.1 "Nederlands is een moeilijke taal, maar je moet leren."[145]

In this section I want to describe two different social strata groups that have high motivations for learning Dutch soon after arrival. The first group is working-class women who married Chinese men, either working separately or running Chinese restaurants together; the other group is middle-class women with a higher educational level who married native Dutch men. Most of them had been working as international professionals for several years before arrival. I also give illustrations of how Dutch integration and immigration policy impacts those who came to the Netherlands after 2003 in the third part of this chapter.

---

[143] Before that, the official language in Taiwan was Japanese as Taiwan was a colony of the Japanese Empire from 1895 to 1945.

[144] If we take postcolonialism into consideration, we see that diglossia is more vivid in Taiwan, Hong Kong, Macao, and Singapore where Japanese, English and Portuguese still a have higher symbolic power than Mandarin, the official language itself. (For related studies, please see Bray & Koo, 2004 and Silver, 2005). In the Netherlands, diglossia of migrant minorities, in particular for Surinamese, also exists. (See G. Wekker and H. Wekker, 1992).

[145] This sentence was directly quoted by Polly in her interview (in Eindhoven, April 2012). She told me in Dutch to express her viewpoint that learning Dutch is difficult but is the only way for working-class Chinese to survive in the Netherlands.

Financial need

Financial need is the biggest motivation for working-class mothers to learn Dutch within a short period. Most of them have no college diploma and work in restaurants as wait staff and bar staff. They followed the Chinese chain-migration pattern to the Netherlands that started in the 1980s. Marriage was not the purpose of their migration but a way to stay legally in order to earn more money.[146] Most of them are in their 50s and 60s. They told me that under the severe selective educational system in China and Hong Kong, if they had not dared to emigrate, they would have been poor and stayed at the lowest scale of society all their life. However, life was not easy in the Netherlands either: as mothers and daughters responding to filial piety, they had to take care of their children, support the family business and send a remittance back to elderly parents[147] or sponsor younger family members in China and Hong Kong. They carried desperate financial burdens, especially in the early phase of migration. Most of them are grandmothers now; they have either sold the restaurants to younger immigrants or passed the business on to their children. Take Wendy's case, for instance; after failing the College Entrance Exam three times, Wendy considered her future career in China would be as a farmer's wife, so 30 years ago she decided to help her sister, who'd married a Chinese running a restaurant in Rotterdam. Now she is a successful restaurant owner. She told me how important it was to be able to speak Dutch in the workplace:

> I had two goals when first coming to the Netherlands. First, work. Second, sending money back to China, fulfilling filial piety for mama and papa. I noticed that waiters made more than kitchen assistants so I made myself learn how to count from 1 to 100 and remembered how to pronounce everything on the menu within one week. I carried a dictionary with me all the time. The boss really liked me, the basic salary of the first month was *f*700 but the boss gave me *f*800 because of my hard work. In the third month I earned *f*900, not including tips yet.

---

146 On the migration pattern and marriage of working-class Chinese in the Netherlands please see chapter four.

147 In China, there is no compulsory health insurance; once elderly parents are sick or injured, treatment costs become a huge burden for family members, especially for a son. However, I found that if their parents in China are in need of money, almost all working-class Chinese women, even if they'd already been married for decades, they would try their best to save or borrow money for them. They proudly told me that this is how a filial Chinese daughter should perform, even with "*meidushu*" (receive little education).

Since Dutch proficiency has a direct positive influence on salary, learning Dutch became the first priority for ambitious Chinese working-class women. Before 2003, there was no free compulsory Dutch course for immigrants: Chinese women learned Dutch in the restaurants. The owner or restaurant manager[148] taught and trained employees in basic Dutch; whoever was recognised for her Dutch oral proficiency could serve the customers. Wait staff shared more tips than kitchen assistants. Some of them learned Dutch on Sundays in Chinese churches. According to my interviewees, there was one Chinese church in The Hague 30 years ago that provided a free Dutch course for Chinese immigrants, but it was in Cantonese.[149] I also found that due to the gender division of labour in the restaurant, a shift in gender power relations occurs among working-class Chinese families as time goes by. The gender division in a Chinese restaurant is usually like this: the man is in charge of the kitchen and the woman is in charge of serving customers. She must speak Dutch to greet and to serve the customers. As a result, the woman often handles all the financial expenditure and makes decisions regarding the children's education because she knows more Dutch than her husband. As time goes by, the Chinese woman is the de facto head of household and business. After being a mother and working as a waitperson for two years, Wendy wanted to open a restaurant of her own. She told me how significant it is for an immigrant to be fully independent by learning Dutch:

> I wanted to open a restaurant but you must have horeca diploma. I bought a book to self-study. My husband told me that we could rent the diploma from another. I didn't like his idea. It meant that your fate was controlled in other hands, what if they suddenly took it back? My husband couldn't speak any Dutch then, I only spoke little. We hired an interpreter to help us to register the first time in City Hall. Only a few minutes cost me *f*100. The second time she didn't even show up. So I decided to do it myself.

---

[148] Given the fact of the Chinese chain migration pattern, the owner or the manager of the restaurant and the waiters are either relatives or friends with connections from the same province or district in China or Hong Kong, thus they are considered as "Zìji ren" (one of us). They can easily access all resources from the older Chinese immigrants, including the acquisition of Dutch.

[149] In further correspondence with Kitty (July 2013), she told me that church was not only for Cantonese speakers: as long as you want to learn Dutch, anyone could go. She considered it a very good chance for new migrants to learn both Dutch and Cantonese at the same time. She also emphasized that she treasured every Dutch course very much; as a young immigrant who came alone in her early 20s, the weekly church gathering consoled her nostalgia and loneliness.

> Although I couldn't fully understand, I tried very hard to communicate with all the Dutch I had. The first step was always the most difficult, after that I felt more confident and tried to learn Dutch whenever I was free. I constantly had a quarrel with my husband, I was really angry about that; I told him "Why don't you learn Dutch since you have been here longer than me? Although Dutch is really difficult, we will live here for a long time, you must learn it. No one will come to solve your problem forever! You must be independent, be brave. You must learn Dutch or you are an idiot. There's nothing bad about learning a new language or do you want to be an illiterate in the Netherlands?"

The gender hierarchy among working-class Chinese families transformed in both the public and the private domain after decades of postmigration. As women became more capable in speaking Dutch, the men became more dependent on them to manage their business and family chores. Several interviewees mentioned that they felt they are considered the man in the private domain because the children obeyed and respected them more than their fathers. In the public domain, they felt customers and employees in the restaurants respected them more than their husbands; it was as if they were the real bosses. The working-class Chinese migrant women seem to adjust quicker and better than the men in my study. For them, Dutch acquisition and proficiency is a cultural capital for women's emancipation. It could reverse and change the traditional Chinese patriarchy and gendered hierarchy in the family after migration.

Being independent

To be emotionally and financially independent and have access to information are the main motivations for middle-class Chinese women to learn Dutch. Before moving to the Netherlands or before marriage, most of them had had a full-time job for years and they were used to thinking and making decisions. Most of them are in their late 30s to 40s with a higher education diploma, from Taiwan and China, and married native Dutch or second-generation Chinese Dutch men. They could not accept being uncomfortable, vulnerable and isolated to the outside world because they could not speak or read Dutch in the early phase of migration. Most of them seldom use Dutch in the work place but communicate in Mandarin and English. However, they all showed great concern that they do not want to totally rely on others' help.[150] Some of them even showed great

---

[150] According to the Directorate General of Budget, Accounting and Statistics, Executive Yuan, 2012, the female labour participation rate in Taiwan was 50.19%.

sympathy towards Dutch women, denoted in the male-breadwinner and female-caretaker or the "1.5 model[151]" that hinders women's career development and made Dutch women mostly financially dependent on men. Most of them paid to learn Dutch at the basic or intermediate level within the first year after migration. Some of them decided to settle in the Netherlands for a better living environment for their children after years of working in other areas of the world.[152]

Helen, a 45-year-old mother, holds a US master's degree and works as a human resource officer in a British business company. Basically, Dutch is not a requirement in the workplace but English is. She has several Dutch friends, the parents of her children's classmates. She leads a trilingual daily life. At work, she mainly uses English. She communicates with her husband and Dutch friends in Dutch. She speaks Mandarin and Taiwanese with her children and friends from Taiwan and China. She told me her personal opinion about learning Dutch:

> I couldn't really understand why people refuse to learn the local language after emigration. I have an American friend who has also been married to a Dutch guy for years; she simply thinks there's no need to learn Dutch. For me at least you can read a newspaper, understand radio news, you know what's going on and you feel like one of them. You can get correct information by depending on no one. I never thought of whether I should learn Dutch one day. Somehow my identity reveals the fact that I am a Taiwanese. Even if I could speak Dutch fluently; they still would consider me an outsider, that's fine with me. Most of the Dutch people are so surprised about my Dutch proficiency and they are kind of happy about that. As long as I respect their language and culture and they respect me as a person legally living here. I am a Chinese that's an undeniable fact, let it show on my name, no problem.

From Helen's point of view, for middle-class Chinese career women, social integration is more important than the financial need to learn Dutch. They want to fully participate in their husbands' social network and be a responsible mother for their children's scholarly performance. Learning Dutch enables them to directly communicate with teachers and other parents. They also want to be a part of Dutch society, and to be fully in charge of acquiring the information they need. They learn Dutch out of

---

See: http://www.dgbas.gov.tw/ct.asp?xItem=30304&ctNode=3246&mp=1 (sheet 3), access date June 15, 2013.

[151] See chapter three.

[152] I elaborate more on Chinese social norms and motherhood ideology in chapter three.

respect for their husbands' culture within a very short period. These younger, highly educated, professional Chinese women were raised in the economic take-off period in both Taiwan and China. Two-thirds of them recalled how the teachers at school said that the girls had to be thankful to their parents for giving them the opportunity to receive a higher education, equal to boys.[153] They were trained to be able to defeat male counterparts in the College Entrance Exam. The most popular political slogan at that time to promote gender equity was "*Nuren chengqi banbiantian*" (Women hold up half of the sky). Growing up in this political atmosphere, these interviewees really value their autonomy in the relationship and in the family. They are eager to take total control of their life as soon as possible after migration, and learning Dutch is the first and the most critical step for them.

Another particular point that shows their independent characteristic is that interviewees within this generation do not change their family names into their husbands' after marriage. They told me they found no need to change their family name to denote who they are after marriage. None of them called themselves feminists. Some of them challenged the Western gendered order to IND officers when being asked if they wanted to change their surnames while applying for new IDs. Helen told me that a Chinese surname is easily identified in Dutch society. Sometimes people have stereotypes toward Chinese; she considered it is their loss to be so narrow-minded. Middle-class Chinese women have a strong ethnic identity. They either grew up in a modernised, democratised, post-war Taiwan or economic take-off, post-Mao China where several gender equality policies were implemented.[154] Transnational marriage made them more aware of their own ethnic identity as a minority in the Netherlands. Keeping their Chinese surname and retaining their individuality are some examples of that.

---

[153] This collective memory is contrary to those of the older generation from Hong Kong. They all came from big families with six or eight children. Most of them were forced to drop out of school after they turned 14. Because going to high school was not free, only boys were entitled to study.

[154] The earliest example of a woman not having to change her surname into her husband's was from the 1919 May Fourth Movement in China. Taiwanese women were forced to change their surname into their husband's during the colony period under the Japanese Empire (1895–1945). After 1945, the new law leaves the choice to women to freely decide whether they want to change their surname into their husband's or not. Basically, the act of changing your surname your husband's is considered extremely old-fashioned, conservative and backward in both Taiwan and China nowadays.

People who came after 2007

From the previous analysis, it is clear that working-class or middle-class Chinese women showed great determination and perseverance in learning Dutch in order to improve their life, fulfil their filial piety as a daughter, and to be fully grounded in the host country. Most of them can speak fluent Dutch for daily communication;[155] especially middle-class Chinese women, who can read newspapers, follow news reports and watch Dutch soap operas with their husbands. Despite their strong personal motivation, some factors in life can hinder their plan, especially the newcomers who immigrated to the Netherlands after 2007[156] and encountered the ongoing Eurozone crisis. To reduce expenditures, local governments cancelled free inburgering (civic integration) classes. Apple (39) married a Chinese Dutch second- generation man who runs two restaurants. She lives in the south of the Netherlands where no Chinese church offers free Dutch lessons. She told me her dilemma:

> Actually. I wanted to learn Dutch right away while arriving, but my husband told me it's very expensive. I knew if I had a child, then the situation for learning Dutch would be difficult and tough. He told me to wait for the letter from gemeente (city hall) then I would have the free Dutch course. I had been waiting and waiting until I was pregnant. And you know what; they don't provide free Dutch course anymore because of no money. I really wanted to learn but the tuition for the whole course and the transportation are expensive, about 2000 to 2500 EUR. There is no Dutch cram school nearby.

Here we see the dilemma of a new immigrant woman. She is eager to learn Dutch after arrival; however, there is no social welfare support to help her. Learning Dutch became a personal responsibility, to show loyalty

---

[155] Ten interviewees reported that some Dutch people (strangers in the open market or restaurant customers) teased their accent or wrong pronunciation, making them embarrassed and frustrated.

[156] Although the Integration Law has been implemented from 2007, for those who only hold permanent residence if they want to naturalize as a Dutch citizen, they also have to pass the inburgering exam (civic integration exam). According to Dutch cultural theorists Marc de Leeuw and Sonja van Wichelen (2014), the inburgering exam is a tool of civilization (p. 350) which is a legitimated discrimination sanctioned by the government because it targets only certain nationalities. Moreover, the inburgering exam and its political justification also represent a forced culturalism and an object of political instrumentalization (Pp. 346–350).

and determination to integrate into Dutch society, especially for non-Western migrant women (niet-westers allochtone migranten vrouwen) (Roggeband & Verloo, 2007). This policy shift failed to see the new immigrant women's difficulties and needs as a financially dependent, cultural minority, and mothers in a host country. For those who live far from Chinese self-supporting community areas like Amsterdam, The Hague or Rotterdam, free Dutch classes are rare. It will definitely take them longer to integrate into Dutch society because of the lack of opportunities and insufficient social welfare.

Learning Dutch is a necessity during the process of acculturation. For working-class Chinese women it is a way to survive, earn money and improve the living conditions for the family in Hong Kong or China. During the process of Dutch acculturation, there is a possibility of emancipating women from traditional Chinese patriarchy. Working-class women gradually turn the power relation in households. For middle-class Chinese women, learning Dutch means integrating into mainstream society quickly and being independent in decision-making. However, the ongoing retrenchment of the welfare state and the increasing neo-liberalism are already making immigrant women more vulnerable and financially dependent. From the experiences of learning Dutch, and the experiences of first-generation Chinese mothers of different age and class groups, one can see how people living in an alien field are being influenced by various powers. The official language (Dutch) not only comes with economic and cultural capital, it gradually transforms into representing a national symbolic power authorities use as a tool to label and distinguish so-called "qualified" immigrants.

The narratives and Dutch-learning experiences of first-generation Chinese migrant women in the Netherlands reveal three points. First, they are all eager to learn Dutch soon after migrating, either by spending one year in a Dutch language school or through the help of Chinese communities. They know Dutch is social-economic capital with which they can find a job and become less economically dependent. Second, as a minority ethnic group, Chinese women try hard to participate in the labour market, either formally or informally. However, their need (i.e. free Dutch lessons, affordable day-care service, or job searching assistance) is often negated by the Dutch government's minority policy, especially the abridged subsidised Dutch lessons, which makes women more dependent financially on their Dutch partners. Third, the retrenchment of the welfare state has a direct negative impact on the speed newly migrated Chinese women integrate into mainstream Dutch society and the opportunities they can find there. After the Netherlands Nationality Act in 1985, the Dutch government uses the Dutch language test as an immigration control with which to select "desired and qualified" future Dutch citizens. According to Rick van Oers' research (2008), both naturalisation and integration tests are a high profit business for the government; furthermore, the test itself is a tool as a barrier to those "unwanted" immigrants by the Dutch government, especially for family reunification and asylum seekers (p. 41). The government assigns individual responsibility for learning Dutch but ignores the gender and ethnic inequality structure of new immigrant women. Learning Dutch in a private language institution costs a fortune; this policy shift only makes immigrant women more financially and emotionally vulnerable, and physically restricted to the household, which, moreover, is contradictory to the women's emancipation policy, aimed at autonomy and empowerment for migrant women. The basic free Dutch course is at least a welcome gate for the immigrant women to participate in Dutch society and interact with other immigrants regardless of race, class, age, country of origin, and educational level. Unfortunately, under the neo-liberalist political ideology, the basic welfare of migration is always the first to be sacrificed. Life as a young migrant Chinese mother is tougher than ever. In the next section, I enter into the discussion about Mandarin education, to see how the heritage language of the mother plays its part in motherhood practice for Chinese women.

5.4.2 Mandarin education as a family struggle

Historical background of Mandarin education in the Netherlands

Before beginning the analysis of Mandarin education, I want to briefly introduce as a background the history of the Onderwijs in Eigen Taal en Cultuur (OETC, which translates in English as Minority Language and Culture Teaching) policy in the Netherlands. The OETC policy was first implemented in 1967. According to Geert Driessen (1996), OETC only involved children of foreign workers from Mediterranean countries (including Turkey and Morocco), Moluccan children, and the children of officially recognised refugees (p. 316). Surinamese and Antillean children were excluded from OETC because the official language of these former colonies is Dutch. Chinese OETC was not subsidised either because Chinese do not fall under the official minority policy. From the policy design of OETC, the social position of immigrant Chinese groups is excluded and marginalised from mainstream Dutch society. This is why first-generation Chinese immigrants could only depend on themselves to teach their children Mandarin in the early days. Most of the weekend

Chinese schools in the Netherlands were founded by parents, and the teachers are usually Chinese mothers who hold university or master's degrees. They rent classrooms from regional public schools and ship the textbooks directly from Hong Kong, China or Taiwan. However, the quality and stability of teachers have been a problem for parent-supported Chinese schools.[157]

Teaching children to learn how to read and write Mandarin requires a lot of effort from mothers. Here I want to show a photo (figure 5-1) as an example of how Chinese immigrant mothers teach their children Mandarin in daily life. Jessie, 37 years old, is a widow whose husband passed away in the second year of their marriage, and at that time her daughter was not even one year old. For the past five years, she has taken several part-time jobs so she can raise her daughter on her own. She proudly showed me how she teaches her daughter to recognise and write Chinese characters: at least five phrases a week.

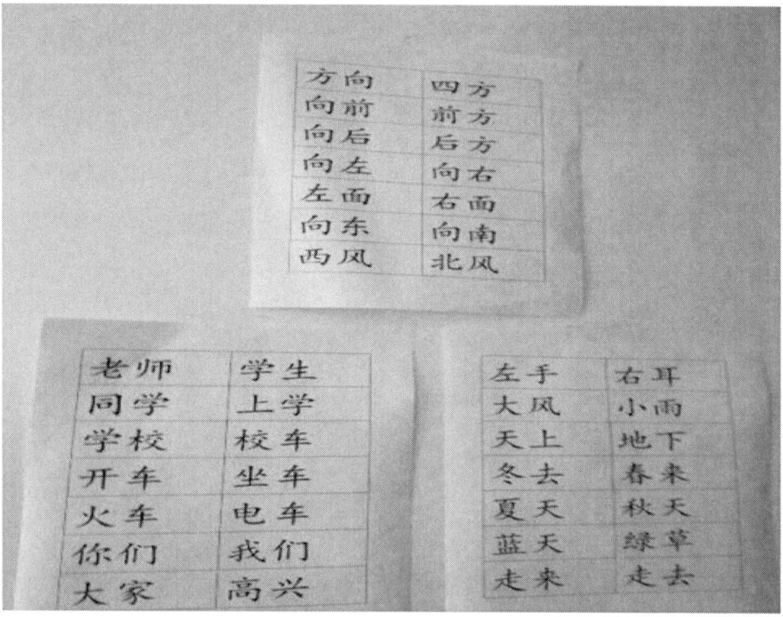

Figure 5-1 Weekly Mandarin work of Jessie's daughter; photograph by Shu-Yi Huang. February 29, 2012

[157] The same problems also occur in the United States despite the Chinese population being bigger than that of the Netherlands; see Li, 2005.

We can see there are three sheets of paper with various Chinese phrases.[158] Once a week, Jessie attaches each sheet of paper on the kitchen wall and teaches her daughter two phrases a day. In the morning she explains the meaning of the words and then she teaches her the pronunciation of the phrases. At night, she demonstrates to her daughter the order of writing these characters and then asks her to write them with her. Jessie told me that maybe one day she would go back to China if she could not meet her goals in the Netherlands. She does not want her daughter to be left behind in her studies. She checks Mandarin classes for children on the internet and follows the instructions step by step. Her daughter, now almost six years old, can communicate with me in correct Mandarin vocabulary, and she can write at least 100 Chinese characters without looking at books. Jessie is not the only Chinese migrant mother who tries to teach her children Mandarin at home. I noticed at least 15 mothers displayed Mandarin-learning papers like Jessie's at home. However, without any government support, only those who received standard Mandarin education after 1949 in China and Taiwan are capable of doing this. For the older generations from Hong Kong with a lower educational level, it is impossible for them to teach children Mandarin on their own.

Analysis

At first, I did not notice that this is one of the most significant issues for my interviewees. From the first three pilot interviews, all interviewees immediately mentioned parent-child communication and Mandarin education problems for their children when asked the question, "What do you consider to be the most difficult thing as an immigrant mother in the Netherlands?" I still remember how Cathy, who has four children, expressed her resentment by saying with a trembling voice, "They (referring to her two younger sons) don't even know how to write their own name (in Chinese)." Cathy's strong reaction suddenly reminded me of my childhood. At the age of nine in 1990, I was elected as "Mandarin promoter" in class. It was a noble honour at the time the Kuomintang (KMT) Party first ruled Taiwan and all people were forced to learn to speak correct Mandarin. Only the one who had the best Mandarin proficiency could be selected as the candidate. Back home, I announced this news to my grandmother with pride; however, she gave me a very sad

[158] For example. the top sheet of paper says "direction, move forward, move backward, turn left, turn right, left side, move toward east, western wind" in the first column.

and worried look. She then asked me, "Do you know how to say your name in Taiwanese?"[159] Of course my grandmother got a negative answer because then pupils would get fined or receive physical punishment for speaking Taiwanese in school. I did not realise back then, however, why she and I spoke different languages under the same roof or why she did not want to learn Mandarin, which was regarded as a modern and advanced official language.

Besides better career development concerns, the fear of identity loss from my grandmother's and Cathy's perspective is embedded in the ability to write and speak one's heritage language. It is a symbol of who you really are and where you really come from. For first-generation Chinese immigrant women, teaching children Mandarin is a way to keep ethnic identity and culture intact; it seems necessary so why do they fail? What causes this heritage language loss for Chinese immigrants? Why does the second generation lose their heritage language during the process of assimilation into Dutch society? Are the reasons that cause heritage loss among second-generation Chinese related to gendered relationships inside the family? How can we make sense of the interaction between immigrant Chinese mothers fighting for children's Mandarin education and mainstream society? In order to answer these questions, I elaborate on them from two dimensions: one is Bourdieu's language and symbolic power theory and the other is the intersectionality theory. Before that, I first review some research done in essentially English-speaking countries, namely the United States and the UK, related to heritage language loss for second-generation Chinese immigrants. To retain and teach a heritage language in a monolingual society is not an easy task. In this section, I am also curious about the language loss issue in the Chinese-Dutch community.

Language education for second-generation immigrants seems to be gender-neutral. Ideally, it happens naturally and parents make their decisions under equal and balanced power. However, although women play mainly caregiver roles and so spend more time with children than men, little relationship has been found between women's bargaining power and symbolic dominant language power in previous studies. By stating that, I mean that scholars paid little attention to how first-generation immigrant mothers interact with their husbands and school teachers when they decide to make their children learn Mandarin in Western societies. Besides the peer pressure to speak the dominant

---

[159] Before Taiwan became a Japanese colony and the governance of KMT Regime, Taiwanese was the most common dialect in Taiwan for the Han ethnic group.

language and the lack of opportunities to speak Mandarin outside the home for children, the process of decision-making that mothers undertake, and the actions of the mothers themselves, are also intertwined with power mechanisms. In my study, I discovered that two power mechanisms play a role, namely, patriarchy and symbolic language power.

I found that the opinion of male spouses plays a vital role in whether mothers can teach children Mandarin or not. Two Taiwanese mothers used the three-month summer vacation to enrol their children in an intensive Chinese summer class in Taiwan. Not all the mothers succeeded and besides the resistance from their children, the attitudes of their husbands were also crucial. In the following discussion, I will divide the analysis into two parts. The first part will give examples of unsupportive husbands who hold negative opinions about children learning Mandarin and how mothers struggle and feel. The second part will provide counter examples about supportive husbands and how couples manage to negotiate with resistant children. I will provide narratives on how women feel, the difficulties they experience, and the rejection by their children of Mandarin education both inside and outside the family. It also reflects that the decision to learn a heritage language is not totally autonomous for immigrant mothers. They must bargain with both the unequal gender power they have with their husbands and with the symbolic power of the society they live in.

Unsupportive husbands

I offer two examples from transnational families. For the definition of transnational families, I mean the husband and wife who have different countries of origin and speak different mother tongues. The most common language they use to communicate is English in this research. Mothers also use English most of the time to talk with their children. The average age of their husbands is over 60. Rachel (58) has two children in their 30s. She married a Dutch husband in her early 20s. Before marriage, she had no working experience; after marriage, she followed her husband to the Middle East and later went to the Netherlands for the primary education of her older daughter. She identified herself as an extremely lonely mother dedicated to the education of her children, and she felt angry toward her unsupportive husband for not letting her teach her children Mandarin. She could not look me in the eye when talking her resentment. For several years she proposed taking her children back to Taiwan for the summer Chinese intensive classes but all her suggestions were rejected by her husband. Now her two children only understand very basic conversational

Mandarin and cannot read or write any Chinese characters. Sometimes she shed tears and grabbed my arms, reminding me not to make the same mistake if I plan to raise children in the Netherlands:

> Every year before the start of summer vacation, I would ask his permission to take our children back to Taiwan to study Mandarin, but he always said no. He didn't want us to be separated for three months and he said there is no need to speak Mandarin in the Netherlands. At that time, I was too young. As long as he disapproved, I would follow his decision. But now I really hate him for that, it is very important to me, as a mother. That is one missing piece in my life. My children are totally Westernized, language is a way of thinking, and I feel so distant to them. Like *xiaoshun* (filial piety) although he (my son) knew this vocabulary in English, he couldn't understand the deeper meaning of it. It is beyond translation, it is culture, isn't it? Now I saw you nodding because you know exactly what I am talking about. I wish my son could have had the chance to learn Mandarin then he could at least realize my feeling as a mother.

We can see the significant connection between Mandarin learning and motherhood practice. The Chinese culture lies and embeds itself in every single Chinese character. Without the opportunity to teach children to write Chinese characters, a Chinese mother cannot truly convey her culture to her children, and that causes her pain and losing her Chinese identity in motherhood practice makes her angry. Let me elaborate more on the connection between Chinese character writing and motherhood. When both Betty and Rachel expressed their disappointment about their children not knowing even how to write their own names in Chinese, I could not help thinking that their wishes for their children were gradually carried away in the process of heritage language loss. Take my name as an example; *shu* (淑) means ladylike, docile and virtuous; *yi* (怡) means happy and joyful literally, but the structure of this character represents a standing heart facing Taiwan. My mother wants me to be a cheerful, virtuous lady with a passionate heart toward her roots whenever I write my names. Chinese parents put their expectations for the next generation into the name of the child and the child carries those wishes all their life, whenever the names are being called and written. Let me continue to examine the characters of *xiaoshun* closer so we can understand Rachel's feelings more. *Xiao* (孝順) means filial. The structure of this character is a (子) child standing under the roof (土). *Shun* means follow. The structure of this character is running water, a stream (川) standing next to a page (頁). If we combine these two characters, the true meanings of *xiaoshun* unfold. To become a filial child, you must not forget which roof you were raised under. You need to study from the books through constant ongoing knowledge accumulation and thus you can fulfil the filial piety. From Rachel's narrative, I argue that Chinese motherhood is deeply grounded in the epistemology of Chinese characters. This happens mainly through teaching children to write Chinese characters and to speak Mandarin, and then a mother can really practice Chinese motherhood and establish a cultural bond with her children.

Rachel's husband is 11 years older than her. As a young wife who spoke no Dutch and earned only a little money from a part time job, she had to get financial support from her husband for flight tickets and tuition for Mandarin classes in Taiwan. Thirty-five years ago, there were few weekend Chinese schools in the Netherlands, and none of them taught Mandarin with traditional Chinese characters. Rachel lived in the countryside outside Utrecht, and the only Chinese school in Utrecht taught Cantonese, not Mandarin. The unequal positions in age, finance, language, and gender power kept Rachel from being able to make autonomous decisions. Whatever her husband disliked, she would refrain from. Although she kept fighting for almost ten years, her husband still denied her and regarded Mandarin as useless. In a monolingual society, people take for granted that the dominant language is the only correct choice for children. Rachel shared an anecdote from her conversation with a neighbour on children's language development:

> My daughter couldn't talk well when she was two. I asked my neighbour's opinion about that; she told me that was because the languages we spoke at home were too complicated. Sometimes Mandarin, sometimes English and sometimes Dutch, that's why my daughter felt confused. She strongly suggested that I only speak Dutch and keep one single language at home. At that moment, I tried to learn and speak only Dutch or English to my children. Years later, I finally found the answer from an article in a newspaper about children's early linguistic development. It explained that children can distinguish different languages on their own as long as parents create a constant bilingual environment for them. (She sighs and takes a deep breath). That report really came too late, too late.

One can imagine a desperate immigrant mother seeking help from a Dutch neighbour. From daily linguistic exchanges, Dutch, when compared to Mandarin and English, has a superior hierarchical position in people's daily life. The public tended to believe that children should learn only a single language at an early age otherwise they would become confused by different linguistic systems. However, in the 90s, a new theory and new discoveries broke the myth of a single language. Jim Cummins, in his

Dual Iceberg theory, argued that bilingual proficiency implies that experience with either language can promote the development of the proficiency underlying both languages, given adequate motivation and exposure to both, either in school or in the wider environment (1992: 22).[160] The earlier linguistic studies only focused on surface language proficiency and most educators in schools prevented students from speaking heritage languages, resulting in unfortunate consequences for language minority students. We can see here that this way of thinking made one mother suffer for years.

The second example comes from Bonnie (59), who has been living in the Netherlands for 30 years. She met her Dutch husband in the United States. It was her second marriage. When she lived in the States, before marriage, she could speak English and Mandarin freely to her son. She told me things changed after moving to the Netherlands:

> My husband said to me and my son to our face, "From now on we can only speak Dutch at home. Since right now we are in the Netherlands, we must speak Dutch. Forget Mandarin and you will learn English later in school anyway…". I was in total shock that he made that decision without asking me. … I am really glad my son bought himself a series of Mandarin self-learning DVDs at the age of 18. He told me he wanted to find his roots. Now we can communicate many ideas in Mandarin.

This is another example that shows how unequal gender power, along with dominant language symbolic power, leads the decision making on what language is spoken at home. Only Dutch, the father's language, the official language, is legitimate and correct. One can interpret the husband's "Dutch-only" discourses from Pierre Bourdieu's theory (1983, interpreted by John B. Thompson, 1991) regarding the symbolic power of an official language and field. Home can be seen as a field of a unit of society. When a husband regards Mandarin as useless and declares that all family members should start speaking the official language, Dutch, in Bourdieu's theory, he is making a political statement to purify his language. This action gives him power over his wife by subordinating and devaluing her heritage language. This action declares his unquestioning role at home and also his role in mainstream society.

I also want to point out here that Chinese husbands are not unequivocally supportive of children's Mandarin education either, they simply react in another way. Six of my interviewees, married to Chinese husbands, all

---

160 Cummins, Jim. 1992. "Language Proficiency, Bilingualism and Academic Achievement." Pp. 16–26.

working-class families, reported that their husbands cared nothing about their children's education. Indifference is also unsupportive. Leaving all education burdens to their wives made these immigrant mothers feel alone and isolated. Like Betty, the woman I mentioned at the beginning of this chapter, who told me that her husband was busy running a Chinese restaurant all day long. He simply put all the responsibilities of caring for her children on her. She does not have the privilege of being a stay-at-home mother – she still has to help in the restaurant at the same time. She sent all four children to weekend Chinese schools for at least four years; unfortunately, she could only spend a little time with her children and all of them complained all the time about their extra Mandarin homework and weekend school. Since there were no signs of improvement in their Mandarin, she gave up in the end.

Supportive husbands

In the second part of this section, I shall show a comparison with those husbands who are supportive of their Chinese spouse's decision to teach their children Mandarin. Some husbands are very supportive and let their children learn Mandarin; most of the husbands are in their 30s to 50s. They see bilingual education as good for their children and the harmony of the family. I will begin with an example of a transnational family to see the discourse behind the father's supportive attitudes. Fanny has a nearly three-year-old son. Due to her husband's job, they have to live for four months in the Netherlands and eight months in Taiwan every year. Her husband, a native white Dutch man, majored in Mandarin in the Netherlands and the languages they use daily to communicate are Mandarin and Taiwanese. Her husband came to Taiwan to learn Mandarin as an exchange student for one year while studying in university. Here comes a very interesting phenomenon when they live in the Netherlands with her in-laws:

> We tried to speak only Dutch in front of my in-laws because they asked us to. They said it is better for my son when he comes back from kindergarten. But my husband wants to raise our children in Taiwan. He likes the weather and food there. He also considers Mandarin has more potential than Dutch in the future; if we raise our son in the Netherlands, it is very difficult to master Mandarin.

We can see the typical reason for fathers who support children's Mandarin education. This focuses on the market capital value for their children's future career. Three interviewees told me they reached a consensus with their husbands to let their children go to weekend Chinese school for at least five years before high school. In this way, they can speak Mandarin to their mother and Dutch to their father at home. Parents cooperate to maintain a bilingual environment in which their children can persistently learn two languages. Quentin told me that peer pressure outside of the home came when children reached a certain age. They wanted to be the same as their Dutch classmates. No one spoke Mandarin at school and since they were young, they could not foresee the future potential of learning Mandarin. When their children started to resist learning Mandarin, she was very fortunate to have her husband as an ally:

> My husband respects me when it comes to our children's education. My son hates to learn Mandarin although he has been studying it for six years. He came to negotiate with his father several times because he knew it was useless to talk with me. Sometimes my husband almost gave in but he kept telling my son that he must respect his mother's culture. Besides, Mandarin will be very useful and important in the future. He also tried to comfort him by telling my son he will be free from weekend Chinese school after two years.

Another interesting phenomenon happens with Chinese immigrant families. When both parents are Chinese, the decision about their children's education with regard to learning which languages has priority. Twelve interviewees told me that as the Euro crisis becomes worse, and the political atmosphere in the Netherlands becomes more conservative and unwelcoming towards immigrants and their children might have a hard time finding jobs here. So, with concerns about their future career, they must learn Mandarin to at least a basic level. Then, in order of priority, comes English, and Dutch is the least important language. Doris (50), a Taiwanese woman, followed her husband to the Netherlands after her husband's promotion. Thirty-one years went by, and with the uncertainty of transnational work for her husband, Doris sent two of her sons to international schools to develop a better English proficiency. She also continued sending her children back to Taiwan for six years for intensive summer Mandarin classes. Of course, she encountered great resistance and arguments with her children as she tried to convince them about the economic capital of Mandarin:

> When you apply for a job in the future, people assume you can speak Mandarin because you are Chinese in appearance. No matter how well you can speak Dutch, people will never see you as a native speaker. The only advantage you have is your Mandarin ability. The market in Asia is a hundred times bigger than in the Netherlands so how will you find jobs in

> Taiwan, China and Hong Kong if you speak only Dutch and English (as a Chinese person)?

Here we see the clear language hierarchies from the standpoint of an immigrant mother. She knows that mainstream society regards immigrant children as Other no matter how good their Dutch proficiency is. Unlike the Chinese in America, the Chinese community in the Netherlands views Mandarin education for children as an investment for the future. They chose to rely on the bigger social and market symbolic power of Mandarin in the Asian Chinese network. This also reveals the flexibility of the Chinese education strategy. As a result, the priority of language learning can be seen as an investment, and those that have the most market value come first. These worries do not come out of nowhere but rather from parents' personal experiences in the Netherlands. Among 38 interviewees, ten reported that their husband left Dutch companies after working for some years[161] because of an invisible ethnic ceiling or because of subtle ethnic segregation. Twelve reported they felt happier and more respected working for American, British or Chinese companies. Eight told me they never think about working for Dutch people because of the bad experiences of other Chinese friends. Recently, a news report also confirmed the phenomenon that youngsters from an ethnic minority background face occupational discrimination in the Netherlands. Native Dutch young applicants were offered a job in 44% of the cases; those considered as an ethnic minority were only offered a job in 23% of the cases, despite the fact that they had the same CV, accent and clothing.[162] When I asked Betty about her new daughter-in-law's job hunting, she gave me the following commentary:

> No, she doesn't have to go out for paid work. She can just help her husband's business. They own a restaurant and a little shop, the couple earns money together, no matter they are rich or poor, the money all belongs to them. Why does she need to go out making little money by looking at Dutch people's faces?

From this argument one realises that for first-generation immigrant Chinese mothers, teaching their children Mandarin is a complex issue. For the early immigrants, when information and Mandarin resources were hard

---

[161] The mean number is 4.8 (years).

[162] Information cited from DutchNews.nl: http://www.dutchnews.nl/news/archives/2012/12/ethnic_minority_youngsters_do.php, access date December 20, 2012.

to access, women found no materials to teach their children Mandarin. At the same time, when husbands held superior power over their wives and claimed that Dutch was the only legitimate and correct language for their children, immigrant wives could do nothing but obey because they were in a comparatively financial, cultural, linguistic, and gender inferior position, both in the family and in the host society.

For the fathers who support their children's Mandarin education, such action comes more from career concerns rather than the Chinese identity of their mothers. The job market can also be seen as a field, and parents' decisions on language learning depend not simply on personal preference but rather on the symbolic market value of capitalism. Although Dutch is the official language in the Netherlands and has its own national legitimate symbolic value, parents with Dutch Chinese second-generation children see the world from a more globalised perspective where English and Mandarin are valued more than Dutch. The boundary between home and society is vague. Decision-making on a child's language acquisition at home is also a field controlled by different powers. Parents and children all struggle to interact with the outside fields such as mainstream society and symbolic market value.

5.5 Conclusion

As discussed in this chapter, both Dutch (the mother tongue of husbands and the dominant language of the host country) and Mandarin (the heritage language of the Chinese migrant mother) cause burdens and have impacts on motherhood practices from a macro-political point of view. For working-class Chinese women, learning Dutch is an imperative requirement for earning a living. It is also a tool for upgrading social class. The gendered division in a migrated working-class Chinese family became a potential for Chinese women to rotate the power division of patriarchy. For middle-class Chinese women who married native Dutch men, learning Dutch is less for financial need but more for social integration, and to be independent in information gathering and decision making. Both working-class and middle-class women benefit from Dutch learning. However, at the same time, Chinese mothers are aware of the xenophobia in the Dutch labour market and the rising economic and political power of China. Making children learn Mandarin is indispensable. It is not only a way to fight against Dutch xenophobia but also a way to carry out Chinese motherhood by teaching children Mandarin. Chinese mothers themselves can remain, in a small way, culturally Chinese through their children's Mandarin education. In this research, I found that migrant Chinese women, especially those under 50 in the Netherlands, prioritised their children's language education. English is the first then Mandarin, and Dutch is deemed the least important. Chinese women foresee their children's future careers from a global Chinese vision. In sum, I connect the Mandarin education of Chinese migrant families to a global Mandarin fraternal network and material counterpart to understand how the rising of "the Greater China" hegemonic discourse directly results in the "Chinese must speak Mandarin" ideology that reconstructs and reshapes the transnational motherhood practices. Mandarin ability for the second generation of Chinese immigrants has positive meaning for both future careers and the social/cultural symbolic. Teaching second-generation Mandarin also becomes a significant task for first-generation Chinese migrant parents to keep their children competitive and connected to the Mandarin-speaking world. From the narratives of my interviewees, I can point out at least three power mechanisms, namely, patriarchy, the rising Dutch nationalism and Mandarin supremacism.[163] Motherhood is forcibly reshaped and reconstructed as far as its contents are concerned and the ideas intertwined with them. But most of them do not question Mandarin supremacism; they do not question that "a Chinese must speak Mandarin" is also an oppression that functions in transnational Chinese motherhood practice. Thus, I argue that the first-generation Chinese migrant women in the Netherlands must negotiate and struggle with these three power mechanisms on the language issue.

---

[163] The so-called Mandarin supremacism is still not a fixed academic jargon. I use this to refer to the rising discourses of "as long as you are a Chinese, regardless of your nationality and living country, you must speak Mandarin." I personally think this phenomenon is another product of the rising Greater China Discourse.

CHAPTER SIX

"TOO MUCH RICE, NO POTATOES?": DEALING WITH EVERYDAY RACISM AND DISCRIMINATION

"*We are strong and enduring. We are also deeply scarred.*"
—Audre Lorde, 1984: 151.

6.1 Prelude: The Very First Souvenir from the Netherlands

This chapter focuses on how first-generation Chinese immigrant mothers deal with everyday racism and discrimination inside and outside the private domain. This chapter emerges from my own personal encounter in the Netherlands. Before analysing the event and the narratives, I want to share an educational scenario that I had during a class in Taiwan. As an ambitious Asian student who had made up her mind to purse an advanced diploma in the West, I was warned by my teacher about the issue of race.

About ten years ago I took a course called "Intermediate Seminar on Homosexuality" at National Taipei University, taught by Professor Dr Wang Ya-Ko. In the first class, he asked how many of us would like to pursue a doctorate diploma abroad in the future. After counting the numbers, he reflected on his own experiences in the Department of Sociology, Loyola University, Chicago. He then posed a question to five of us who were holding a PhD dream and were eager to hear his opinion on how to move forward academically, which was: "There are only two kinds of people in white Western eyes, one is white, what is the other? If you don't have the courage to accept the answer, then you had better start to read some critical race theories now." None of us had the correct answer to his question. As far as he was concerned, the answer was "non-white". It was not until I, an Asian immigrant woman, came to study and live in the Netherlands that I fully realised the scope of Professor Wang's question. The inhospitable and uncomfortable reception I received from the Netherlands began way before the initiation of this research. I went to the Immigratie en Naturalisatiedienst (IND)[164]in Rijswijk for residence registration on the third day after arrival. The IND officer asked me some questions while reviewing my documents. "Has anything changed for you?" the female officer asked. I was kind of confused by this question and replied: "What do you mean by 'changed'?" She said: "Are you seeing anyone or are you pregnant maybe?" I shook my head and said no. She continued: "Do you plan to get married with a local here in the future?" I was very shocked by this rude and direct personal inquiry and responded: "No, I am here to study." She replied: "You never know, most single Asian girls end up marring locally." Compare my experience with my white Canadian colleague: she arrived one month later and she also went to the IND for immigration registration. The IND officer simply greeted her with "Welcome to the Netherlands"; there were no questions about any personal conditions regarding pregnancy or an intimate relationship. Both of us brought the same letter of acceptance as a PhD candidate enrolled in Utrecht University, and both of us are government-sponsored scholarship holders. Even though I emphasised that my purpose in the Netherlands was to pursue an academic diploma, the IND officer still kept labelling me as a husband hunter, and I was suspected of wanting a marriage of convenience, or even being a prostitute, rather than as a foreign student who is willing to fly across half the world to achieve self-realisation in Western academia. What are the reasons for this hugely different treatment between me and my Canadian colleague? We concluded that there are at least two reasons for this. First is the country of origin: She comes from a so-called "developed country", Canada, unlike "the developing country" of Taiwan where I am from. Second, we agreed that even more significant than the country of origin is "race". She is defined as white and I am an Asian. After exchanging our experiences[165] at the IND, I truly began to understand what it means to be a single Asian woman through Dutch eyes.

Please understand that the concept of "race" I use throughout this book is framed between quotation marks to indicate the racism connotation and prejudiced social construction itself. The very word "race" is an inappropriate and taboo word to use in the Netherlands while using the

[164] The English translation for IND is "Immigration and Naturalisation Service", which is affiliated to the Ministry of Security and Justice.

[165] Apart from the questions being embedded within sexism and compulsory heterosexuality, my Canadian colleague actually also felt discriminated against by the different treatments of the IND. She told me in a serious tone that: "If those questions are the standard procedures to check the single foreign woman who plans to live in the Netherlands, why didn't they ask me if I am seeing anyone or will I plan to marry locally? Is it because I am too old?"

word "ethnicity" seems to be more acceptable academically. I will discuss these two concepts in the second section in this chapter. Nonetheless, one must realise that for me as an Asian and my colleague as a white Canadian, while discussing this daily scenario, we immediately used the word "race" instead of "ethnicity", which indicated that our cognition of the power dynamics involved in my IND experience were directly linked to racial concerns. This is also an example of how people outside Western Europe recognise the sensitivities of race.

Let me first make a quick review of the two main reasons (nationality and race) which resulted in different and unequal treatment. I find the distinction between "a developed country", "a developing country" and "an underdeveloped country" problematic. First, it is only possible from an unproblematised Western standard to decide the value for the rest of the world, which amounts to economic reductionism. Secondly, these labels function not only to produce a We (modern/ advanced/powerful/rich), and an Other (crude/backward/vulnerable/poor) in a dichotomous construction, they also define the global hierarchies of geopolitical linguistic power. Thirdly, the use of the word "develop" with its colonisation connotation equals what Mohanty (1984) stated; that the "Third World" category invented by the Western powers implies a relation of structural domination and violent suppression which masks the heterogeneity of the subject(s) in question (p. 333). In the conversation with the IND officer, I felt my power of speech was taken away and the symbolic value of me as an international student was compulsorily objectified into a sexualised and *Orientalised Chinese woman* by a *white Western woman.*

While recalling this unpleasant encounter with the IND of nationality and race, I realised that there is a double standard of sexism in those questions. Would she ask the same question to a single young Asian man? Would she assume that he will end up marring locally? Why did she ask three separate single questions regarding my sexuality? What lies behind her questions is the prejudice and sexism of many Dutch people towards non-white, non-European citizens and Third World Asian women like me. It not only implies that I could be a prostitute cloaked by a student status but also presumes me to be a husband-hunter who uses pursuing higher education in the Netherlands as a stepping stone. No wonder that a half-year later, when I discussed my research idea with Professor Rosemarie Buikema, director of the Graduate Gender Programme at Utrecht University, she replied: "Watch out, many white Dutch women think Asian women come here to steal their men." Briefly, from my third day here in the Netherlands, I started to realise that my environment actually put triple intersecting discriminations on me, viz., nationality, race and gender.

The excitement and joy I felt that my dream was coming true came very near to being destroyed by the IND encounter. I even questioned my own judgement and whether choosing the Netherlands instead of the United Kingdom was the wrong decision. Ironically, I got a scholarship for Gender Studies and, looking at the situation I put myself in, there was absolutely no gender equity at all in view of those IND questions. My previous impression of this country from the mass media in Taiwan was totally overthrown. The information and media representation of the Netherlands is that of a modern advanced European country with higher moral standards of human rights protection than in Chinese society and full social welfare. As an immigrant European country, they are more tolerant and liberal with multiculturalism than where I come from. Then, how can I make sense of the gap between this Dutch representation in Northeast Asia and my own experience? Either the mainstream media in Taiwan merely chooses the positive and bright side when reporting about Western European countries, and perhaps their knowledge about Dutch national culture is outdated, or the Dutch government is very good at promoting and establishing utopian images internationally. If the IND's attitude towards single Chinese women is common and generally applied to all Chinese here, what is the situation of my Chinese sisters as immigrants in this country? And how do they deal with these daily instances of racism and discrimination as an immigrant, a mother and a woman?

In line with my encounter at the IND, the topic of dealing with everyday racism surfaced spontaneously during interviews. I did not come up with the theme of racism myself, as I mentioned earlier in chapter two; the conversation referring to racism and discrimination began from the word "but" or a sigh. All interviewees, regardless of age, class or educational level, responded quickly and spoke precisely, using such terms as "racism" and "discrimination against Chinese" while describing their or other family members' daily unpleasant encounters with Dutch mainstream society. Interestingly, before sharing experiences, most of them would praise the positive aspects of the Dutch people first. For instance, the most common interview situation evolved like this: "*Do you think Dutch people are friendly to Chinese?*" asked the researcher; *Ja…, most of Dutch people are friendly to Chinese, but…*", and significant utterances came after the word "but". Moreover, I also noticed that after saying "but" there were various emotions, especially when discussing Dutch racism. Some were excited; they raised their voice and tone when describing how ridiculous and unjust the experiences were. Some showed a little embarrassment in the beginning; they lowered their voices and made sure their Dutch husbands or cleaning ladies were not around, then some excitement surfaced: "*Now, we are going to talk behind Dutch people's backs, haha, let me tell you...*". Still others even paused to make another pot of tea and brought some snacks before continuing because they thought this would be a long conversation. During the interview, I did not feel that "race" and "racism" are taboo words or topics among first-generation Chinese immigrant women but rather that it is a liberating and empowering process for them to speak out.

The knowledge and conception about Dutch racism towards Chinese in this study is a novel epistemological contribution by bottom-up voices, which are seldom heard or studied in this country. To combat racism, one needs to understand how its hierarchical and relational power is demonstrated and performed in real-life situations. It requires one to interrogate the cultural narratives of women who have less of a voice. I do not treat these Chinese migrant women as passive and victimised by Dutch racism. On the contrary, they are full of agency and have the creativity to deal with this issue. I want to borrow American feminist Ann duCille's opinion on scholarly integration of racism against non-white women, that they are capable of becoming cultural producers rather than "as objects of the racial gaze" (1994). In honour of women's situated knowledge, this chapter has two aims. First, it intends to make visible the lived experiences of everyday racism among first-generation immigrant Chinese women in a Dutch context. I will describe how everyday racism penetrates their lives, inside and outside the families, especially in their daily individual encounters and interactions with mainstream Dutch society. I will also focus on the women's responses as mothers to racism toward their children. I found that dealing with individually experienced everyday racism and racism toward their children are inherent in motherhood practice for Chinese women. Their reactions and reflections on Dutch society prove that the very power relation of everyday racism is not unidirectional, just as Susan S. Friedman argues: "which contradictory subject positions allow for the possibility of connection across racial and ethnic boundaries" (1995: 38). Thus, anti-racist thinking and the discourses women produce are key elements to analyse and conceptualise in immigrant motherhood studies in white-dominant Western society. The second aim is that this chapter tries to implode the silence around gendered discrimination inside Chinese communities through their testimonies and, in particular, patriarchy. I will give two examples as case studies. Through these accounts of Chinese women going about their daily encounters with racism and patriarchy at home, this chapter tries to problematise and call attention to everyday practices that the majority of the Dutch people take for granted and are therefore aloof. Moreover, the experiences of first-generation Chinese dealing with Dutch racism are seldom told and need to be studied. Racism towards Chinese in the Netherlands can be put into a broader scheme of racism as it functions against other Asian groups and non-white immigrant groups in the Western European context.

This chapter is divided into three sections. In the first section, I want to discuss the contested concepts of "race" and "ethnicity" in the Dutch context from their historical background and its outcome of inventing new categories to construct We and Them by not mentioning "race". In the second section, I first introduce Philomena Essed's "Everyday Racism" approach which I use as an analytical tool; furthermore, I elaborate on why I think it is useful to apply her theory. Then I conduct a brief literature review on the relationships between the experiences of Asian women dealing with daily racism and motherhood practices in Western society. In the last section, I provide the results of my analysis of everyday racism, paying strict attention to the perception and discrimination of Chinese communities, both in private and public domains in the Netherlands. In addition, I situate myself in the location from which I use my voice because, in some ways, I am also in the same boat with my interviewees. It does not make any difference that I am a researcher; I am also a migrant woman.

6.2 Speaking Out a Problem Without a Name: Dutch Racism

"The price of increasing power is increasing opposition."
—Audre Lorde 1984: 158.

6.2.1 Racial Europeanisation and denial of racism

Generally speaking, the definition of racism is the cumulative instantiation related to prejudice (Essed, 1990, 2002; Barker, 2002[166]), arbitrariness (Said, 2002[167]), and power (Essed, 1990) resulting in the inherent superiority to justify the right to dominance (Lorde, 1984), which always leads to institutional inequality (Omi & Winant, 2002[168]). Within this unequal power relation, certain ethnic/racial groups are defined as inferior to the

[166] Barker, Martin. 2002. "The Problem with Racism", Pp. 80–89.
[167] Said, Edward. 2002. "Imaginative Geography and Its Representations: Orientalizing the Oriental." Pp.15–37.
[168] Omi, Michael & Winant, Howard. 2002. "Racial Formation." Pp. 123–145.

dominant ethnic group because of their different cultural origin (Wekker, 1995[169]). Racism is a constructed discourse which routinely reproduces itself within different forms;[170] it convinces and legitimates stereotypes and prejudice of a racial minority among a white majority which results in the justification of right-wing-oriented policy implementation. According to Henriques et al. (1984 in Bacchi, 1999: p. 94), it is common in the West that whenever the problem is seen to be racist, it will immediately be reduced to a kind of personal attitude of the perpetrator, or as an individual aberration of the perpetrator, which suppresses recognition of the institutional and structural dimensions of discrimination (ibid: 94).

Due to the German occupation of the Netherlands during War World II and given the circumstances of the Jewish Holocaust, talking about and discussing racism in the Netherlands became taboo (Essed, 1990, 1995 in Lutz et al.[171]; Wekker, 2015). According to Wekker (2009: 72 in Franken et al.[172]), in this post-WWII social atmosphere, whoever mentioned race was considered as highly uncivilised and a disgrace. From the Dutch government to the mainstream media and academia (Essed & Trienekens, 2008), people cautiously avoid using the term "race" (Wekker & Lutz, 2001 in Botman et al.[173]). The very word "race" signals and represents an atrocious past where racism and power performed in an absolutely cold-blooded way to take the lives of mainly one certain group as well as Others. Thus, in order to move on and forget the tragic past, "race" is unmentionable and unspeakable in every public domain; furthermore, it has its specific indication, referring to the Holocaust and Anti-Semitism only. David Theo Goldberg calls this pattern of racial avoidance and general denial of race in Western Europe racial Europeanisation (2004: 343).

The denial of racism not only happened in the Netherlands but also throughout Western Europe (Zick, Pettigrew & Wagner, 2008; Van Dijk,

---

[169] Wekker, Gloria. 1995. "'After the Last Sky, Where do the Birds Fly?' What can European Women Learn from Anti-Racist Struggle in the United States?" Pp. 65–87.

[170] Van Dijk concludes at least five forms of the denial of racism that the press generally quote to sustain and strengthen the racist discourses, viz., 1) positive self-presentation; 2) denial and counter-attack; 3) moral blackmail; 4) subtle denials and 5) mitigation. Please see Van Dijk, 1991, 1993, 2002.

[171] Essed, Philomena. 1995. "Gender, Migration and Cross-Ethnic Coalition Building." Pp. 48–63.

[172] Wekker, Gloria. 2009. "Into the Promised Land? The Feminization and Ethnicization of Poverty in the Netherlands." Pp.65–77.

[173] Wekker, Gloria en Lutz, Helma. 2001. "Een hoogvlakte met koude winden. De geschiedenis van het gender- en etniciteitsdenken in Nederland." Pp. 25–49.

2002[174]). As Van Dijk (2002) argues, it is a major strategy to disclaim antiracist criticism. On the one hand, unlike the United States in the 1960s, Europe never had large-scale ethnic minority civil rights movements. On the other hand, European states generally did not consider themselves as immigrant countries until the very late 1980s or 1990s. One critical consequence of this is that European ethnic minorities typically have severely limited political influence (ERCOMER, 1997 in Zick, Pettigrew & Wagner 2008: p. 234). Ethnic minorities in the 1960s and the 1970s from outside the EU were seen as temporary sojourners so their progeny is still very often considered as outsiders, and they encountered institutional racism in everyday life, i.e. education, housing, employment, and health insurance. In a nutshell, as Zick, Pettigrew & Wagner state, the refusal to accep the fact that European states are in-migration countries not only resulted in institutional racism in many facets but also sustained the state's power to an often arbitrary categorisation of ethnic minorities for its political interest (p. 234). Moreover, there is a passive tolerance of racism in Western Europe (Essed, 2002: 183). Recently, Dutch racism, as Essed and Hoving (2014: 13) argue, has been transformed from a "carefully fabricated image of tolerance" in the 20th century to the "right to offend" in the 21st century. This trend is precipitated especially by right-wing, anti-Muslim Dutch politicians such as Pim Fortuyn, Rita Verdonk and Geert Wilders, who claim that their freedom of speech (Article Seven of the Dutch Constitution) is more important than Article One (freedom of religion). This kind of starkly explicit and open public discourse makes "native Dutch citizens feel entitled to make racist remarks without excuse or introduction" (ibid: 17–18), which means native Dutch people can express their dislike and hostility towards any non-Dutch because it is protected by law. However, I found Wilders' argument unconvincing. Let us look at Article One more closely. According to the Dutch Government website, overheid. nl, the content of Article One in English means "All persons in the Netherlands in similar cases should be treated alike. Discrimination on the grounds of religion, belief, political opinion, race, gender, or any other grounds whatsoever shall not be permitted.[175]" In the second sentence, the elements of discriminations are separated by commas,

---

[174] Van Dijk, Teun A. 2002. "Denying Racism: Elite Discourse and Racism." Pp. 307–324.

[175] The Dutch text is "Allen die zich in Nederland bevinden, worden in gelijke gevallen gelijk behandeld. Discriminatie wegens godsdienst, levensovertuiging, politieke gezindheid, ras, geslacht of op welke grond dan ook, is niet toegestaan.", see website: http://wetten.overheid.nl/BWBR0001840/geldigheidsdatum_27-02-2015, access date Feb 27, 2015.

which in the legal system indicate that every mentioned element is equally important without any hierarchy in legal effect. Unfortunately, in the current situation, it seems the Dutch legal system favours more the pro-white political opinion, and if this is the case, what are the circumstances that Chinese migrant women have to face and deal with on a daily basis? Are migrants also entitled to equal freedom of (racist) speech with native Dutch citizens? The phenomenon of the "right to be racist" is speeding up racial Europeanisation, which excludes and silences the immigrants because of their non-European origin, religion and physical features. Particularly in the Dutch context, racism is often seen as an individual problem (Essed, 2002) but not a social issue. Perhaps my claim of being discriminated against by the IND is not convincing at all for a general Dutch audience. In seeking a common language to discuss the contested concepts of race and ethnicity academically, Essed mentions that "after WWII, the old colonial model of "race" exploitation and cultural oppression rationalized with pseudoscientific "race" is losing ground and it transformed into a more cultural oriented racism" (1990: 13). At the same time, the term "ethnicity" emerged by a strong nationalistic identification with the cultural heritage of the (same cultural) group (ibid: 13)". Dutch historian Marga Altena later made a clear-cut defining line between these two words used in different geographical contexts. She argued that after 1945 in Europe, except in the UK, since the term "race" is no longer acceptable in academia, the focus on biological difference was replaced by ethnicity (2012: 28), in contrast to the North American context where "race" is still a dominant language to describe people with different skin colours. Altena's reading seems to suggest that the use of "race" and "ethnicity" are coterminous in Europe and the United States; nonetheless, she fails to point out that the specificity of racism can also work on the notion of ethnicity (Anthias & Yuval-Davis, 1992). Dutch social science scholar Albert W. Musschenga (1998) points out that there is no consensus in academia regarding how to give a neutral term to the minority groups in Dutch society because "each term reveals what the user regards the main difference between groups and the rest of society" (ibid: 204). Thus, as an Asian feminist, in this chapter, I still insist on using the term "race" not only to stress that the Chinese are presented as non-white in physical features but also to emphasise the stereotyped cultural differences that are imposed by the dominant ideology. Moreover, from the perspectives of the women who are the subjects in this study, it is the term "race" instead of "ethnicity" that they used to define the cause and the origin of racism. In the next part, I discuss how the Dutch separate Us from Them without mentioning the R-word; instead they created new terms: *allochtoon* and *autochtoon*.

6.2.2 Allochtoon vs. autochtoon: The Construction of "Otherness"

Goldberg noted that racial Europeanisation had as a consequence swept away the concept of "race" after WWII; it was thought that the silencing of the Holocaust could bring peace and the wound would heal eventually. However,

> This is a wishful evaporation never quite enacted, never satisfied. A desire at once frustrated and displaced, racist implications always lingering and diffuse, silenced but assumed, always already returned and haunting, buried but alive. (Goldberg, 2006: 334)

The denial of racism avoids using the sensitive word "race", and some controversial public policies were even implemented or new terms invented to avoid race sensitivities; for example, the invention of the binary terms *allochtoon* and *autochtoon*, which have been widely used from the 1980s until now. The racist connotations were denied by the Dutch government and by the majority of white Dutch, thus, the whole society is a variant of the sense of denial of racism (Essed, 1990, 1991; Wekker, 1995 in Lutz et al., 2006; Goldberg, 2006; Vasta, 2007). Generally speaking, *allochtoon* literally means "those coming from elsewhere" and it indicates migrant, foreigner, alien, or outsider, and is particularly used to refer to people or their parents originating from outside the EU, the non-white, the non-Westerners. Opposite to *allochtoon*, *autochtoon* literally means "those who are from here" and it symbolically has a higher position. It stands not only for native and local but also indicates a more favourable connotation. It is more valued, and considered without problems (Wekker, 2009: 71).

In recent years, the concept of *allochtoon* has particularly referred to Islamic people, i.e. Turks and Moroccans and their descendants. They are currently constructed as the "Ultimate Other" who cannot possibly be integrated into Dutch society (Wekker, ibid: 72). The construction of Otherness through naming outsiders *allochtoon* justifies their second-class citizenship (Essed, 1995: 52 in Lutz et al.). It draws a clear line to separate those different from "Us" and it sustains white supremacy in the Netherlands along with the white identity of Europe (Essed, ibid: 53). The innovation of new words based on one ethnic or racial background is not just bloodline but the intertwining of culture and blood to separate one from another in the framework of social hierarchy, and can be understood as a kind of "racial project" (Anthias and Yuval Davis, 2012) which preserves ethnic exclusivity and privileges the dominant ethnic group within the nation state (p. 5).

The ideological climate behind *allochtoon* versus *autochtoon* is rooted in the two Dutch vocabularies. As Essed (1991) points out, the first form of Dutch racism is a paternalistic remnant of colonialism, which could be realised with these outsiders and foreigners as the past "Dutch burden". As many immigrants migrated to the Netherlands from the former colonies (Indonesia, Antilles and Surinam), a certain kind of paternalism came out of the "good intention" to "help" blacks, or non-white Others, to join "modern" Dutch society (p. 16). However, during the 1980s recession, workplace discrimination was common and many Blacks were unemployed, and therefore public opinion turned to blaming these *allochtonen* for their laziness and flaky attitudes, abusing the welfare system and wasting white Dutch taxpayers' money. In short, *allochtonen* are considered a threat to society and bureaucratic systems. The differentiations in the *allochtoon* and *autochtoon* dichotomy not only exclude non-white and non-Western migrants from mainstream society but they are also particularly gendered. According to a study of the transformation of Dutch minority policies, Verloo and Roggeband (2007) argue that Dutch minority and integration policies have shifted from degendered to gendered policies (p. 286) in which migrant women, especially Muslims, are constructed as the most problematic *allochtonen* in Dutch society because of their cultural background and their backwardness, which obviously interferes with Western democracy and women's emancipation. The responsibilities lie heavily on them to decide whether they are willing to abandon their Islamic culture or fail to integrate into Dutch society, and it is a threat to the majority because women are the cultural carriers for their children. While framing Muslim *allochtone* women as the ultimate and urgent problems, the native *autochtone* women are considered free from patriarchy and liberated. Ellie Vasta (2007) also criticises the Dutch political discourse shift from multiculturalism to assimilation, which reveals the pervasive institutional discrimination and cultural racism that will only further deepen ethnic societal divisions. Simply put, Muslim migrant women are framed as a "problem" to be solved because the contents of their motherhood are "dangerous" and "backward" to modern Dutch society while the existing gender inequity among native Dutch groups are dismissed and ignored. The privileges and dominance of Dutch patriarchy itself remains unchallenged and taken for granted.

Over the recent decade, some Dutch people have become aware that the state construction of the *allochtoon* and *autochtoon* dichotomy is harmful to social harmony and national development in the long run. In 2008, Justice Minister Ernst Hirsch Ballin has tried to make a proposal in parliament to end the use of *allochtoon* because of its negative effect on national identity formation; however, he failed to get any support.[176] In November 2009, the integration minister, Eberhard van der Laan, suggested to MPs that the term *allochtoon* be replaced by nieuwe Nederlanders (new Dutch) to make people feel more welcomed and more integrated into the mainstream.[177] Unfortunately, his suggestion has yet to be accepted.

Only in 2014 did the Amsterdam city council, headed by Mayor Van der Laan, announce it will no longer be using the term *allochtoon*. As far as I am concerned, it is a good start that Amsterdam, the most advanced and modern Dutch metropolitan city, is willing to take the lead in the effort to welcome all immigrants and the future new Dutch regardless of ethnicity, race, religion, and nationality.

In Dutch eyes, Chinese are considered *allochtonen* and so are their descendants, even though some Chinese have already been living here for over a century, speak no Mandarin and their national identity is Dutch. I shall give a short review historically and elaborate on the daily impact regarding the construction of Chinese as Other by media representations in contemporary Dutch society. I will first briefly depict the Dutch attitude towards Chinese in Indonesia during the colonial period, as I found a connection with the contemporary Dutch prejudice. To realise how the mainstream Dutch treat immigrants, the word "tolerance" must be discussed first. Dutch tolerance is an axiom the general public use to indicate how open-minded Dutch people are. However, it reveals a hierarchical system and unequal social status between *allochtoon* and *autochtoon*. As Essed (1990) argues, tolerance is based on the rejection of biological determinism and egalitarianism (p. 17). Nevertheless, the norm of tolerance has its power-hierarchy connotation. It is in the mainstream Dutch society, the so-called *autochtonen*, who are so generous to show

---

[176] Please see:
http://www.dutchnews.nl/news/archives/2008/02/minister_wants_to_ditch_term_a.php#sthash.GicLMw7P.dpuf and
http://www.dutchnews.nl/news/archives/2008/02/allochtoon_too_established_to.php#sthash.hWEgY45s.dpuf, access date January 24, 2014.

[177] Please see:
http://www.dutchnews.nl/news/archives/2009/11/integration_of_immigrants_is_g.php#sthash.oaKtlCLm.dpuf, access date January 24, 2014.

their goodwill to "tolerate" these outsiders and foreigners to "our" country. Thus, the responsibilities for accepting mainstream social norms, languages and religious values, are on the *allochtonen* alone. As a result, "those (outsiders) who desire to achieve in society usually have to pay the price of first adapting to and accepting the dominant culture" (ibid: 17). Besides the power dynamics, Dutch tolerance is not unconditional. I will give two women's narratives to sustain my argument later in the third section. This finding may explain why the Dutch Chinese community is much more socially and politically isolated than other ethnic minorities in the Netherlands.

Now, let me give a quick review on how the Dutch dealt with the Chinese during the colonial era in Indonesia. According to Waaldijk (2003), in the 19th century, the Dutch colonial state increased its emphasis on racial differentiation in order to distinguish between the indigenous population and "Europeans" (p. 103). The Chinese and the so-called peranakan (native-born Chinese in the Dutch East Indies) were subdivided as "Foreign Orientals", basically referring to Arabs, Chinese and other Asians living in the colony (p. 103). During the debate about which groups in the colony were to be considered as Dutch citizens between the 1880s and the early 1890s, the Chinese were denied their rights because among the "Foreign Orientals" groups, they were often considered a danger for both colonial rule and the indigenous population (p.107) because they seemed to be more loyal to China and not to the Dutch colonial state. Along with the indigenous population in Indonesia, they were declared to be "Dutch subjects, not Dutch nationals" (p. 105). Waaldijk states that the declaration in 1910 introduced a new concept in Dutch legislation (p. 105). [178] Another instance of unjust and discriminatory treatment of Chinese in the Dutch East Indies was the limited access to education. Even though Indonesia had served as a colony of the Dutch Empire for at least four centuries, not until 1908 did the first *Hollandsch-Chinese School* (Dutch-Chinese secondary school) in the Dutch East Indies start to accept Chinese students who had excellent academic performance during their Dutch basic education (Li, 1998: 168–169 in Sinn[179]). The representation of Chinese in the Dutch East Indies was socially constructed as a potential threat to the colonial government, thus they could not be treated equally as

---

178 Waaldijk, Berteke. 2003. "Subjects and Citizens: Gender and Racial Discrimination in Dutch Colonialism at the End of the 19th Century." Pp. 101–118.

179 Li, Minghuan. 1998. "Living Among Three Walls? The Peranakan Chinese in the Netherlands." Pp.167–183.

citizens. As Homi Bhabha (2002 in Essed and Goldberg[180]) argues, "The colonial mimicry is the desire for a reformed, recognizable Other, as a subject of a difference that is almost the same, but not quite" (p. 114). The creation of Chinese as one of the Dutch Subjects is a kind of ambivalence based on the mimicry of the dominant Dutch nationals. Besides political concerns, the social representation of Chinese in the Dutch East Indies also reflected a certain racial prejudice. While studying Dutch popular magazines from the mid-19th century to the mid-20th century, Altena (2012) found that they generally depicted Chinese in the Dutch East Indies as poor and primitive. They lived "penned up[181]" like the "ghetto of an old German town" (p. 56), while the economic inequalities and unequal treatment by the colonial State were left unmentioned. Even though some Chinese were highly educated, middle-class, and had led a European lifestyle, positive images never appeared in these Dutch folk magazines. Altena concluded that because of the magazines' racial prejudice and novelty, the majority of the Dutch people only received the eccentric aspects of China and Chinese people, the "unfathomable language, bound girl's feet, and edible birds' nests" (p. 55). In short, Chinese representation in the Dutch media and political discourse until the middle of the 20th century was that of a completely exotic Other and took the form of Orientalism and sexism.

From the representation of Chinese in Indonesia I now want to turn to what was the social representation of the Chinese in the Netherlands itself at that time? Two studies showed that Chinese workers in Amsterdam and Rotterdam at the beginning of the 20th century were deported during the years of the Great Depression because of state racism and xenophobia (Wubben, 1986 and Zeven, 1987, cited in Essed, 1991). As was mentioned earlier in chapter four, based on Mak's research (2000), Chinese men were considered as abandoned, poor, ill, and potentially harmful to public health, and morally dangerous to Dutch society in the 1930s. To sum up, the general attitudes towards Chinese either in the Dutch East Indies or in the Netherlands were less positive than before WWII.

In the next section, I will discuss why Philomena Essed's Everyday Racism Approach (1990, 1991, 2002) is the main theoretical framework of this chapter.

---

[180] Bhabha, Homi. 2002. "Of Mimicry and Man: The Ambivalence of Colonial Discourse." Pp. 113–122.

[181] According to Altena, "penned up" is a phrase usually reserved for animals and suggesting an unhealthy and immoral atmosphere (p. 56).

6.3 The Everyday Racism Approach of Philomena Essed

I use Essed's "everyday racism" as the main theoretical framework in this chapter. I find her approach very inspiring and helpful while interpreting and conceptualising the daily experiences of Chinese women in dealing with racism. Moreover, I am more interested in how racism functions as a power mechanism, which has pervasive impacts on people's ordinary life in various cultural dynamics, rather than in an economic analysis of racism (Hall, 2002[182]). Hence, I am more aware of the political considerations and struggles behind interaction and decision making while women deal with racist encounters.

Here I want to give a brief outline of the definition of the "everyday racism" approach. According to Essed, "the concept of "everyday racism" connects structural forces of racism with routine situations in everyday life. It links ideological dimensions of racism with daily attitudes and interprets the reproduction of racism in terms of the experiences of it in everyday life" (1991: 2). Essed points out that the "everyday racism" approach shows "the frequency (on a daily basis)" and the "systematic structure" of racism (1986: 24). Thus, the everyday racism approach is to conceptualise and generalise the personal experiences of non-white people encountering racism in the white dominant Western society in order to understand the practices of power and white supremacy that penetrate public/ private domains and reinforce the status quo. Essed (2002) argues that everyday racism can be defined as a process, whereby

> (a) socialized racist notions are integrated into meanings that make practices immediately definable and manageable, (b) practices with racist implications become in themselves familiar and repetitive, and (c) underlying racial and ethnic relations are actualized and reinforced through these routine or familiar practices in everyday situations (p. 190).

Thus, while generalising and conceptualising the "everyday racist" experiences of Chinese women, I especially focus on those common racist encounters and denials of racism that were mentioned continually by most of the interviewees in daily encounters with Dutch society, because everyday life is not only where people live but it is also an environment full of regulations composed by dominant power mechanisms. These regulations form a system according to the interest and norms of the dominant majority. The value of the system is passed on to individuals by

---

[182] Hall, Stuart. 2002. "Race, Articulation, and Societies Structured in Dominance." Pp. 38–38.

socialisation processes through which people internalise and come to obey dominant propriety. In fact, as Anthias & Yuval-Davis point out, racist practices do not necessarily connect with institutional power, but its effect matters. Thus, "these practices may exacerbate or even produce exclusions and subordinations which are coterminous with supposed 'racially' different populations" (1992: 13). In short, racist practices can be carried out by everyone in every facet of daily interactions between racial majorities and minorities.

Essed (1991) mentions that this internalisation process takes time and needs a stage where everyday life serves as a place for both the reproduction of the dominant social norms and individual internalised transformation. The denial of racism further makes racism a process operative in everyday life (Essed, ibid, p. 47). By applying the "everyday racism" approach, I can generate and conceptualise the characteristics and types of Dutch racism towards Chinese from women's day-to-day life experiences. Alternatively, I can also elucidate how dominant social values work on women's motherhood practices inside and outside the domestic domain, and how women negotiate and interpret this power mechanism. In the next paragraph, I delineate previous research regarding the experiences of how racism in Western societies affects Northeast Asian women's motherhood practice.

6.3.1 Motherhood practice and racism experiences

The influx of Asian immigrants has changed the demographic landscape of the West. Nevertheless, the experiences of Asian immigrant motherhood practice with racism are still limited to only a few specific academic fields, especially psychological and educational studies. While studying Korean immigrant mothers' perspectives on their involvement in American schools, Soomin Sohn & Christine Wang (2006) reported that all interviewees felt at the receiving end of racism and discrimination when communicating with American teachers. In contrast, the majority of white American teachers are aware of only black and white racial conflicts, and claim to have no racial sensitivities towards Asian immigrants in schools, which resulted in the denial of racism or the ignorance of racist reports from children and mothers. In Nordic European countries, Svendsen (2014) pointed out that there is a general paradox between textbook knowledge and the real-life experiences of teachers' cognition of racism. The "racism" topic in the textbook is described as a remote, fictional, historical, and foreign concept (p. 10), while the Asian students' daily experiences with racism in schools are seldom recognised by white native

Norwegian teachers. Svendsen suggested that students learning racism in the absence of "race" is an urgent problem that should be dealt with in the educational system. Leibkind et al. (2004) found that immigrant boys are more likely to become the targets of racist bullies in school than girls, and parental support has a positive impact on children's school adjustments. Social-psychological studies have focused on the relationships between immigrant children's psychological adaptation and parenthood practices. Sabatier & Berry (2008) point out that parenthood practices play a vital role for immigrant youth in the process of acculturation and adaptation in both Canada and France. Parents' reactions to the perceived discrimination in the receiving country have a direct impact on children's psychological adaptation and socialisation. However, this research failed to further explore the gender difference on how mothers and fathers reacted to the perceived discrimination. Another research focused on the motherhood practice of first-generation Hongkonger middle-class women dealing with structural discrimination in the host country. Man (1995) noted that first-generation Hongkonger middle-class women devoted themselves to children's academic performance because of generally being out of employment and out of frustration of having no financial independence after emigration. Most of them reported that their relationship with children largely improved after emigration.

In sum, the previous studies show, either in America or in Nordic Europe, that teachers have a different perception and lack of recognition of racism towards students. While the majority of teachers in schools are native white, they lack knowledge about and sensitivities towards racism directed against Asian students. Asian mothers in general feel discriminated against while communicating with school teachers. Migrant women shift their focus to children's education because of the lack of equal access to the labour market and social discrimination in the host country. In the next section, I show the empirical studies on how first-generation Chinese immigrant mothers deal with everyday racism and discrimination inside and outside the private domain in the Netherlands.

6.4. Chinese Women Dealing with Everyday Racism and Discrimination

Before entering the analysis, I want to explain where and when Chinese learn the concepts of race and racism and how they conceptualise them in Chinese culture. Dutch historian Frank Dikötter argues that the invention of racial hierarchy and the myths of origin, ideals of blood and the formation of Chineseness as the descendants of the Yellow Emperor and

Dragon have emerged since the late 19th century because of the rise of the nationalist movement and imperialist invasion of the Qing Dynasty (1994: 404). This nationalist movement was a Westernised reform movement that aimed to rebuild the weak late Qing Dynasty through learning the advantages of Western knowledge, such as military technology, philosophy, medicine, and science.

As I mentioned in chapter one, which was about three discourses of Chineseness, before the late 19th century, Chinese considered themselves as Middle Kingdom, and the criterion to distinguish We (Chinese) and Other (Barbarians: nomadic tribes outside Middle Kingdom) was the Confucian culture. Nomadic barbarians could turn themselves into Chinese by learning Confucian Classics and practising Confucian culture. Dikötter considers this cultural assimilation and China-centric tradition was broken by Qing's defeat by the British (Opium War, 1839–1842) and by the Japanese (Sino-Japanese War 1894–1895). Thus, in order to call for solidarity and reconstruct people's confidence, reformers like Qichao Liang (1873–1929) and Youwei Kang (1858–1927) started to create Chinese as a "yellow" race by using the literary meaning of the first Chinese emperor's family name, Huang. By calling all Chinese a "yellow" race, these reformers encouraged people to study and work hard in order to compete with the "white" race, defeat white racism and racial humiliation and take back China's old glory (Dikötter, 1994: 410–411). This is how and why the Chinese started to learn and domesticate the concept of race and racism. Dikötter argues that Chinese are not passive victims of Imperialism and racism but rather active reformers localising a global trend by combing the original culture and Western discourse (2005: 177–178 in Nyiri and Breidenbach[183]). The concept of Chinese as a yellow race also affects how Chinese migrant women react to everyday racism in the Netherlands.

In this section, I provide a description and analysis of how Chinese deal with everyday racism and discrimination inside and outside the family in the Netherlands. I divide this section into two different parts to distinguish the negative experiences and treatments based on its roots. In the first part, I discuss the everyday racism Chinese women routinely face inside and outside the family with regard to their motherhood experiences. I focus on the interaction and relationships between everyday racism and motherhood practice. In the second part, I reflect on sexism and patriarchy inside the Chinese family itself and focus on how it affects women and their motherhood practices. To make a comparison between transnational

---

[183] Dikötter, Frank. 2005. "Race in China." Pp. 177–204.

families and Chinese families, I separate women's racist experiences inside transnational families from the experiences of those who marry endogamously because the perpetrators represent different cultural and racial backgrounds. I hope to show the intersectionalities by making these distinctions. After analysing the narratives of women's experiences, I argue that the motherhood practice of Chinese immigrant women serves as a method to combat, resist and negotiate racism and discrimination in a white dominant society.

6.4.1 "Mama, kijk, Chinezen!" Everyday racism at school

When the second stage of Chinese emigration to the Netherlands started after World War II, they became visible while joining in every facet of society. Chinese are easily singled out in a white dominant environment by their physical appearance. At the age of five, children begin with their compulsory education. As mothers, Chinese women also engage with children's scholastic performance and social events. Both mother and child become visible in daily interaction with school teachers, other parents and their children. The title of this part "Mama, kijk, Chinezen!" (Mama look, Chinese!) is a direct quote from Gina's narrative. She is 54 years old and has two teenage children; she is a middle-class full-time housewife married to a native Dutch man and living in a Dutch neighbourhood with few immigrant families. Ten years ago, on the first day of school, as she biked her son to the gate, a child saw them and said to her mom in a loud, surprised tone, "Mama, kijk, Chinezen!" "… as if we were some animals she had never seen. It was really a culture shock (to me) that in 2003, people could still marvel while seeing Chinese," Gina told me with incredulous laughter. This anecdote became Gina's family joke, either her husband or her in-laws joke regularly about this "first-day-of-school" encounter. I chose the surprise of a little Dutch girl seeing Chinese as a symbol to show that the presence of Chinese in a white dominant society did attract attention and trigger reactions from the majorities. What happened next to the Chinese after they were seen by the majorities?

Besides the nine women whose children were still under school age at the time I conducted the interviews, the remaining 29 mothers all reported that their children suffered different levels of racism at school,[184] while

[184] Except for one mother who reported that her child was bullied outside the school, bullying often happened on the way to school or on the way back home. Because the perpetrators were her child's classmates or senior schoolmates, I still consider that this case belongs to racism at school.

only five teachers corrected and gave warnings to the offenders. This means that Chinese students must face racism and bullying as ethnic minority members in school. As racism is a taboo and not mentioned in the Netherlands, understandably most teachers either told the parents they did not witness the event or they denied that the offences were racism. "They were just playing" is the most common comment by teachers. Two mothers chose to transfer their children to international schools in the end. For those women whose children are under the school age, six of them reported that they have already registered their children or that they were waiting in line to enter the international schools to prevent them from harm because of other Chinese children's racist experiences and the indifference of teachers towards racist bullying behaviours.

While typing and coding all the transcriptions and narratives, I found one shocking and extremely sad truth – that my introduction to Dutch profanities came from their experiences with everyday racism. Furthermore, I never really knew that there are so many aggressive and hostile words that people and their families could be exposed to in everyday situations, just because they live in a Western society as immigrants. Here are all the terms that mothers reported their children were exposed to at school or in the street: *poep Chinezen* (shit Chinese); *kut Chinezen* (cunt Chinese); *vieze Chinezen* (dirty Chinese); *ching-chang-chung* (a meaningless pronunciation used to mock Chinese[185]); *Chinees studeer varken* (Chinese study pigs); *loempia* (spring roll); and *babi pangang* (Indonesian grilled pork). These negative terms range from inferiorising one's race and degrading one's diligence to Asian food and peculiar pronunciation. Verbal racist attacks are the most common form of bullying that the Chinese students encounter in schools. The racist bully behaviours are also gendered. For boys, these often turn to physical violence. For girls, some verbal racist attacks end in sexual harassment. I want to analyse two cases to show that the ruthless denial of racism results in serious racist attacks on children.

At the beginning of this chapter, I used Gina's daughter's first day at school as an opening. Here I describe the experience of Gina's second son, Gimmi,[186] who is 13 years old, one year younger than his sister. In 2004, Gimmi went to the same school as his sister; they were the only two Chinese students. Compared to his sister, Gimmi looks more Chinese in appearance. From the first week at school, Gimmi reported several times

[185] But the truth is there is no single Chinese term pronounced as *ching-chang-chung.*

[186] To protect the privacy of the children mentioned in this chapter, pseudonyms are used.

being mocked or sworn at by schoolmates. Gina mentioned the racist verbal attacks of both children to their teachers by email, phone calls or face-to-face, but the teachers replied that it was nothing serious, just "children playing". Gina also told her Dutch husband that she wanted to transfer the children to the international school, but her husband insisted that the children must stay at a Dutch school to mingle with Dutch children. Her husband told her that children need to learn how to deal with this matter by themselves, and this is the Dutch way to teach children independence. Gina has no other choice but to tell her children that they have to learn to talk back and, unless necessary, not to use violence to solve the problem. At first, her children just ignored the racist swearing. After his parents' encouragement, especially Gimmi, started to talk back. However, talking back is a very risky way for minority students. One time, Gimmi was called *poep Chinees* and *kut Chinees* during the class break. Gimmi shouted back "fucking *vies Nederland* (fucking dirty Netherlands)" but ended up with six to ten students surrounding him in the corner and pushing and yelling at him. Fortunately, other students told the school teachers to intervene. About two days later, Gimmi was chased by the same students who always bullied him at school on the way back home on bicycles. They threw balloons filled with water towards him and kept swearing at him with all kinds of unbearable slang. As soon as Gimmi arrived at the door, he jumped from his bike and slammed the front door. It happened to be a holiday break for Gimmi's father, and when he looked through the window, he witnessed around eight children throwing water balloons and pebbles at his living room window and shouting "*poep Chinezen*, fucking Chinezen". Gimmi's father opened the door and grabbed two children. They told him that they were also throwing water balloons at other families and they were just playing with Gimmi. After this event, Gimmi refused to go to school for a week and he became very emotionally unstable. Gimmi's father finally realised how bad and serious the racist attacks that his children suffered at school were. In the end, they transferred both children to the international school and they moved to a neighbourhood in Eindhoven where more expat families lived. Gimmi and his sister had to go through one year of treatment by a child therapist; their unstable and hostile emotions towards school became more controlled but one never knows how it still might impact their sense of self in adult life.

Another example happened to Iris's daughter, Nikki. Iris has a Taiwanese husband. She decided to bring both children to the Netherlands after being seven years apart from her husband. Before 2012, her husband lived and worked alone in the Netherlands so they thought that maybe it was time for both children to try a Dutch education and living environment.

However, things did not go very well for Nikki. After three months studying in Dutch language schools, she entered a local Dutch school. Nikki felt very frustrated in the beginning because of the language barrier. Her classmates often made jokes at her expense and she failed to make friends. The racist bullying did not take place at school but on the school bus. In the beginning, some badly behaved boys touched or pulled Nikki's long black hair. Nikki was very frightened because she was taught at schools in Taiwan that you could not touch another person's body unless you get the other's consent. Nikki told her mother when she returned home, and Iris emailed the schoolteacher. The teacher said she was not on the school bus so she did not know what happened exactly. Iris then asked to talk to the teacher who was on that school bus but the teacher told Iris that Dutch children are friendly and open so they will have some physical contact, which is good for Nikki to make friends. Things became more serious after the teacher told Nikki that touching was a way Dutch students show goodwill and friendliness. Nikki told Iris that maybe this is a cultural difference. However, the school bus teacher made the wrong judgement because he or she lacked racial and gender sensitivities. Two months later, Nikki screamed out loud on the school bus because, whilst sitting on the back seat, she was touched on her breasts and pinched on her crotch. The school bus teacher at that moment immediately separated the perpetrators from Nikki and corrected their behaviour. Iris could not believe that her daughter would suffer this pain in such a modern country.

Although Nikki changed to a front seat next to the teacher of the school bus after the sexual assault, at the time I conducted the interview, she was already going to another international school. Iris told me that both she and her husband were very upset and hurt by this event and by the teacher's carelessness. They are considering moving back to Taiwan as soon as the company finds a successor.

The two cases show how severe the consequences of the denial of racism at school can be. The fact that the majority of Dutch schoolteachers lack racial and gender sensitivities is also a contributing factor. Gina and Iris represent relatively powerless immigrant mothers. They reported racist bullying repeatedly, not only once to the schoolteachers, but in vain. They tried to teach their children to assimilate into Dutch culture by talking back or by accepting physical touch as a symbol of friendliness which resulted in their children suffering more harm. Their cases show an urgent requirement for all Dutch schoolteachers to be trained and re-educated on racial and gender sensitivities. At the same time, all schools should teach pupils to respect the diversities of race since migrants from all over the globe will keep joining Dutch society because of globalisation. If the state or politicians refuse to break the ice to talk about racism and sexism towards ethnic minority students at school and work out how to deal with racist and sexist bullying behaviours against ethnic minority students at schools, the same situation and harm will happen repeatedly without being treated seriously.

6.4.2 Dealing with everyday racism with pity and being above the racist

Most mothers told me that they teach their children to deal with racism by pitying the perpetrator. They think that this is the safest way and their children will be not harmed by talking back; it is also a way to build their sense of confidence. Some Chinese mothers from transnational families do not agree with the way their Dutch husbands or in-laws teach children to talk back or fight back by giving the perpetrator a punch or a kick. They need to negotiate with their husbands and in-laws to stop the risky ways of teaching their children to deal with racism. Chinese mothers in transnational families must educate their Dutch husbands and in-laws by making them clearly understand that their children or grandchildren are not considered by the majority of Dutch as people like them. As an ethnic minority at school, talking back or punching back can risk the children's safety. Thus, in general, Chinese mothers would not suggest that their children deal directly with racism; instead, they teach them to pity and be above the racist.

The contradictory attitudes in dealing with racist encounters between Chinese mothers and their Dutch spouses and family members reflect the starkly real-life alterity because of racial differences. From my own personal experience, I can totally understand and relate to these women's violence-avoiding decisions in dealing with racist attacks. On Christmas Eve, 2013, I was walking alone after a long day working in the Utrecht University City Library. It was nearly dark and I was about 200 metres from my accommodation in the Burgemeester Reigerstraat when two white teenagers crossed over from the opposite side of the road. They started to yell loudly at me "ginger duck, ginger duck", I was furious and thought, "For God's sake, it is Christmas Eve, you Dutch people." So, for the first time in my life, I yelled back "F**K YOU" after they had passed me. I thought my action would silence them; unfortunately, they started to mimic my high and feminine tone by moaning "Oh, f**k me, ja f**k me." To my surprise, when I was running away from their filthy humiliation, I saw a woman smoking on the street corner and laughing at this "street drama". I felt no sympathy or mutual support in that minimum eye contact.

It was the worst Christmas Eve I had ever had. Thus, from my own racist encounter, I now know why Chinese women decide not to talk back or fight back at that moment because it could bring more humiliation and risk to oneself, and no one is going to intervene. Their decisions are out of careful calculation and Chinese women have developed a unique life philosophy to reverse the negative emotion.

There is a psychological shift necessary here to put oneself above the racist by pitying and laughing at their stupid and uncivilised behaviour. Yolanda is a 70-year-old Taiwanese woman who married a Dutch man. They have been living in an upper-class Dutch neighbourhood for 40 years. In the 1970s, their daughter was the only half-Dutch half-Taiwanese student at school. Yolanda told me that her daughter was constantly being laughed and sworn at in school because of her half-white half-Asian appearance. She constantly came home crying, and this was what Yolanda taught her girl:

> Don't you cry, my daughter; in fact, some Dutch people are like the frog living in a well. Their worldview is only Europe. They can only see the sky above their head. Now the (public) transportation is so convenient, you can go to different countries in a very short time. You have to understand some people can only see themselves; their worldview is so narrow. Don't let their narrow-mindedness affect you; these people aren't so lucky like you to be born in a family with broader global perspectives. So, you must learn to be your own master, to be independent, then you can survive in any place (in the world). Before that, you need to cultivate yourself, don't let others beat you down with these boring discourses. What matters is your wisdom and knowledge.

Yolanda is very proud of her only daughter. She is now working as a doctor in Germany. From Yolanda's words, it is clear that she taught her daughter as a global person to deal with racism by lifting her position beyond the Netherlands, beyond Europe, beyond race issues. Conversely, she looked upon those racists by pitying their fates for they, with their narrow-minded worldview, are not among those lucky enough to be born in a transnational family. Thus, what they thought and what they said are boring discourses which do not serve her daughter and which only means that she has to study harder to be her own master.

I found the discourses on encouraging children to surpass racism by studying hard as well as pitying the racist are not only shared by middle-class mothers but also by their working-class sisters. For example, Wendy, a 51-year-old restaurant owner, has three male children. Her first son had a fight that cost the opponent a tooth because this boy constantly harassed him physically and swore at him, such as "*ching-chang-chung*" or "*poep*

Chinees" in public at school. Fortunately, the schoolteacher witnessed the whole event, and the boy's parents accepted Wendy's apology. Back home, Wendy gathered all three boys together and disciplined them;

> You have to realize the fact that Dutch people don't like Chinese. Your father speaks no Dutch and mother speaks only *klein een beetje* (a little). If you really made some serious trouble, that will be a big problem. Oh, don't waste your energy fighting and being angry with idiots. How can you *duiniutanqin* (play music to the cows)? After that, all of my children ignored those boring children.

Here we can see the two themes that were also present in Wendy's narratives. First, she asks her children to not cause trouble for their parents by picking fights with the perpetrators because of their minor language abilities, which also implies the relatively powerless social position by telling children the fact that Dutch people do not like Chinese. To avoid more trouble caused by responding to racist action, Wendy chose to teach her children to deal with daily racism by ignoring the insults and staying silent. I found that this is the Chinese survival strategy in the Netherlands, which is correspondent to Blakely's theory on the behaviour code of Dutch tolerance, being invisible, keeping a distance and acting harmlessly. Allison Blakely (1993) points out that there is a common conception of behaviour code towards blacks or other Others in the Netherlands. The general consensus of Dutch tolerance sees diversity as not a problem as long as it stays politically invisible and harmless socially.

Second, in these two cases, Wendy and Yolanda also shifted their position to a higher moral ground by teaching children to save their energy because you cannot educate those people. For example, Wendy used the Chinese classic four characters idiom *duiniutanqin* (對牛彈琴) to persuade her children that it is no use reasoning with those persistent people because they will not appreciate your opinion. Hence, they do not deserve your time and energy. In sum, firstly, when dealing with everyday racism at school, Dutch teachers in general keep their distance from this sensitive issue. They either deny students' hostile behaviour is racism or they lack the knowledge and cognition on racism and sexism towards immigrant students. Secondly, mothers often felt powerless to deal with children's experiences of everyday racism at school because of the general denial of racist attitudes of schoolteachers or even their Dutch spouses. Nevertheless, being an ethnic minority themselves in Dutch society, women often encounter everyday racism and from their own perceptions, Chinese mothers teach their children to deal with everyday racism by putting children's self-esteem in a higher moral position, to disgrace and pity those uncivilised and undereducated racists. This is a carefully calculated method to protect children from further direct (physical or verbal) confrontation at the moment of being discriminated against. In the next part, I discuss everyday racism in the workplace, how it affects motherhood practice and how women deal with it.

6.4.3 Everyday racism in the workplace

In this part, I discuss the relationship between workplace racism and motherhood practice experiences. Three main findings are presented in this part. First, middle-class women have more difficulty finding white-collar full-time jobs than their working-class sisters. Second, for those who work in a Dutch company, whenever they encountered everyday racism, they chose to keep silent to protect their position. Third, especially the middle-class women value children's language education in English and Mandarin more than Dutch in their motherhood practice. For more description on how Chinese mothers arrange children's language education as a strategy to deal with racism in their future workplace, please see chapter five. In this part, I only elaborate on the first two findings.

Unlike the working-class women, the middle-class women, especially those who do not have previous Dutch or international working experiences and who obtained their final diploma in China and Taiwan, generally have a hard time finding a white-collar job in the Netherlands. Besides the language barrier, these women said that their previous working experiences are considered useless for a Dutch company and their Chinese diplomas are not officially recognised. This downward job-hunting phenomenon happens not only for Chinese migrant women. According to a news report from DutchNews.nl, married migrant women often end up jobless in the Netherlands, especially well-educated women.[187] Some of them were extremely frustrated after being discriminated against in job agencies. The attitudes of coordinators in job agencies often show impatience, disrespect or ignorance. For instance, Candy shared her job-hunting experiences of nine years ago with me. Candy holds an MBA diploma from a famous university in China; she came to the Netherlands because her husband got a full scholarship as a PhD candidate in 2004. After graduation, her husband has been working as a post-doctorate researcher. Candy had two children before coming to the Netherlands; she

[187] Please see http://www.dutchnews.nl/news/archives/2014/10/foreign-partners-more-likely-to-be-jobless-isolated-in-the-netherlands.php/, access date October 29, 2014.

worked as a manager in a manufacturing company in China. In order to integrate into Dutch society and find a job to make life better, Candy went to a Dutch language cram school and passed the NT2 exam[188] in 2006. In the beginning, Candy went to the career-day events in Amsterdam several times to have direct interview chances with employers, but in vain. She got some feedback and suggestions for her strange accent when speaking Dutch and English. To improve her accent, Candy hired a native Dutch teacher to tutor her and her two daughters in the correct Dutch pronunciation. Candy thought if her accent was a barrier in finding a job, then her two daughters must have the same problem and they might be discriminated against. After six months, the Dutch tutor approved their pronunciations. Candy was more confident about returning to job-hunting. This time, Candy found a job agency to help her. However, things did not go very well. Candy complained that the attitudes of the agency staff were really impolite and she could tell this from the way they talked and the way they looked at her. Candy tried to find a part-time job as an administrative assistant but the job agency told her that she had better apply as a *schoonmaak* (cleaning) lady. She then emotionally expressed her anger.

> *Schoonmaken*! After all these years of studying Dutch so hard, they think I only deserve schoonmaken! Can you believe that? This country gives no opportunities to immigrants and they blame us for (our own) laziness!

After this humiliation, Candy gave up trying to find a business-related job. She joined the training of overseas Mandarin teacher programmes organised by the Chinese government. She has been teaching Mandarin in several weekend Mandarin schools and high schools since 2008. Candy's is not a unique case. As I mentioned in several research reports earlier in this chapter, ethnic minorities are more likely to be out of work than the native Dutch even if they have the same qualifications. Recognising workplace racism in Dutch society, women adjust their disappointed feelings and arrange their everyday life in positive and creative ways. Some of them start their own business with the lowest amount of capital by opening online shops. They sell second-hand European antique furniture or famous luxury brands to Taiwan or China. Some online shop

---

[188] The NT2 Exam is a simplified jargon referring to Staatsexamen Nederlands als tweede taal (State Examination of Dutch as a Second Language), often abbreviated as Staatsexamen NT2. It is an official Dutch proficiency test for non-Dutch native speakers as proof of their linguistic command of the Dutch language. The test result can be used to apply for a job or for college entrance in the Netherlands.

owners sell their home-made Chinese cuisine to the Chinese community in nearby countries. Some of them are happy to be a full-time mother and put all their energy in their children's education. Some of them go to Chinese companies, and still others join the training of overseas Mandarin teacher programmes to become part-time Mandarin teachers. In short, Chinese immigrant mothers are practical in their dealings with workplace racism. They create their own ways to make money without being dependent on the Dutch job markets.

The second finding came from women's working experiences and encountering everyday racism in a Dutch company. They chose to keep silent to protect their positions in that moment. Polly is a 37-year-old woman who has a four-year-old boy. She married a Dutch man, who was her contact person in a branch of a Dutch company in Guangzhou City. After emigration, Polly found a job in a trading company because of her previous working experience with a Dutch company in China. She is one of only two Chinese people in that company. Polly told me that her colleagues often directly criticised the other Chinese colleague as "*domme Chinees* (stupid Chinese)" in front of her, and she immediately becomes very angry. However, she holds her temper because of her son; for his sake she must keep calm. The following is Polly's opinion towards everyday workplace racism.

> I often feel that they deliberately say *domme Chinees* nearby. In appearance, they are pointing to the other Chinese but I know they also laugh at me from their heart. They really dislike Chinese; they think we took their jobs... I came here only for making a better life for my son and I don't care what they say. Without us two stupid Chinese, how can they do business with China?

Polly's silent reaction to the racist comments towards Chinese does not mean she agrees to or submits to the dominant power. On the contrary, she draws a clear line in her mind that she knows she is irreplaceable to this company. As a mother, this extra income is to provide a better life for her son. To keep this position she chooses silence towards racism but she puts herself above it. The negative comment does not damage her self-esteem.

To conclude, I found that middle-class women with no previous Dutch working experience and no Western higher education diplomas have a very difficult time finding white-collar jobs in the Netherlands. The general discrimination and racism in employment towards immigrants makes them frustrated and disappointed. However, some middle-class women start their own business, some develop their second professional training in Mandarin teaching, and still others devote themselves to their children's education. For those who work in a Dutch company, they choose to deal silently with workplace racism. Nevertheless, they consider their contribution to a Dutch company as irreplaceable and unique, which allows them to negotiate the degrading racist speech. After personally experiencing the Dutch workplace racism, Chinese mothers arrange their children's language education as a strategy to deal with racism in their future workplace. They value English most, then Mandarin, and Dutch is the least important one. In the next part, I provide a description and analysis of women's everyday racism experiences with their children in other public spaces and how they responded to racism at that moment.

6.4.4 Everyday racism in the shops

Being the main caregivers in the family, women spend more time shopping than men in daily life. The chances that they will encounter everyday racism in the shops are also high. Many mothers reported that racist encounters in the shops often happen when they are alone without the company of their Dutch husbands. Women living in small townships encounter less racism in shops than women who live in the metropolitan cities. The common forms of racism women encounter individually while shopping are: being followed everywhere in the shops until they pay, their handbags and pockets being checked by the security guards, being told "you can't afford it", being deliberately run into with shopping carts by teenagers; and being rejected and yelled at when they try to return purchases as allegedly damaged within two days. Just as they teach their children not to talk back directly to confront the racist at that moment, most women look down on the racists and never shop again at the same store. For mothers, the most intolerant racists are those who perform their discriminating actions while children are present. I want to take Fanny's experience as an example. It happened during the summer vacation: Fanny took her three-year-old son to Amsterdam and she'd promised to buy him a Miffy toy that day. When they walked into a toyshop near Dam Square, Fanny told me she encountered the most intolerant racist in her life.

> It's the store with a pair of massive wooden shoes in the front door; my son wanted to see one Miffy in the top shelf. Because I am quite short, I tried to reach it but in vain. I asked the saleslady to help me. At first she gave me a long face, and we waited. When she finally approached, she directly told me "That one is expensive, they're "all[189]" very expensive, I don't

[189] Fanny told me the sales lady deliberately emphasised the word "all" with louder and longer sound.

think you can afford it." I immediately walked out of the shop. I was furious. That really pissed me off, what a bitch! Outside the shop, my son asked me "Mummy, don't we have money?"

How did you reply?

Of course we have money. Just the aunt in the shop was in a very bad mood today.

Why didn't you tell your son she was a racist? Or she doesn't like Chinese?

Please, my son is not even four years old yet. You want me to tell him what? Do you want me to tell him that he was being discriminated in his father's own country and (that) is because he has a mother with black hair and yellow skin?

Fanny was very emotional in response to my questions and I realised that I should not question her motherhood practice directly without any linguistic modifiers. I was being too rude and too impolite. I was overwhelmed by my eagerness to know the "correct" answer from my own presumptions on racism and at that moment triggered another confrontation. I should have noticed that she was furious with that racist encounter. I should have been more sensitive to the fact that she even cursed the saleslady with a word "*jia* 賤" in front of me. That word is used to disgrace a woman as a despicable evil-minded whore in Chinese society. I not only did not notice her anger but I further questioned her motherhood authority. I'd forgotten the Chinese hierarchy codes in personal relationships; in Fanny's eyes, I am a junior sister, not a researcher. My carelessness could have stopped the whole interview so I immediately apologised to her for my impoliteness and ignorance. Fanny was my seventh interview and I learned a valuable lesson from this experience. From the eighth interview onwards, I would think twice or wait a little bit longer before returning to any sensitive topic.

In order to ease the confrontation and embarrassment, I told her she is not alone in encountering everyday racism in the Netherlands, and I shared two of my experiences with her. Fortunately, the topic was still around racism; Fanny told me what she did after that day. She told this story to everyone she knows and she shared her experience in the Dutch Taiwanese group on Facebook. Another mother forwarded her post to the Dutch Chinese online community. Fanny felt that it is a good thing that more Chinese people know this story, then other Chinese mothers will not have to suffer similar discrimination. Fanny commented with this sentence:

"If Dutch people want to make money from Chinese, they better not hire a racist."

To avoid a direct confrontation at the moment of encountering racist treatment is how Chinese mothers deal with everyday racism. But as an old Chinese maxim goes "*Yazihuashui* (鴨子滑水)" – while ducks skimming on the water look calm and peaceful in appearance, the feet are busy below the surface. Social media is a powerful tool linking the Chinese community, especially when encountering everyday racism. Fanny found comfort and encouragement from Facebook friends and other Chinese on the internet, which resulted in many people deciding to boycott that store. Fanny showed her agency both in protecting her boy from racist harm and taking her power of speech back via her motherhood practice to confront and negotiate everyday racism in an indirect but powerful way. In the next part, I talk about everyday Dutch racism inside the transnational family.

6.4.5 Everyday racism inside the transnational family

In this part, I focus on everyday racism inside the transnational family. As I mentioned in chapter five, by transnational family I mean the family composed of a Chinese woman and a Dutch man. I was advised by female friends and also my interviewees not to write about this highly sensitive topic; however, I would like to highlight that everyday racism not only happens in the public domain but also in the private. Compared to public everyday racism, private everyday racism has more negative impacts on immigrant women. In the transnational family, some migrant women must face patriarchy with racist oppression together on a regular basis, which sometimes relates to their motherhood practices. I am not saying all transnational families are problematic; indeed, among the 17 women who are married to Dutch husbands, only 3 reported that they felt discriminated against by their husbands or in-laws. I appreciate their courage and trust in sharing with me, and it is my duty to make this problem visible especially in this interdisciplinary study regarding diaspora, gender and family life. I dedicate this part to their epistemological contribution and if I do offend some people, please accept my most sincere apology.

In chapter five I mentioned Bonnie's experiences on the issue of the language education decision. Bonnie's husband declared his will in forbidding the use of Mandarin anymore at home without respecting Bonnie's feelings and opinions as a mother. As an immigrant spouse, Bonnie encounters triple intersecting dominant powers, viz., racism, patriarchy and nationalism. She is deprived of her rights of decision making on her children's language education by her husband, which can be seen as patriarchal discrimination. On the one hand, the ideology behind the husband's action is supported by racism, which considers Mandarin and the mother's Chinese cultural background as useless in Dutch society. On the other hand, only the official Dutch language is the right and useful one for children.

The second case I want to offer is the confrontation resulting from cultural differences between the Dutch mother-in-law and the Chinese daughter-in-law, Fanny. The speech uttered by the Dutch side made her Chinese counterpart uncomfortable and Fanny felt she was being discriminated against. Because of her husband's work, they often have to live in the Netherlands for three or four months annually and they do not have their own house here so in order to save money, they sometimes live with their in-laws. Fanny's son is physically more Asian: his body is smaller and his eating habits Chinese in appetite. Contrary to this, Fanny's in-laws are typically Dutch; they eat a warm meal once a day in the evenings. Breakfast and lunch are often simple and cold. Fanny and her husband forbid their son to eat junk food, such as coke, hamburgers, chips, coloured candy, concentrated juice, or any fast food in Taiwan. However, every time Fanny's family comes to stay at the in-laws, they prepare a lot of junk food for their grandson. Fanny tried several times to communicate with her in-laws by telling them that such food is not healthy for small children but her mother-in-law took her action as deliberately distancing her son from his grandparents. Some misunderstandings occurred because of the low language proficiency on both sides and the atmosphere at home is somewhat tense. Fanny asked her husband to reason and explain with his mother, but her husband asked her to endure these trivial things and let his parents be happy since they only get the chance to be with their grandson once a year for a short period. But last summer Fanny told me she was pushed to her limit and decided that from then on, they would only stay with her in-laws for one week and then rent temporary accommodation while staying in the Netherlands. This scenario occurred at the dinner table while Fanny and her family were spending their holidays at her in-laws' house during the second week.

> I was preparing the dinner in the kitchen then; my mother-in-law came to see what I was cooking. She saw me cooking rice in the pot and then she murmured "Rice every day, rice every day" twice. My husband was able to have a dinner with us on that day then my mother-in-law first spoke some Dutch and then she grabbed my son's arm and spoke in English, "Why is my grandson so thin? Too much rice, no potatoes?" I felt that she didn't want me to feed my son rice.... The second day, I bought a bag of potatoes

> for dinner and I found her cooking the rice. She has no clear standard and I really don't know how to cooperate with her. I wonder if she would say the same words or not if I were Dutch?

Here we can see that Fanny is in a relatively lower position as a daughter-in-law in a transnational family. When contradictions and misunderstandings happen because of different eating habits, parenting style and low language proficiency on both sides, Fanny's Dutch husband asks her to keep calm and make his parents happy, without trying to make things better or to bridge a mutual understanding. He puts his family's interests first, without supporting his wife. Fanny must face an uncomfortable environment by herself without breaking the surface harmony; however, those sarcastic words deliberately spoken in English to question her motherhood practice by her Dutch mother-in-law made her feel discriminated against. Fanny compared her own experience with that of other friends; she told me that in general, Dutch in-laws do not interfere with their daughter-in-law's motherhood practice. They respect their decisions on childrearing, but Fanny does not feel the same support from her mother-in-law.

Maybe some people think that I am being controversial about a simple conversation around a dinner table. However, rice and potatoes represent opposing symbolic meanings beyond eating habits from East and West. The conversation directly points to the specific lifestyle differences between two cultures. Here I want to take a recent news event as an example to emphasise my argument that using rice as an innuendo to question a Chinese daughter-in-law's motherhood performance is an act of racism. On November 17, 2013, Xiao Wang, a young Chinese PhD candidate who studies economics at Erasmus University, participated in the wildly popular "Holland's Got Talent" live show. Before Wang's performance, Wang told judges that he was going to sing an Italian opera song "La donna è mobile" from Verdi's Rigoletto. A Dutch judge called Cornelis Willem Heuckeroth,[190] nicknamed Gordon, responded, "Which (Verdi) number are you singing, number 39 with rice?" After Wang's wonderful performance, Gordon continued to give his feedback to Xiao by saying, "Honestly, this is the best Chinese I've had in weeks, and it's not a takeaway." Gordon seemed to be very pleased with his humour and kept going by turning to the audience and saying in Dutch, "He looks like a waiter from a Chinese restaurant." At that moment, an American judge, Dan Karaty, intervened and told Gordon directly, "You're really not supposed to say things like that to people." Gordon still could not stop

[190] Mr. Heuckeroth is famous for his sarcasm in the Netherlands.

giggling and laughing in front of the camera, repeating "Number 39 with rice, number 39 with rice" several times. Gordon's "number 39 with rice" utterance soon became international news, especially in the United States and in almost all Chinese mass media, invoking the white innocence (Wekker, 2015) characteristic of Dutch racism. At first, Gordon tried to defend himself as he thought that "number 39 with rice" was a way to show how well Dutch Chinese integrate into Dutch society. His reply triggered more criticism; young Dutch Chinese and several Chinese associations in the Netherlands did not keep silent and clearly expressed their anger. On the website gogodutch.com,[191] users immediately launched a petition asking Simon Cowell[192] to fire Gordon.[193] Also on Facebook, a group of second-generation Dutch Chinese established a fan page called "nr39metrijst" (number 39 with rice) to condemn Gordon's racist speech. Within a week, Gordon apologised. During President of the PRC Jingping Xi's visit to the Netherlands, Wang was invited by the Dutch Royal family to participate in a dinner party with President Xi.[194] Apparently, Gordon's racist speech was turned into a political and diplomatic issue that needed to be handled with care. As I mentioned earlier in chapter five, according to Bourdieu's theory, language has symbolic meaning, from this number 39 with rice event back to the sarcastic "too much rice no potato?" uttered by Fanny's mother-in-law. Since rice is referring to the Chinese and potato is referring to the Dutch in Fanny's mother-in-law's speech, Fanny read the music beyond the melody, which means that she got the offensive and hostile connotation using potato as a vivid metaphor to attack and question Fanny's Chinese motherhood performance, which does not meet the standards of a Dutch mother-in-law. One can tell there is a hierarchal link

---

[191] This website, www.gogodutch.com is the biggest Mandarin website for migrant Chinese and Chinese international students who currently live in the Netherlands to find all sorts of information they need, such as immigration policies, Dutch language tests, housing problems, insurance services, looking for a date, a Mandarin tutor, shops. Users will also share their experiences in applying to Dutch universities for a master or doctorate diploma, their transnational marriage issues or restaurant evaluations. In general, it is a website that provides all kinds of information and personal experiences of Chinese migrants and international students in the Netherlands. People outside the Netherlands can also browse this website and communicate on line with all users.

[192] Simon Cowell's corporation is the main sponsor of "Holland's Got Talent".

[193] See http://bbs.gogodutch.com/forum.php?mod=viewthread&tid=719250&highlight=Gordon, access date November 24, 2013.

[194] This event also was reported in the gogodutch website; see, http://bbs.gogodutch.com/thread-768164-1-1.html, access date March 30, 2014.

between rice (Chinese) and potato (Dutch) in that question. Too little potato makes him thin, and this equals too much rice, which is not sufficient, and also implies that the Dutch way of raising children is better than the Chinese way. This connotation made Fanny upset and discriminated against, and it also shows that for migrant women everyday racism often occurs not only outside but also inside a transnational family.

In the first part of this section, I discussed the everyday racism relating to motherhood practice that Chinese migrant women have to deal with. Not only outside the family, such as at schools, in the workplace or in shops but also at home they all interact with and negotiate these regular and routine racisms. I found that Chinese women do not talk back or fight against racism directly for safety concerns. They also teach their children not to risk their personal safety when dealing with racism. They generally put themselves above the racism in their mindset, and they perceive themselves as having a higher moral status than the racists. In the second half of this section, I concentrate on the discrimination inside the Chinese family to explore how women perceive it and how they deal with it.

6.4.6 Everyday discrimination inside the Chinese migrant family

In the final part, I want to discuss the /gender discrimination inside the Chinese migrant family. Apart from racism, this discrimination is rooted in Chinese traditional *patriarchy chong nan qing nu* (重男輕女), which literally means place importance on the male and belittle the female. *Chong* is used as a verb, which means to put weight on something, contrasted by the second verb *qing*, which refers to disdain or to look down. This sexism, which is based on parents valuing male offspring more than female, happens most especially in the Chinese working-class migrant family. Compared to only one middle-class woman, all the working-class women mentioned they were being neglected or that they sacrificed their opportunities for higher education to make a financial contribution to their natal families. After emigration, most of them made up their minds in their own motherhood practices to treat their children equally regardless of their gender. They do not want their daughters to suffer the same prejudice and oppression they had experienced. However, those women who emigrated to the Netherlands at a very young age still felt unequally treated because of their gender. Here I want to take Grace as an example to illustrate how a daughter's rights are sacrificed under the *chong nan qing nu* patriarchy.

Grace (44) was born into a farmer's family in Hong Kong. She told me her hometown is an island village; people have to take a little wooden boat for commuting. She is the youngest daughter after three brothers. Her family is the typical chain-migration immigrant: her father and the older brothers left for the Netherlands first and then years later her mother took the other two sons. When Grace was 14, her mother could finally bring her to the Netherlands. She was mainly raised by her grandparents and had little feelings for her own parents. Grace had a very hard time after emigration. Learning Dutch from commencement was difficult for her and her parents could only help her a little. She was also bullied and isolated at schools and she had no friends to talk to. She decided to give up studying and help the family business. Three years later, Grace's parents told her that they had officially retired and that they are going back to Hong Kong. They told her she could stay with one of her brothers until she married and then they left. Grace was very angry and upset with her parents; she still cannot forgive them.

> I feel like my parents abandoned me twice, once in Hong Kong, once in the Netherlands. They left three restaurants for every sons, but not me. Only a son can take over their business but not a daughter. I was not in their hearts at first at all. In fact, what my brothers are capable of (running a restaurant), I am capable of, too… I was abandoned (by my parents) … (My parents) they are really very traditional.

Grace finally chose not to depend on any of her brothers and went to live with a man at the age of 17. She is 44 years old now and has two daughters, who all chose her family name after a painful divorce. Grace must work two shifts to make ends meet. She works as a cleaning lady during the day and as a waitperson in a friend's Chinese restaurant at night. In order to save more money for her two daughters' future tuition for higher education, Grace sacrifices most of her holidays to babysit for other colleagues' children. She repeated "I feel so tired; life is so difficult" eight times during her two-hour interview. Grace always teaches her girls not to trust anyone and to be strong. Do what you want to do and as your mother I will support them in almost every way. Grace's case reflects how Chinese sexism and patriarchy can destroy one's life in a diasporic context. Being a youngest daughter, she was left behind alone in Hong Kong during her entire childhood. After emigration, she was not only deprived of her educational opportunities because of the language and cultural barrier but also her non-paid domestic physical labour contribution from 14 to 17 years of age was taken for granted. She was treated as a temporary guest at home – under the traditional Chinese *jiaqu* (嫁娶) concept, raising a daughter is a waste of time and money because she cannot carry the family blood. One day in the future she will "marry out" to another family where her "true" home is. Ironically, Grace not only carries her family blood by changing both of her daughters' surnames into hers but she does not depend on her brothers, as her parents planned.

In short, Chinese migrant women face patriarchy and sexism inside the Chinese family different from the everyday racism they deal with in the public domain or in the family as it is a discrimination resulting from unequal gendered values.

6.5 Conclusion

In this chapter I made a short review of Dutch racism theories and the mass media representation of Chinese both in the Dutch East Indies and later in the Netherlands during the first half of the 20th century. The origin of Dutch racism is rooted in its imperial and colonial past. The racial perception towards people of colour in overseas Dutch colonies is still consciously being reproduced by the state and the mainstream white society in every facet of life as a taken-for-granted ideology. After the Nazi occupation during WWII, the terms "race" and "racism" became taboo in public discourse. It only happens somewhere else in the world, but not here. In the Netherlands, "race" and "racism" no longer exist, they belong to the past. Nevertheless, the ideology of white superiority and dominance still prevails in the Dutch mainstream society, which considers non-white immigrants as outside intruders. The general attitude and political speech on "racism" policy or language is denial. The country depicts itself as an innocent victim of Nazi racism and is satisfied with its smug ignorance at the same time (Essed and Hoving, 2014).

In the third section, I divided everyday Dutch racism experience from Chinese patriarchy and sexism. I elaborated how Chinese mothers deal with racism and the way it affects their motherhood practice. I found that mothers often felt powerless to deal with children's everyday racism at school because of the general denial of racist attitudes of school teachers, or even their Dutch spouses. Nevertheless, being ethnic minorities themselves in the Dutch society, women often encounter everyday racism both in the public and the private domain. Based on their own perception of racism, the way Chinese mothers teach children to deal with everyday racism is to put children's self-esteem in a higher moral position, to disgrace and pity those uncivilised and undereducated racists. This is the result of careful calculation to protect themselves and their children from further direct (physical or verbal) confrontation at the moment of being discriminated. After analysing women's narratives, I argue that the motherhood practices of Chinese immigrant women serve as a method to deal with, to resist, and to negotiate racism and discrimination in a white dominant society. The relationship between motherhood practice and racism in migrant women's daily life experiences from different racial/ethnic groups still needs to be explored and be recorded globally. From empirical studies, researchers can conceptualise the discourses on women dealing with racism and sexism.

In the next chapter, I present the experience and feelings of Chinese migrant women giving birth in a host country, and how its unique social welfare helps migrant women start their motherhood in an unfamiliar social environment.

CHAPTER SEVEN

FIRST-GENERATION CHINESE IMMIGRANT WOMEN'S EXPERIENCE OF USING KRAAMZORG (MATERNITY CARE SERVICE) IN THE NETHERLANDS

While conducting field research on the motherhood practice of first-generation Chinese women in the Netherlands between 2011–2014, the interviewees always praised the country's kraamzorg system. Out of curiosity, I looked into this unique maternity care service and found it humane and worth recommending. Kraamzorg means maternity care service, which is covered by the basic state health insurance and can be enjoyed by every female resident living in the Netherlands regardless of her nationality. The rationale behind this service system is the belief that motherhood and fatherhood are not natural instincts but require learning and guidance. In the Netherlands, the majority of families are formed by heterosexual parents but some families have same-sex parents or novice adoptive parents with adopted newborns. The duties of kraamzorg nurses are to help novice parents to adjust to the postpartum period and instruct the partner how to take care of the mother and the infant.

7.2 Introduction of Childbirth-related Insurance in the Netherlands

7.2.1 Background

Policy Background

After the Millennium, in response to the shortage of medical personnel, the reduction of medical resource waste and the inclusion of the midwife system that had been separated from the Dutch medical system since 1950 into the medical care industry, the Dutch government implemented a series of drastic reforms in the health care system and medical insurance policy, aiming to save expenditure as well as increase sources of income. Thus, related tangible and intangible facilities were established and the training of human resources was finalised by September 2005. In January 2006, a compulsory basic health insurance system (basisverzekering) was introduced to cover all residents of the Netherlands, both foreigners and citizens. In this new health insurance system, kraamzorg (maternity care) was added, apart from the medical care during pregnancy, which is accessible to all female residents of the Netherlands regardless of their nationality and citizen status.

Market mechanism was introduced in pregnancy and maternity health care services, and the care service was separated from the medical service. There are four main purposes for adding kraamzorg in the insurance coverage: (1) reducing postpartum depression, (2) assisting novice parents to be adept at taking care of newborns, (3) separating childbirth and maternity care services to reduce the waste of medical and social resources, and (4) increasing women's labour force participation rate.

Service Content

Once female residents of the Netherlands get pregnant, they must periodically visit the verloskundige (midwifery centre) located in their neighbourhood to undergo prenatal testing conducted by professional midwives.[195] When necessary, midwives refer the pregnant women to hospitals for precise examinations. At about the seventh or eighth month of pregnancy,[196] midwives confirm with the women whether to give birth at home or in hospital and help them to make appointments with the nurses responsible for postnatal care. According to a news report in 2012, one in eight newborn babies in the Netherlands was born at home, which is the highest rate of home births in Western Europe.[197] If a woman chooses to

---

[195] The Royal Dutch Organisation of Midwives (KNOV – *Koninklijke Nederlandse Organisatie van Verloskundigen*) provides open data regarding the evaluation of pregnancy and childbirth services for the general public. Those who are interested can search for the information about the practices of midwives in their neighbourhoods: http://www.knov.nl/samenwerken/tekstpagina/489/midwifery-in-the-netherlands/.

[196] Some local governments ask midwives to confirm with pregnant women their choice of home birth or hospital birth in the third month of pregnancy because of the lack of wards in hospital. The public can also check the childbirth and hospitalization regulations of hospitals close to their place of residence on the internet: http://www.nfu.nl/.

[197] Source: http://www.expatica.com/nl/healthcare/Having-a-baby-in-the-Netherlands_107665.html, retrieved on September 27, 2016.

deliver at home, the midwife gives her a *Home Birth Handbook*, that provides information regarding the must-do preparations for home birth. For example, the bed must be elevated to 90–100 cm in accordance with the height of the maternity nurses to prevent the nurses from incurring occupational injuries. The childcare environment (e.g. indoor temperature and cleanliness) and utensils (e.g. number of feeding bottles, towels, baby bathtubs and other appliances) should also meet the requirements stated in the handbook. In addition to the midwife, a maternity nurse will also be present on the day of childbirth to provide necessary assistance. In case of any unexpected emergency during the delivery, pregnant women who choose to give birth at home must dwell in an area where the ambulance can arrive within 10 minutes.

Competition Mechanism for Marketised Childcare Services

The maternity care service covered by basic health insurance is provided for 8–10 days with a total of 49 hours following the birth, which must be reserved online in advance. The purposes of such service are to enable mothers to have sufficient rest, provide physical and psychological support and a social network during the 8–10 days following child delivery when the mothers' body is weakest, and to help the family to adapt to life with newborns. Maternity nurses visit the family every day for three hours; the number of hours can be adjusted according to individual needs. If a mother develops postpartum depression, has other complications or requires special health care, she can make a reservation with a qualified maternity nurse for live-in services but such services are paid at her own expense. If a mother is unsatisfied with the reserved maternity nurse, she can ask to change a nurse immediately and can reserve a specific maternity nurse who has a high reputation in her neighbourhood. Also, a mother can decide not to receive these free maternity care services due to personal privacy concerns. Services provided for postpartum families covered by maternity care insurance are as follows:

1. Instructing mothers to breastfeed
2. Instructing mothers and their partners how to bathe their babies
3. Changing bed sheets for mothers
4. Cleaning the home environment and teaching all family members how to create a childcare environment suitable for newborn babies
5. Preparing simple meals and shopping daily necessities
6. Checking babies' health condition and mothers' recovery status
7. Making early intervention and identify dysfunctional families as early as possible so that they can be reported to social welfare departments

If a mother considers the basic 49 hours of maternity care as insufficient, she can also choose maternity care services with various hours and service content covered in the postnatal medical insurance package provided by private insurance companies.

In the Netherlands, kraamzorg reduces the time postpartum women stay in hospital. Childbirth and postnatal care are separated. Physicians only intervene when necessary or in emergency situations, otherwise all the services are provided by midwives and maternity nurses. The Dutch people consider childbirth as a natural process instead of regarding pregnant women as diseased bodies that require medical procedures. Numerous women choose to give birth in their comfortable home with familiar surroundings. The care work of maternal protection provided by kraamzorg is covered in the state basic health insurance.

7.3 Methodology

Because the policy of free maternity care service in the Netherlands was implemented in September 2005, this study was able to compare the postnatal experience between different generations, namely, users of this free service and immigrants in early times. Among the 38 interviewees, 16 were users of the aforementioned maternity care service. Among the remaining 22 interviewees, 6 gave birth in their home countries, 12 hired Chinese or Indonesian babysitters to help with their postpartum confinement (or "zuo yue zi", a Chinese ritual of postpartum care), and 4 did not receive any postpartum care because of the need to work for their restaurant business. Through examining the differences between generations as well as between cities and rural areas and different educational levels, I investigated whether the Netherlands' maternity care service benefited the first-generation immigrant women who gave birth in a foreign country, with an attempt to portray the service users' actual experience.

7.4 Literature Review

Although the maternity care service policy has been implemented for over a decade, studies on the experience of first-generation immigrant women users are rare, especially those on Chinese women. Existing studies on this policy have primarily focused on maternity nurses' clinical experience regarding the care for first-generation immigrant women who were not from the European Union or Western countries, or did not use English as their first language.

The language barrier constitutes a major hindrance stopping immigrant women from receiving services. For example, Kupper (2010) found that the inability to communicate in Dutch and English is the most crucial obstacle during service provision. Other major obstacles include cultural conflicts and insufficient numbers of maternity nurses in non-urban areas. Moreover, because midwives and maternity nurses have to take shifts and be on call 24 hours, many of them frequently encounter a conflict between work and family life. Boerleider (2014) and her research team interviewed 15 maternity nurses who had provided services for first-generation immigrant women who were not from the European Union or other Western countries and whose first language was not English. Her study indicated that the largest difficulty for the nurses to provide services in such immigrant families was communication. Immigrant families' unfamiliarity with the medical process in the host country and the cultural differences easily resulted in misunderstanding and conflicts. Therefore, maternity nurses must be more flexible when providing services and more creative in communication. Boerleider (2014) also suggested that the Dutch government should provide cultural diversity training for first-line medical personnel.

7.5 Research Findings

The findings of this study differed from that of other Dutch studies on maternity nurses' clinical experiences. I found that the communication problem resulting from the language barrier did not annoy immigrant women too much. Among the 16 interviewees, only one reported that the maternity nurse who took care of her could not speak English; therefore, they could only use body language or ask her husband to be the interpreter. I found that first-generation Chinese immigrant women's largest trouble regarding their childbirth experience and use of maternity care service in the Netherlands was the cultural conflicts due to different cultures and customs. The interviewees generally had three attitudes when facing these conflicts: accepting them, resisting them and attempting to reach consensus through communication.

Cultural Shocks During Childbirth

The Chinese immigrant women primarily experienced the following three cultural shocks during their childbirth. First, 22 interviewees, regardless of whether they gave birth at home or in hospital, all reported that the standard operating procedure in the Netherlands is that midwives and nurses help the puerperal women to bathe (including washing their hair) immediately after child delivery in all seasons. This contradicts the Chinese culture that asks puerperal women to avoid bathing. Therefore, all the interviewees were in shock when washed involuntarily but did not have the strength to resist this practice. Second, 17 interviewees mentioned that immediately after they gave birth, their newborn was presented to them without being washed. Therefore, they were more shocked than touched when they saw their babies covered in blood and fluids. Third, eight interviewees reported that the Dutch people consider childbirth a natural physiological behaviour and thus tend not to use unnecessary medical procedures. These eight interviewees had requested for caesarean section at their own expenses to advance the timing of their delivery, surgical cutting of the perineum to lessen the severity of tears, or a uterotonic injection to accelerate the child delivery process, but their requests were all rejected by midwives or physicians. Therefore, the eight interviewees all perceived that they suffered from childbirth more in the Netherlands than in their home countries and experienced cultural shock.

Cultural Shocks Experienced When Receiving Maternity Care – from Uneasiness to Acceptance

The attitudes of the interviewees who faced cultural shocks when receiving maternity care can be generally categorised into three types: accepting them, resisting them and attempting to reach consensus through communication. Examples are delineated as follows. The accepting attitudes were mostly adopted in response to the practice of breastfeeding. Because breastfeeding is highly encouraged in the Netherlands, the primary task of a maternity nurse is to instruct postpartum women on how to breastfeed their babies, including the nursing position, timing, keeping record, and how to pat the baby's back and help them to get hiccups. These instructions put the novice mothers who have given birth in a foreign country at ease. Maternity nurses carefully and patiently give instructions and demonstrations; they also teach the mothers breast care and how to cope with the pain caused by breast engorgement.

When giving birth to her first child in the Netherlands, Quentin (45 years old) was 38 years old, which is regarded as an advanced maternal age in Taiwan. Quentin chose to give birth at home. The midwife she booked arrived at her home and stayed with her when she began to have labour pain, and constantly encouraged and soothed her during her labour. In the first few days of breastfeeding, she produced only a small amount of milk. Knowing the benefits of breastfeeding for the infant but not having sufficient milk, Quentin became emotionally unstable. Under this situation, her midwife continuously encouraged and instructed her with great patience. The maternity nurse also helped her to clean the environment, making her home a cosy and warm space. This indicates that the patience and sincerity shown by midwives and maternity nurses can increase immigrant novice mothers' willingness to adopt the culture of the host country. Quentin vividly depicted the situation.

> I think breastfeeding is convenient and healthy and can prevent the baby from getting sickness. In particular, kraamzorg continuously told me that breastfeeding is a happy thing; it enhances the connection between mother and child and cannot be replaced by formula milk. However, in the first two to three days of breastfeeding, I produced no milk. I was very worried and even asked my husband to find pork knuckles. Kraamzorg asked me whether I wanted to try the Dutch way of increasing breast milk production: drinking beer. Although drinking cold beer contradicts our concept (of not drinking cold after childbirth), I decided to believe her because she is experienced. I would give it a go for my baby.

Resistance

The strongest resistance regards the postpartum confinement taboo against having cold food and contact with cold air in Chinese culture. For example, 16 interviewees mentioned that the maternity nurses only gave them cold sandwiches and cold juices and drinks. Some of them asked the nurses to make hot soup while others asked the nurses not to prepare meals for them because their parents came to help them with the confinement practice. Some interviewees conflicted with the nurses due to ineffective communication regarding the cultural concepts. Laura (36 years old) described the experience of interacting with her first maternity nurse after giving birth to her first child.

> I gave birth in the afternoon and went back home at 10:00 on the next day. The kraamzorg covered by the insurance came to take care of you at your home immediately after you gave birth. My insurance covered 48 hours of maternity care service. In the first few days, the kraamzorg stayed 8 hours a day to teach you how to take care of and bathe the baby. On the third day, it was snowing and the outdoor temperature was about 0°C. She told me that I should bring my child to have a walk outside instead of lying on the bed all the time. How can this be possible? It's snowing outside! I insisted that I would not go out, but she just fetched me a coat and a hat and asked me to bring my baby outdoors to adapt to the weather. My Dutch was not good but I still argued with her. I told her that Chinese women can't be exposed to wind within one month after delivering child,

> but she insisted that Dutch women can go outside on the first day after childbirth. So I changed another nurse on the next day.

Attempting to Reach Consensus through Communication

With the culture of avoiding having cold food and being exposed to cold wind, some interviewees tried to use their cultural capital to persuade the Dutch maternity nurses. Although such persuasion may not have been successful, the two parties sought to establish a collaboration pattern. Jessie, a 37-year-old woman from Hong Kong, shared her experience.

> My mom brought traditional Chinese medicine. Dutch people's postnatal care practice differs from Chinese people's confinement practice. She (the maternity nurse) believes that drinking cold water can facilitate wound contraction. Here in the Netherlands, if you do not have obstructed labour, you can get out of bed and go home two hours after the childbirth. I was hospitalized for two days because I had obstructed labour and underwent the surgical cutting. On the first day after childbirth, the nurse wanted to take me to have a shower, but Chinese women can't take a bath; we can only have a sponge bath with ginger water. Therefore, I compromised by telling her not to wash my hair. Also, she told me to drink cold water, but I asked her could you please give me warm water? She said we only had cold and boiled water, no warm water. I told her to give me both, and I can mix them by myself. That's it. Kraamzorg did what Dutch people do, whereas my mom followed the Chinese practice. She asked me to eat a boiled egg every day, while my mom asked me to drink longan-jujube tea. She asked me to go out taking a sunbath for an hour every day, but my mom asked me to sit in the garden wearing hat, mask and sunglasses. For the entire seven days, I received care that combined Eastern and Western approaches!

7.6 Conclusion

Focusing on 38 first-generation Chinese immigrant women, this study reviewed their experiences of giving birth and receiving maternity care service implemented by the Dutch government in 2005 in the Netherlands, attempting to understand the influence of the kraamzorg system on first-generation immigrant women. I found that not all women know how to be a mother and take care of newborns right after they get pregnant. If well-trained and experienced regional maternity nurses can provide home care for postpartum mothers 8–10 days after the childbirth, and such service is covered by basic health insurance so that the mothers do not need to spend a large amount of money on staying in the confinement service centres, immigrant mothers can more easily and quickly adjust to the postpartum period. In particular, the maternity care service system enables early intervention in, prediction of, and reporting of high-risk families; thus, it can be regarded as a favourable mechanism to facilitate social harmony and maternal protection. This system renders the Netherlands one of the European countries that best realise safe childbirth and maternal protection. Facing the cultural shocks resulting from different concepts of maternity care between Chinese and Dutch cultures, first-generation Chinese immigrant women were still able to develop their response methods.

CHAPTER EIGHT

DRIFTING LILIES WITHOUT ROOTS: DIASPORIC SUBJECTS AND REFLECTION ON MOTHERHOOD

"Dare I speak to you in a language that will move beyond the boundaries of domination—a language that will not bind you, fence you or hold you?"
—bell hooks 1989: 16.

8.1 Introduction

This chapter focuses on the reflective narratives regarding the intersectionalities between diaspora, the sense of belonging, nationhood, and motherhood of first-generation Chinese immigrant women in the Netherlands. Seldom do Chinese migration studies pay attention to how women perceive themselves as transnational subjects, especially towards the issue of the politics of diaspora. This chapter aims to break the silence and to speak from the margins to problematise the hegemonic discourse of Chinese nationhood, the so-called "Greater China" discourse. This very discourse, as I discussed in chapter one, intertwines a patriarchal bloodline imagination as decisive, and as the ultimate centripetal force that takes up all global Chinese, and on their descendants places a single plane of sameness and homogeneity.[198]

Let me take the contents from a music textbook from Taiwan's compulsory education as the starting point of my analysis. I still remember that in my fifth grade at school everyone had to learn to sing a patriotic song called "*long-de-chuanren*, 龍的傳人 (Descendants of the Dragon)[199]".

[198] About debates around the three discourses of Chinese, see chapter one.
[199] Later, in 2000, it was reorganised by a Chinese pop star Leehom, Wang, the cousin of Gien-Fu, Lee. In 2001, the renewed version was elected The Best Single of Taiwan in Hong Kong.

This song was written by Der-Gian Ho[200] and was sung by Gien-Fu Lee in 1978. Later, this song was officially recognised by both governments of China and Taiwan as one of the recommended patriotic songs. The second paragraph of the song represents the imposed Chineseness and the idea of nationhood as follows:

> In the ancient East, there was a dragon named China.
> In the ancient East, there was a group of people; they were all the descendants of dragon. Under the feet of this giant dragon, I was brought up as the descendant of the dragon. Black eyes, black hair, yellow skin. Forever and ever are the descendants of the dragon.

It is telling to realise why this song was part of compulsory education and an officially recognised patriotic song. It constructs a national identity and calls for the solidarity of all global Chinese people to never forget one's roots, which are from China. From the 1930s onwards, this sentiment has been promoted and reinforced from the "centre" (China) to the "peripheries" (Southeast Asia, North America, and around the world) through systematic and deliberate efforts by the government to strengthen nationhood domestically and to link Chinese identity globally. Chinese historian David Wu points out that, from the 1960s onwards, overseas Chinese identity construction through financial and material support to global Chinese schools became a mutual competition between the pro-Kuomintang (National) government in Taiwan and the pro-Communist government in Beijing (Pp. 152–153 in Tu, 1994). No matter where diasporic Chinese find themselves, the process of identity construction of Chineseness itself, as Ien Ang argues, is almost a utopian and emotional project (2003) that provides an imaginative bond beyond geographical proximity, language barriers and nationalities "no matter how remote one's ancestral links can still be defined as Chinese" (ibid: 142). This single and homogenous Chineseness discourse is not only for economic benefits but also a transnational promotion of a single identity politics that aims to establish a global Chinese nationalism (Ang, 2001).

In this patriarchal nationhood discourse, women function as the cultural and biological producers of the "descendants of the dragon" – they are educated to sing the song, which was written by men, accept the imposed Chineseness identity with its inherent nationalism, and, most important of all, to deliver and reproduce the "black hair, black eyes, and

[200] Der-Gian Ho (1 October, 1956-) is a Taiwanese songwriter, composer and singer from Taiwan. His songs are always in relation to Chinese culture and Chinese mentality.

yellow skin[201]" Chinese. Notwithstanding, within diasporic Chinese motherhood research, women's narratives on the relationship between how they perceive themselves as migrant subjects and how they reflect on the dominant ideology, women as mothers of a country, are seldom noticed or taken academically seriously. I take the absence of women as the starting point of this chapter and I seek to put the hegemonic patriarchal nationalism and women's own thoughts on their responsibilities as mothers into dialogue. I aim to deconstruct this homogeneous "Greater China" discourse and myth based on the voices of first-generational diasporic women in the Dutch context.

This chapter is divided into three sections. In the first section, I review the critical Chineseness theories that problematise and question the statist production discourse. Then I turn to feminist theories pertaining to the relationship between gender and nation and their arguments on the possible resistant strategies against the statist discourse production. In the second section, I provide a narrative analysis of the Chinese mothers' statements to show how they make sense of their motherhood practice in bringing up the second generation, especially on how they see their children's national identities and belongings. In the last section, I give an analysis of the self-reflective narratives of the Chinese mothers to see how they describe their own positions as migrant subjects and their relationship with transnational motherhood. This study shows that first-generation Chinese women of different historical backgrounds and regions hold various views regarding motherhood and nationhood as their individualities are enmeshed in both East and West. Their self-reflections and opinions have significant contemporary and generational meanings in deconstructing and breaking gendered nationalism and they work against assimilating the "Greater China" ideology.

8.2 Diasporic Subjects: Deconstructing the State-Propagated Nationhood Discourse

In this section, I first give a brief review of the critical Chineseness theory, which criticises the unequal relation between women and nation biologically, culturally and symbolically. Then I read from Rosi Braidotti's nomadic subjects theory, and Ien Ang's becoming "hybrid" theory, to serve as the theoretical framework to confront and deconstruct the hegemonic patriarchal Chinese nationalism on women.

---

[201] About the reverse of racist and negative "yellow skin" in the political movement in contemporary China, see chapter six

The Unescapable Chineseness

After the Reform and Open Policy from the 1980s in China, as was mentioned earlier in chapter four, the Communist Party was eager to attract more overseas capital and techniques to boost the economy and improve domestic technology; their first target population was the wealthy and successful overseas Chinese in Southeast Asia, including Hong Kong and Taiwan. Later they extended to the Chinese overseas in North America, using patriotism and Confucianism as the promoting tool, calling for the global overseas Chinese to come back to their roots. The term "come back" here refers to encouraging overseas Chinese to virtually bring back material (money, technology, advanced knowledge, and human capital) as well as symbolically bringing back culture and national and racial identities. According to Aihwa Ong's research (1999) on the state propaganda on global Chineseness construction in China, from 1990s onwards, China's press emphasised the significant material and cultural contribution of the overseas Chinese to their *muquo* (母國; motherland) inasmuch as they represented an embodiment and a model for China's capitalist modernity. Let me explain first why Chinese Diaspora Studies uses the term "motherland" instead of the common term "fatherland" to describe migrants' original countries. I draw on the motivation of creating a global Chinese fraternity after the 1980s. The creation of the new term *haiwai huaren* (海外華人; overseas Chinese) functions as a symbol of the inseparable racial and cultural links to their origin. Second, to shape what distinguishes being Chinese, the elite intelligentsia once again brought back the importance of Confucianism, which was degraded as old-fashioned feudalism during the Maoist reign. This was called the revival movement of Confucianism, which indicates, in Ong's words,

> Cultural solidarity, filial piety, and everlasting loyalty to the motherland are key elements in the language of overseas capitalism… . The enduring symbols of Chinese roots stress the indestructible nature of ancestral home and kinship ties, thus casting the ultramodern flexible relationships of capital accumulation in the timeless and unchanging representation of Chinese culture (1999: 254).

The revival of Confucianism and the call for overseas Chinese to come back to their motherland have a political intention behind them, which creates a kind of Chinese hegemony to establish a unique racial group contrary to the white West. This statist production on "authentic" Chineseness also has a certain impact for all Chinese immigrants in their daily life. For example, in her critical and reflective autobiography, Ien

Ang (2001), an Australian-based, Dutch-Indonesian peranakan and cultural studies scholar, illustrated her own childhood memories of the Netherlands and later of her short visit to Hong Kong, China and Taiwan. Ang felt oppressed by this imposed, compulsory and unescapable Chineseness imagination. Her Chineseness was questioned in the Netherlands; she was considered a "fake Chinese" because she did not speak Chinese during her childhood (p. 30). She found herself recognised as a quasi-national citizen in Taiwan but people were confused and troubled about her inability to communicate in Mandarin. She then questioned the dominant thinking of not only Chineseness but also diaspora politics. In this respect, overseas Chinese have no freedom to choose their cultural and national identity. Besides, it is this overwhelming Chineseness discourse and imagination that makes Chinese minorities overseas a constant object being Orientalised as a single collective – as people of China by the West and by China as well.

Now I want to discuss the specific use of the term motherland in Chinese Diaspora Studies. Scholars from this field use motherland rather than fatherland to signal the state-propagated discourse on the relationship between overseas Chinese and the Chinese government. In her research on the impact of Japanese migrants on Chinese migrant workers in the United States during the early 20th century, Taiwanese historical scholar Wang Show-Hui (2001) found that the Chinese entrepreneurs in the United States at the time called China their *muguo* (母國; mother country) to imply that being Chinese in appearance and keeping Chinese cultural practice is similar to the infant connected to its mother through the umbilical cord. Ong (1999) also recorded elite Chinese narratives on describing overseas Chinese as "marry-out daughters". In sum, the ideology behind the state-propagated discourse on Chineseness and the relationship between overseas Chinese and the motherland is a hybrid combination of Foucauldian biopolitics and Confucian kinship imagination. The family concept, with the "mother country" and "marry-out daughters" metaphors, is to strengthen the global Chinese bonding beyond languages and nationalities. These two metaphors stressed the implicit meaning of offspring to their mother, which implies filial piety to parents and absolute loyalty to the family. Women's responsibility as Chinese (no matter whether native or overseas) is once again intensified through the state-propagated discourse. The following section discusses the relationship between gender and nation in a Chinese context.

Women as the Mother of the Nation

Simply stated, in the context of the patriarchal nationhood ideology, women are positioned in the private domain – a subjective "naturalised" position as mothers. Women are not considered national subjects: they have been largely deprived of or excluded from their rights of participation in the public debate on nationalism and nationhood (Yuval-Davis, 1997). Women's first priority is to produce the (male) heir of the nation because of their naturally given characteristics. Although both women and men are members of the nation, the women's role is always defined by the national interest and "their reproductive ability, sexuality, and life cycle positionings are under the national project" (ibid: 38). Through controlling women's wombs, the male-dominant state discourse considers women's role as the mothers of the nation as vital. From a Foucauldian biopolitical perspective, people are the significant foundation of a nation. Thus, the nation manages its population not only in quantity but also in quality through changing family policies. For example, as I mentioned earlier in chapter four, the hukuo system as a population control mechanism has long been implemented in both Taiwan and China; it decides women's sexuality (compulsory heterosexuality) and fertility rights.[202] Or the Confucius Three Followings[203] is the fundamental principal that regulates and defines how to be a proper and virtuous Chinese woman. Women are the objects and projects to be shaped and manipulated according to the national construction plan. In this respect, as nomadic subjects, can migrant Chinese women struggle and speak their subjective narratives to confront and deconstruct the hegemonic imposed nationalism on them? Can a migrant Chinese woman imagine herself as a human being who has no country or wants no country, as Virginia Woolf (1938) stated? Can diaspora or migration create a space and freedom for Chinese women to carry out their mothering, free from the nationhood ideology?

In her empirical and insightful research on middle and upper-class overseas Chinese elites located in Eastern and Western metropolitan cities, Aihwa Ong (1999) describes the capability of these wealthy overseas Chinese elites to manipulate their symbolic cultural capital through their economic and political networks, accumulated wealth, Western education (either themselves or their children), and their multilingual ability to

---

[202] For instance, the One-Child Policy in China and Family Planning Policy in Taiwan. For the contemporary Family Planning Policy transformation in Taiwan and the national discourse on population control, please see Huang, 2008.

[203] The Confucius Three Followings are "as a daughter, obey your father; as a wife, obey your husband; as a mother, obey your son if your husband is deceased."

"purchase" a Western nationality in an English-speaking country for political security and social status improvements. The male overseas Chinese elites continue their business networks in North or Southeast Asia; they have their family members settle down in the host society for a better education and accumulate Western cultural capital but still live mainly inside the Asian community in the host country. Ong argues that this gaining of dual nationalities or multi-nationalities for family members is a performance of flexible citizenship. It not only shows the agency of overseas Chinese elites in challenging the nation-state's authority but it is also resistance to imposed Chineseness. Nevertheless, first, Ong pays little attention to the gendered aspects of the narratives of migrant Chinese women. How do they make sense of the strategy of flexible citizenship and how do they reflect on their own cultural and motherhood practice in an English-speaking host society? Second, Ong fails to touch on the issue of intersectionality regarding working-class migrant Chinese narratives about flexible citizenship, in contrast to their middle and upper-class counterparts. In this respect, do working-class women hold a different opinion on their inconvertibility regarding motherhood, citizenship and imposed nationalism? I want to answer this question from feminist perspectives in the following paragraphs.

To combat the subjected role of women positioned by the male-dominant nation-state discourse, Western feminists have developed several careful theories to deconstruct nationally constructed womanhood and gendered citizenship. I name three here. First is Yuval-Davis's (1997) transversal politics theory. According to Yuval-Davis, women can cast off the universalist and relativist dichotomy of identity politics. As she argues,

> Transversal politics aims to be an alternative to the universalism/relativism dichotomy which is at the heart of the modernist/postmodernist feminist debate. It aims at providing answers to the crucial theoretical/political questions of how and with whom we should work if/when we accept that we are all different as deconstructionist theories argue (1997: 125).

In short, transversal politics value the importance of dialogue between different people. It calls for international feminist cooperation and solidarity. It is an alternative to identity politics. Yuval-Davis considers that to combat male-defined national identity, women from the global North and South should open up a mutual dialogue for the hegemonic, patriarchal, nationally shaped "identity politics tend not only to homogenise and naturalise social categories and groupings, but also deny shifting boundaries of identities and internal power differences and conflicts of interest" (p. 119). She also noticed that unfortunately transversal politics has its limitations if women cannot surpass their own national identities. For example, she described her own experiences as an eye-witness in several international conferences; some female participants still put national interest over women's rights; as if women must lean on fixed, male-dominant geopolitics and national identity first, then their rights have space to be discussed after. Can women, however, refuse to be placed in a primordial and fixed geopolitically constructed and gendered position in the age of globalisation in which people are itinerant, capital as well as jobs are fluid, everything is uncertain, and even the authority of the nation-state is in a "Scattered Hegemonies" (Grewal & Kaplan, 1994) situation?

In the case of resisting the imposed hegemonic Chineseness, Ien Ang's becoming "hybrid" theory is the second method that I want to discuss. Ang (2003) proposes that overseas Chinese, as all people in the world, should reject the single and uncritical imagination of "motherland" or nation-state thinking. To live together-in-difference, one should surpass the implanted ideology of nationalism or other essentialised discourses on races or gender into a hybrid being. Inasmuch as "hybridization consists of exchanges, crossings, and mutual entanglements, it necessarily implies a softening of the boundaries between "peoples"[204]" (ibid: 147). In other words, one should be aware of imposed external labels such as Chinese, women, whites, or Asians to be able to break nationalism, essentialism and sexism.

How can we make a change from within and start learning to become "hybrid"? I think that Rosi Braidotti's nomadic subject theory can be a third method for individuals to defy imposed nationalism. In her revised feminist postmodern theory, Rosi Braidotti (1994/2011) points out a strategy, a daily 'as if' performance practice is a way of becoming a nomadic subject. She views that nomadic subjectivity has the power to decentralise power, to challenge the phallocentric nation-state authority and discourses. It functions as an act of resistance, both politically and epistemically, inasmuch as "nomadic subjectivity provokes and sustains a critique of dominant visions of the subject, identity, and knowledge, from within one of many centres that structure the contemporary globalized world" (Pp. 7–8). According to Braidotti, it does not have to be a person who is constantly drifting or homeless, but it starts with a state of being from within: to act, to perform "as if" one is a nomadic subject. It is to cultivate and develop an idea, an independent critical thinking, to resist all taken-for-granted, especially masculine authority, discourses.

[204] The quotation mark was added by Ien Ang.

I find that Braidotti's nomadic subject is a very useful methodology to apply to the narrative analysis of diasporic women. Emigration itself is a process of becoming and living as a nomadic subject. Uprooting from their Chinese culture and making a living in a Western society such as the Netherlands is, as Braidotti says, living in a transition (ibid: 64) for "the migrant…is caught in an in-between state whereby the narrative of the origin has the effect of destabilizing the present" (p. 59). Moreover, as time goes by, "the period of relocation and temporary stability are necessary to produce the kind of syntheses and associations that allow for a sustainable notion of nomadic subjectivity" (Braidotti 2006 from 2011: 65). In the examples I will provide in this chapter, I discovered that the longer those women are away from home, the more nomadic their narratives are, regardless of their class.

Before entering the narrative analysis, I want to describe how this topic emerged from the interviews. During one of the first three pilot interviews, Betty shared that after living in the Netherlands for almost 20 years, her mother-in-law insisted on returning to China alone, like a "falling leaf back to its roots". However, Betty told me that she would like to stay in the Netherlands for good, despite her husband's disagreement. This dissonance of the taken-for-granted assumption that all diasporic Chinese, even their remains,[205] yearn to go back to the "motherland" eventually sparked my curiosity.[206] Thus, from the fourth interview, I asked all the interviewees about their future plans – either staying here or going back after retirement. Among 21 Chinese families, four wives have an opposite opinion to their husband's desire to return. Two said they are saving money and planning to buy a house for their retirement in China and Hong Kong. Two women from Hong Kong said they are planning to go back to Asia for retirement, not to Hong Kong but to spend the rest of their life in Taiwan. The other 14, most of whom are below 45, said they are not sure now; it depends on future developments. As for the other 17 transnational families, this question seems not such a difficult one for most of the women; in fact, some of them are practising their nomadic life traversing

---

[205] About the historical research of bones of the deceased Chinese returning to China from the late 19th century, see Sinn 2012, chapter seven: "Returning Bones". Or the superstition from Chinese folklore about burying bones abroad will cause disaster and bad fortune for the offspring. The complex emotional feelings and the punishment from being unfilial is well illustrated in Fae Myenne Ng first novel, *Bone* (1993).

[206] I am indebted to my doctorate supervisor Professor Dr Gloria Wekker's precious and inspirational insights during the discussion of the results of the three pilot interviews.

Europe and Asia annually by spending six to seven months in this country, and the rest in Taiwan, Hong Kong or China.

One thing to be pointed out, because of the different cultural concept of home between Chinese and the West, I did not assume that going back to their countries of origin equals *huijia* 回家 (returning home). On the contrary, I replaced the term "home" with the name of the place they came from. I then asked their opinion about *jia* 家 (home). I find it is necessary to clarify the concept of *jia* in the Chinese cultural context for it is a unique cultural category and not exactly the same as the concept of home in Western languages. According to Chou Wah-Shan (2001), "*jia* condenses the meaning of family and home in the English-speaking world; however, in the Chinese context, *jia* is also a mental space which refers to the ultimate home and roots to which a person belongs" (p. 35). This is to say in the Chinese context, *huijia* (returning home) "means fundamentally searching the ultimate place/space to which one belongs" (ibid: 35). Chou translated *huijia* into "coming home" but I would use the term "returning home" to emphasise the virtual motion and physical action for diasporic women flying from West to East to fulfil the ultimate desire where "a falling leaf goes back to its roots".

Interestingly, their feedback on my invitation to reflect on being a mother in a host country and considering returning home or not creates the significant voices of the diasporic women as subjects questioning and challenging the imposed Chineseness nationalism. Their narratives serve a possibility and a potential strategy for making the motherhood practice itself powerful enough to deconstruct and resist all male-dominant nation-state discourses. In the next section, I first provide women's narratives of how they perceive their motherhood practice and their children's national and cultural identities.

8.3 "S/He Can Be Anyone, the World is my Child's Stage"

In this section, I focus on the relationship between motherhood practice and the national and cultural identities of the mother herself and her children. As I mentioned in chapter five, all Chinese mothers try more or less to teach or let their children learn Mandarin more for practical and career concerns than for Chinese identity construction.

Most of the middle-class mothers told me that they had made up their minds to quit their jobs in Asia and emigrate to the Netherlands to be able to provide a better educational environment which is less competitive and more liberal for children. Only one middle-class family decided to spend most of their time in Taiwan for the children to master their Mandarin, because the Dutch husband considers Mandarin will be more important than Dutch in the future. Six mothers under the age of 40, who immigrated less than a decade ago to the Netherlands, told me that it is their goal to cultivate their children to become world citizens who can survive outside China or Taiwan. Based on this reason, and by making comparisons on educational environments on both sides, they decided to uproot to the Netherlands for their children's sake. Only one middle-class mother in this research, Rachel, who is over 50 from a transnational family, showed resentment about her children's total Westernisation and the loss of the maternal heritage language.[207]

Here I want to take two cases for generational comparison. The first case is Doris. As I mentioned earlier in chapter five, Doris made efforts to have both her sons learn Mandarin by sending them back to Taiwan during summer vacation for intensive Mandarin study camp in Taipei. After six years she eventually had to face their teenage resistance and gave up. She chose to let go of her insistence on Mandarin. Nevertheless, one must understand that her insistence came from fear because of the continual uncertainty of her husband's job contract in the Netherlands. Doris told me that from the first day she moved here, she mentally prepared for the sudden dismissal of her husband by his company. She had to make sure that her sons could keep up their study if they must go back to Taiwan without a choice. Thirty-one years ago, when the IT company offered Doris' husband work in their new Dutch branch, this young couple decided to give it a shot. During the first two years, Doris became a de facto single mother who raised her elder son alone in Taiwan; with a full-time job, she only had a chance of a family reunion twice a year. In the fourth year, Doris considered that the separated, long-distance family life was not healthy for anyone; she quit her job in Taiwan and moved to the Netherlands. However, the headquarters in Taipei could not promise how long the Dutch branch would exist, so Doris's husband's contract is always between two to three years. Not knowing how long they could stay in this country, Doris sent her elder son to an international school in the beginning for English proficiency. Doris thought that even if the branch was dissolved, her son could keep up his study in the international school in Taiwan.

Ten years after the migration, when her elder son applied successfully to a British university, Doris decided to send her younger son to a Dutch middle school to integrate more with the natives. She told me that she has changed her mind on education. The main reason of the attitude shift came

[207] For more information on Rachel's case, see chapter five.

from the ongoing business stability of her husband's company. She sensed that there is a great possibility that they will have to live here until they reach the retirement age. She found that she must alter her education strategy by noticing her elder son's behaviour and realising something she'd never thought of before. As Doris describes to me,

> While we are watching the football match, my elder son always cheers for Britain and we cheer for Orange. He seldom speaks Dutch even though he can understand. He speaks English most of the time…My younger son lives totally like a Dutch person and he thinks of himself as Dutch. It is great but I feel a little unfair for my elder son. Who is he? British or Taiwanese? Definitely not Dutch, I think. After all, I and my husband will eventually go back to Taiwan. I am very worried about his belonging now to be honest; hopefully one day he will find one no matter where he chooses to live.

From Doris's story, one can see two things. Firstly, her narrative directly deconstructs the hegemonic-imposed Chinese nationhood discourse. Although Doris is concerned about her elder son's pending identity as if he is a person without belonging, what makes her views matter is that as an overseas Chinese mother she cares more about her children's localised belonging and daily culturally practiced identity than their Chinese identity. Her children's national identity does not have to be the same as their parents'. Secondly, from Doris's transnational motherhood practice experiences, one can also see that immigrants' decisions about their children's education have a clear connection with capitalism in this age of globalisation. Uncertainty with regard to how long a temporary job would last, highly skilled immigrants such as Doris's family could not send the child to a local school during the first few years. In this respect, she decided to send her elder son to the international school so that she could make sure of his English proficiency, since English guarantees more symbolic market and capital value globally than Dutch. Doris is definitely not alone as a transnational middle-class mother, and I found most of the highly skilled immigrant Chinese families made the same choice by sending their children to English-based international schools in order to lean on a Western-oriented language and gain more cultural capital.

The second case I want to discuss here is Tess, a 32-year-old mother from China, who is married to a native Dutch man. Tess was in her second year as a medical PhD candidate in a famous Dutch university when I conducted the interview. Her opinion about motherhood practice and her children's cultural and national identity represents the most nomadic subjectivity spirit. She laughed so loud in response to my question if she would go back to China after retirement. She challenged me instead: "Can you be sure where you will be after five years? If not, then this question is meaningless, ask me again maybe 40 years later." She then shared her opinion on being a foreign spouse and migrant mother nowadays.

> As far as I am concerned nowadays when life is so competitive and everything changes so fast, a mother's responsibility is to cultivate my child to be mentally healthy first, independent second. Then she will be able to survive anywhere in the world. I even can't make sure will she be Dutch or be Chinese in the future. I can say one thing for certain that I will feed her healthily, educate her well and she can be anyone: the world is my child's stage.

One can tell that Tess is an ambitious mother; she is so confident about her motherhood that she will cultivate her daughter to become possibly anything she decides to be. Tess indeed mentioned one thing that deconstructs the phallocentric national discourse and I consider her opinion has contemporary meaning. That is the uncertainty of the near future, the severe competition of modern society which results from capitalism and globalisation. This uncertainty, at least at the motherhood practice level, challenges and breaks the nation-state's authority and boundary. For those middle-class migrant mothers such as Tess or Doris, regardless of their husbands' nationalities, who are highly-educated, intelligent polyglots, their motherhood strategy is not to educate children to become Dutch or Chinese but beyond the fixed nationality of Eastern or Western culture to become a nomadic subject with all possibilities. Their flexible motherhood practices entail that their children decide their future belongings along with their national and cultural identity. This unfixed and in flux attitude is deeply intertwined with the development of capitalism and globalisation. As the working opportunities of the multilingual, highly-skilled labour market are decidedly unstable and changing, cultivating children to become nomadic world citizens does deconstruct the hegemonic-imposed Chinese nationhood imagination and discourse.

In contrast to their middle-class counterparts, I found that women from working-class Chinese families took more time to let go of the upset and disappointment by recognising the impossibility of educating children according to their own wishes. The main reason working-class women take more time to adjust to their sense of loss, compared to middle-class women, is that unlike their middle-class sisters, they came to the Netherlands mainly to earn more money and improve the living condition of their natal families. None of them claimed that they came here for the sake of a better education for their children. In other words, women from these two class groups had different goals in mind on emigration. I will now describe how working-class women face their sense of loss of mothering and how they narrate the situation.

I mentioned in chapter five, on the issue of heritage language loss, Cathy's indignation when mentioning all her four children knowing zero on reading and writing Mandarin as "they even don't know how to write their own names… they are Chinese but they forgot the roots". She then expressed that her hard work is a bit wasted because her children's Mandarin inability makes them unable to connect to the rising economic opportunities in China. Cathy's case showed a strong resentment from a working-class mother who felt powerless when dealing with her children's identity loss and potential career loss. When I tried to comfort Cathy by saying "But your children, they all have their own shops or restaurants in the Netherlands, isn't that good enough?", Cathy said, "So I gave up (children's Mandarin education) when they said they had no time, suit themselves". One can tell that it is very difficult for a first-generation woman to impose her desire of identity construction or heritage language learning on her children as time goes by in a host country. Not all working-class women feel upset and very disappointed about it; most of them adjust their motherhood practice by adopting the "Western" or "Dutch" parenting style and feel happier and more at ease than before.

I want to take Kitty's experience as an example of self-liberating from the pressure of performing as a Chinese mother.[208] Kitty is a 58-year-old working-class Hongkonger. She told me that when her elder daughter turned ten, she started to resist going to the weekend Mandarin school and they had a big argument. Kitty came to realise that "the Netherlands is definitely not her roots but for her daughter it is." She actually said this sentence with a joyful tone, "They grew up here, they are not Chinese anymore, it is natural for them to be Westernised and they are Dutch." She then told me she is really grateful right now that her elder daughter had the courage to disobey her wish and talk back to her.

> It was totally a shock to me, my daughter was a sweet, docile child…she never says nee (no) to me before.[209]…and you know that it is much easier to teach children in Dutch way (than in Chinese way). To be frank, I found myself happier to be a mother in the Netherlands than my sister in Hong Kong…So I always suggest her *fangshou* (let go) like Dutch people.

---

[208] For more information on Kitty's background, see chapter four.

[209] To keep the original linguistic expression by Kitty, I kept the Dutch word *nee* in her quote.

Kitty's narrative shows an interesting point that practicing motherhood is not unified or culturally, ethnically anchored. The motherhood practice style is flexible and porous according to the different milieus people live in. Kitty and her sister are both Chinese from Hong Kong; however, the longer Kitty lives here, the more flexible she performs her motherhood under the influence of the Dutch milieu. First, from that disagreement with her elder daughter, Kitty became aware that her children's future is actually based in this country and that they will grow up as Dutch although their parents are Chinese. She let go of her wish to make her children learn Mandarin. Little by little, as time went by, she adopted, as she called it, the Western parenting style like Dutch people, and she felt easier as a mother here. She even exported her experiences and the idea of flexible motherhood to her sister; as a first-generation migrant Chinese woman, she introduced the Dutch parenting style to her siblings in Hong Kong. For example, Kitty is against her sibling's obsession on her children's academic performance and the children's tight schedule on extracurricular activities (piano, English and cram schools). She also criticises Hong Kong's parenting culture in which rich people hire au pairs to take care of their children while the real parents spend less and less time accompanying their own children. Whenever she had the chance, chatting with her siblings, she shared with them how Dutch parents spend a lot of time with their children and that she herself also tried very hard to keep up with the Dutch style.

To briefly conclude, migrant women's social class has a significant influence on how they educate children in the matter of ethnic identity. For middle-class Chinese women, in order to survive in a rapidly changing globalised world, they have a clear idea about raising their children in the Netherlands to gain a Western diploma. They care more about children's localised belonging and identity than about their Chinese identity. Their goals are to cultivate children that are capable of living as nomads with good English proficiency. In contrast to middle-class women's determination to bring up a global nomadic subject, working-class women spent more time realising that their children will not follow their wishes. Most of them chose to let go and felt liberated from the pressure of performing as a traditional Chinese mother. One similar idea that middle-class and working-class Chinese women share on the relationship of motherhood practice and children's identity construction in this study is that they have no strong intent to raise their children as Chinese in the Netherlands. Moreover, they know exactly that their children will root differently than they will. In the next section, I come back to the women themselves, to see how they make sense of their perception on the relationship between home, roots and diaspora from their perspective as a migrant subject.

8.4 To Return or Not Depends on Quanxi

In the final section, I engage women's narratives on their perception of home, roots and diaspora. From 38 women's narratives, I found that the alleged hegemonic discourse of the overseas Chinese ultimate desire to return to the "motherland" is losing its legitimacy. On the one hand, this totalitarian image of connecting global Chinese through bloodline and kinship is a masculine, nation-oriented myth. On the other hand, the high living cost because of the rapid economic development in the home country makes migrant working-class Chinese, in particular, homeless and rootless; for example, the incredibly expensive household prices and living expenditure, which resulted from the rapid capitalisation, particularly in Hong Kong. Notwithstanding, the decision "to go home or not" after retirement, from women's perspectives, lies not in patriotism or the idea of "a falling leaf back to its roots" but depends on *quanxi*. Women put more value on their social network and personal connections, which play a vital part in their decision making.

Earlier in this chapter, I mentioned that Betty's mother-in-law insisted on going back to China alone to spend the final stage of her life. She called it "a falling leaf back to its roots". However, even though Betty showed her resentment and disappointment at her children's loss of Chineseness, on being asked whether she will return to China, Betty gave me a different answer to that of her mother-in-law and her husband. She told me that her husband kept saying he wants to go back to Wenzhou after selling their restaurant, which symbolises official retirement among the working-class Chinese community in the Netherlands. But Betty wants to stay here with her children and take care of her grandchildren. She told me, "My family is here, so I want to stay here". Apparently, Betty considers her *quanxi* with children and grandchildren as more important than her husband's desire to go back.

Among 38 interviewees, only five women said they will definitely go back home while others keep an open mind about the future. Whether they will go back or not will depend on the situation of their children or their family members. For those who made up their mind to return home, three of them are Taiwanese who followed their husbands here because of a job switch. Two working-class women, one from China and one from Hong Kong, told me that they came to this country mainly to make more money. The similarity between these five women in making up their mind to go home out of filial piety. They want to fulfil their responsibility and obligation to take care of sick parents or in-laws. For example, Ivy, a 53-year-old woman and a restaurant owner from Hong Kong, reflected on her nearly 35 years in the Netherlands.

> I came (to the Netherlands) mainly for earning money so to speak. I won't call here my home. Hong Kong is my home. I know exactly here is a place for living, for saving money. Although I gradually like the Netherlands more recently, I really like Hong Kong much more. Every time I go back to Hong Kong to visit my parents and in-laws, I feel so warm and so familiar; I feel I am finally home.

Ivy's narrative states that the concept of home in a Chinese context is equal to the concept of one's origin and roots. The English term home is closer to a temporary place for living. There is one thing worth discussing for the three women who revealed their pending decision on whether or not to go back home besides *quanxi*. Two of them from Hong Kong, and one from China, told me that they can never go back to that ideal home because of the rapid economic development and the incredibly high household prices and living expenditure in their home town. For example, Fiona, a 50-year-old working-class Hongkonger, who has been living here for 30 years. Fiona was born in Hong Kong in a big family with traditional Chinese patriarchal values where girls were devalued and boys were treasured. As the second child among six, Fiona followed her elder sister's footsteps, working in a garment factory from the age of 14 until she was 20. After marriage, she came to the Netherlands with her husband and worked in the Chinese restaurant of an acquaintance. Unfortunately, the business was not good and they soon became jobless. Over the past 30 years, Fiona and her husband have constantly changed jobs and they could never save enough money to purchase a restaurant of their own. I conducted the interview with Fiona during her short break as a cleaning lady. Fiona sighed a lot during the interview, especially when talking about the uncertain future.

> Indeed, both my husband and me want to *huijia* (return home). You need to save a lot of money to be able to live out one's life in retirement (in Hong Kong) now. Last year we asked the estate agent in Hong Kong to look for a possible (house) unit for us, we calculated that even if we sell our house (in the Netherlands) plus our savings, we still can't afford it. Household prices in Hong Kong have risen several times (compared to the Netherlands). We are really worried about that we can never go back home in our lifetime.

Fiona's fear of having no chance to return home is not because of the political instability as with early Chinese migrants, but because of the social consequences of capitalisation. Due to the unaffordable household prices and living expenditure for working-class Chinese migrants, it becomes a home that is too expensive to afford and they cannot go back even with all their life savings.

In this section, I discussed women's opinion on home, roots and diaspora. Their narratives differ in many respects from the male-centred, nation-state oriented hegemonic discourse. They put *quanxi* in the centre of their future decision-making concern. The idea of "a falling leaf back to its roots" or the nostalgic thinking of diasporic overseas Chinese coming back to their motherland in the end is changing. In contrast, the migrant Chinese women in this research show more caregiver-oriented characteristics in a diasporic life course. They put more value on their social function as caregivers and daughters in a personal social network, and on their filial piety. Nevertheless, some working-class Chinese migrants found that they could possibly never return to their home even after several decades of hard work in the West because of the consequences of rapid capitalisation in Hong Kong and China. As Fiona sighed, "That ideal home, Hong Kong, I might be never able to go back to." The life course of the Chinese migrant workers at the bottom eventually turns out to be like drifting lilies without roots.

To sum up, this chapter engaged in a sensitive topic on Chinese immigrants' ideals on home, roots, motherhood, and nationhood from the perspective of first-generation migrant women in the Netherlands. From their reflective narratives, women's voices open the possibility to deconstruct the dominant homogenous, hegemonic, male-defined, and nation-state Chinese discourse. Their pragmatic views on children's transnational and nomadic identity in a globalised era challenge the fixed masculine nation-state identity construction project both in countries of origin and in the host country. Besides, from their interactions with Western society, I argue that migrants' motherhood practice is flexible and in flux, like water will change its shape in different vessels. As time passes, migrant women's mothering performance will change in accordance with the social milieu. During the process of letting go of the authoritative Chinese parenting style and of their imposed desire on their children, migrant women also reach self-emancipation as mothers.

CHAPTER NINE

CONCLUSIONS

This research topic comes from an accidental encounter at a festival event of the Dutch Chinese community in Amsterdam. It is a big challenge for me, as a newcomer, to conduct anthropological research in a foreign country. It takes courage and perseverance to complete. I think the most important step as a migration researcher is to walk into immigrants' real-life situations and to pay attention to Chinese migrants who come from different regions. In this study, I was curious to understand first-generation Chinese migrant women's post-emigration adjustments, their motherhood experiences and real-life practices in the Netherlands. This empirical study places women's subjective narratives and conceptions of their post-emigration lives at the centre of analysis, representing the history of Chinese migration in this country, from a gendered and intersectional perspective lens. This study is located at the crossroads of three scholarly fields: Chinese migration studies, Dutch migration studies and gender studies. The research findings provide alternative Chinese migrant women's narratives under a contemporary Western European social context.

My fieldwork focused on Chinese migrant women's real-life experiences of motherhood practices, which are, on the one hand, intertwined with their life cycles and post-emigration adjustment. On the other hand, their subjective narratives on motherhood practices are interwoven with their own backgrounds, which intersect with individual differences of age, class, educational level, country of origin, and regional vernacular belongings. Four themes with regard to Chinese migrant women: mothering strategy; learning Dutch; children's Mandarin education; and dealing with social discrimination and retirement life, surfaced after analysing migrant women's narratives out of 38 interviews and a participatory observation I conducted over the course of three years (2011–2013). Their narratives can not only be read as an epitome of contemporary Chinese migratory life in a non-English speaking Western European country from a gendered perspective but also can be understood as a comparison to their counterparts in English-speaking Western countries. I will summarise my main findings in the following paragraphs.

In the introductory chapter, firstly, I pointed out the lack of scholarship regarding the complexities and contested ideology and theories on the definition of Chinese immigrants within Dutch migration studies. Secondly, I showed the fact of Chinese migrant women outnumbering men and questioned that this missing puzzle has never been taken seriously and explained in Dutch migration studies. As for the former aspect, I illustrated three main discourses in Chinese migration theory (the Greater China, the Cultural China, and the Critical Chineseness discourses) and their intra-relationships. I found that previous Dutch migration studies noticed the regional and vernacular differences of early Chinese migration yet they still comprehended Chinese migrants in the Netherlands as a homogenous "ethnic" group from the concept of the hegemonic Greater China theory. As for the latter aspect, I explained the phenomenon from the pattern of Chinese transnational gendered labour division, which shows how single male migrant workers went abroad for several years, waited for the opportunity to get legal residence, and then returned to their hometown to look for wives through quick match-making by local *quanxi*. Then, when the first child was born, the mother and perhaps the mother-in-law were brought over. Thus, from the discussion of the three discourses of Chinese migration theory and from the macro-politics of gendered transnational movement, I aimed to give an overview of Chinese migration history in boarder perspectives from the beginning.

In the theoretical framework chapter, I conceptualised modern Chinese migrant motherhood practice experiences, which constantly clash with Dutch milieus from two perspectives: Western feminist theories and Chinese Confucianism. All my interviewees, regardless of their backgrounds, believe firmly that it is the women's responsibility to educate "successful" children through strict discipline and mothering. However, their faith in education is contradictory to the Western style. Thus, I think it is necessary to look at the trajectories in which motherhood is defined and constructed between Western and Chinese societies. Conversely, from the historical development of the motherhood debate in feminist scholarship, the focus has been shifting from a white, middle-class and Anglo-centred approach into a multicultural, intersectional and transnational discussion. As a result, transnational motherhood subjects come to the fore due to globalisation and modernisation. Then again, the social norms and motherhood development trajectories under Chinese Confucianism put the sole responsibility of education on mothers; to properly educate "successful" children has been considered an ultimate life-task for Chinese women. Furthermore, transnational motherhood is seen as positive and is encouraged by Chinese society in Northeast Asia to push Chinese mothers to do their best by assisting children to acquire Western cultural capital and, at best, gain foreign nationality in the future. From a feminist perspective, I argue that this very kind of Chinese motherhood social requirement is a continuum of Confucian patriarchy. In contrast, motherhood in Dutch society is perceived as a self-conscious choice out of women's free will that is a voluntary and contented life work. Contrary to Chinese Confucian ideology, Dutch society does not ask women to bring up "successful" children as the primary task of their motherhood practice. By elaborating motherhood discourse development from Western feminist theories, Chinese Confucianism and the social norms of both Dutch and Chinese contexts, I aimed to make sense of modern Chinese transnational motherhood practices in multi-perspective scholarly and current social debates.

My analysis and themed discussions began in chapter four. In this chapter, I illustrated the landscape of motherhood practices' daily-life situations of working-class migrant women. Combining interviews and participation observation, I found that working-class migrant women have developed a unique strategy to cope with childrearing and labour work, which I called "running a restaurant downstairs and raising children upstairs". This strategy requires deliberate geographical arrangements and mutual cooperation with other female workers, or mothers-in-law, to carry out a collective care and labour system. Besides, due to the lack of Dutch education and language skills, working-class mothers all feel powerless to help their children academically. However, they carry out their motherhood from their own cultural capital, namely, "exercise is better than precept", which is a Confucian aphorism. This particular aphorism urges parents to be their children's role models by physically demonstrating hard work and diligence. As a result, working-class migrant mothers value children's moral ethics, such as politeness, benevolence and diligence, more than their academic achievements.

Chapter five presented the most significant issue for all Chinese migrant women in this study, namely, children's Mandarin language education and learning Dutch. The former is connected to the rising economic and political power of China and children's future career opportunities. The latter results from Dutch migrant policy, which stipulates all Chinese migrants that come as foreign spouses must pass the Dutch language exam. As for the children's Mandarin language education, all my interviewees, regardless of their backgrounds, tried more or less to teach, or let their children learn, Chinese's heritage language Mandarin. Heritage language education decision-making and practices largely intersect with individual differences in ages, class, vernacular groups, husbands' nationalities, and neighbourhoods. Among them, migrant women from Taiwan and women from China who were born after the 1980s made the most effort on children's heritage language education. They were willing to spend time and money to send children back to intensive Mandarin summer camps in Taiwan or China for several years. Despite all migrant women acknowledging the significance of Mandarin ability for both children's better career future and their linguistic and cultural connection with the global Chinese community, children's learning motivation and their Dutch husbands' support play a crucial role when it comes to investing time and money on children's Mandarin learning. Meanwhile, regarding the Dutch learning issue for Chinese migrant women themselves, the results show that middle-class women have fewer job opportunities than working-class women after passing the Dutch Integration Exam or NT2 Exam. Some women turn to work in Chinese-owned companies; some try to be self-employed as an internet shop owner; others put all their time and energy into their children's academic performance. In short, chapter five represents how Chinese migrant women deal with two languages (Mandarin and Dutch) as migrants and mothers.

Chapter six focused on two issues, namely, Dutch racism and sexual discrimination inside and outside the private domain, and how these two issues affect migrant women's motherhood practices. The former is a cultural taboo which is usually denied in Dutch society but is constantly mentioned by all migrant Chinese women. By analysing women's narratives, I found most Chinese mothers chose to teach their children not to directly confront the perpetrators but place themselves on a higher moral ground than the perpetrators. I argued this action is a careful calculation that represents how Chinese deal with hostile behaviour in the host country as a social minority. The latter is rooted in Chinese Confucianism, which gives men more social and cultural value than women. In this study, working-class migrant women went through sexual discrimination from childhood; in their motherhood practice, they tried to treat their children fairly regardless of their gender because of reflection on and resistance to their own experiences.

Chapter seven explored Chinese immigrant women's experiences of giving birth and receiving the maternity care service implemented by the Dutch government in 2005 in the Netherlands in an attempt to understand the influence of the kraamzorg system on first-generation immigrant women. I found that not all women know how to be a mother and take care of newborns right after they get pregnant. If well-trained and experienced regional maternity nurses can provide home care for postpartum mothers eight to ten days after childbirth, and such service is covered by basic health insurance so that the mothers do not need to spend a large amount of money by staying in the confinement service centres, immigrant mothers can more easily and quickly adjust to the postpartum period. In particular, the maternity care service system enables early intervention in, prediction of, and the reporting of high-risk families; thus, it can be regarded as a favourable mechanism to facilitate social harmony and maternal protection.

The last theme concerns migrant women's life trajectory about nostalgia, retirement arrangement and reflection on their transnational motherhood in chapter seven. I found that husbands and wives sometimes have different opinions about retirement arrangements. As for working-class migrant women, *quanxi* still dominates their decision to stay in the Netherlands as caregivers for their grandchildren or return to their country of origin to fulfil their filial piety. Moreover, by reading migrant women's narratives about the definitions of *jia* (home), on the one hand, they tend to link it with the concept of roots. On the other hand, they think the Netherlands is home to their children since they grew up locally, but it is not theirs. In other words, migrant women consider the Netherlands a place for making a living and giving a better chance for their children rather than a place for putting down their roots. Home is in the East; however, for working-class women, in particular those who came from Hong Kong, home might be a place where they could possibly never afford to live and to return because of the economic developments. As for their reflection on transnational motherhood, middle-class migrant women tend to prepare their children to become global citizens. "The world is my child's stage" reveals how transnational motherhood practice has the potential to deconstruct the imposed Chineseness and Dutch nationalism. To conclude, from Chinese migrant women's transnational motherhood exercises in interaction with Dutch society, I argued that the characteristics of Chinese migrant motherhood are flexible and in flux, like water can change its shapes in different vessels. Simply stated, from Chinese migrant women's motherhood practices, this research challenges and deconstructs the hegemonic discourse of the Greater China and Cultural China's assumption, which presumes that overseas Chinese always educate their children to remain Chinese and their ultimate desire is to return to the "motherland" in the last stage of their life cycle.

I hope that my study will contribute to further research in three areas: Chinese migration studies, Dutch migration studies and feminist studies. For Chinese migration studies, I think empirical studies about Chinese in non-English speaking European countries are still relatively unknown.

Researchers should leave their own political standpoints aside, open their minds to listen to the voices of people from Taiwan, Hong Kong and China and pay close attention to the intersectionality in age, class, educational backgrounds, and vernacular origins. For Dutch migration studies, I think documentation of the real-life experiences of Chinese migrants and their perceptions of the host country is scarce. Dutch migration studies should pay more attention to migrants' social interaction and their narratives rather than engaging in "fact-finding" statistical research. Last but not least, with the rapid speed of globalisation, feminist motherhood studies have an important role in the future, taking note not only of motherhood practices themselves but also their relationship with social milieu, transnational experiences, intersectionality, and their intra- and inter- power dynamics.

REFERENCES

Absllis, Kevin. 2009. "'From now on we speak civilized Dutch': The Authors of Flanders, the Language of the Netherlands, and the Readers of A. Manteau." *Language and Literature,* 18 (3): 265–280.

Adamuti-Trache, Maria. 2012. "Language Acquisition among Adult Immigrants in Canada: The Effect of Premigration Language Capital." *Adult Education Quarterly,* 63(2): 103–126.

Altena, Marga. 2012. *A True History Full of Romance.* Amsterdam: Amsterdam University Press.

Andors, Phyllis. 1983. *The Unfinished Revolution of Chinese Women, 1940-80.* Bloomington: Indiana University Press.

Ang, Ien. 2001. *On not Speaking Chinese: Living between Asia and the West.* London: Routledge.

Ang, Ien. 2003. "Together-in-Difference: Beyond Diaspora, into Hybridity." *Asian Studies Review*, 27 (2): 141–154.

Angelou, Maya. 1969. *I Know Why the Caged Birds Sings*. New York: Bantam.

Anthias, Floya and Nira Yuval-Davis. 1992. *Racialized Boundaries: Race, Nation, Gender Colour and Class and the Anti-racist Struggle.* London: Routledge.

Bacchi, Carol Lee. 1999. *Women, Policy and Politics: The Construction of Policy Problems.* London: Sage.

Barker, Martin. 2002. "The Problem with Racism", Pp. 80–89 in *Race Critical Theories: Text and Context*, edited by Philomena Essed & David Theo Goldberg. Oxford: Blackwell.

Barlow, Tani. 1994. "Theorizing Woman: Funü, Guojia, Jiating (Chinese Women, Chinese State, Chinese Family)" Pp. 173–196 in *Scattered Hegemonies: Postmodernity and Transnational Feminist Practices*, edited by Inderpal Grewal and Caren Kaplan. Minneapolis: University of Minnesota Press.

Baxandall, Rosalyn and Linda Gordon, eds. 2000. *Dear Sisters: Dispatches from the Women's Liberation Movement.* New York: Basic Books.

Ben, Tan Chee. 2004. *Chinese Overseas: Comparative Cultural Issues*. Hong Kong: Hong Kong University Press.

Benteon, Gregor and Hans Vermeulen, eds. 1987. *De Chinezen*. Muiderberg: Coutinho, Migranten in de Nederlanse samenleving nr.4.

Benton, Gregor and Frank Pieke. 1998. *Chinese in Western Europe*. London: Macmillan.

Benton, Gregor. 2011. "The Chinese in Europe: Origins and Transformations." *Religions & Christianity in Today's China*, 1 (1): 66–70.

Bhabha, Homi. 2002. "Of Mimicry and Man: The Ambivalence of Colonial Discourse." Pp. 113–122 in *Race Critical Theories: Text and Context*, edited by Philomena Essed & David Theo Goldberg. Oxford: Blackwell.

Blakely, Allison. 1993. *Blacks in the Dutch World: The Evolution of Racial Imagery in a Modern Society*. Bloomington: Indiana University Press.

Bleakley, Hoyt and Chin Aimee. 2004. "Language Skills and Earnings: Evidence from Childhood Immigrants." *The Review of Economics and Statistics*, 86(2): 481–496.

Boerleider, Agatha W. et al. 2014. ""Being Flexible and Creative": A Qualitative Study on Maternity Care Assistants' Experiences with Non-Western Immigrant Women." *PLOS One,* 3(9): 1–7.

Bourdieu, Pierre. 1991. *Language and Symbolic Power,* ed. and introduced by John B. Thompson. UK: Blackwell.

Bourdieu, Pierre. 1993. *Sociology in Question*. London: Sage.

Bovenkerk, F., M. Gras and D. Ramsoedh. 1994. *Discrimination Against Migrant Workers and Ethnic Minorities in Access to Employment in the Netherlands.* Geneva: International Labour Office (ILO).

Braidotti, Rosi. [1994] 2011. *Nomadic Subjects: Embodiment and Sexual Difference in Contemporary Feminist Theory.* Reprint. New York: Columbia University Press.

Bray, Mark and Ramsey Koo. 2004. "Postcolonial Patterns and Paradoxes: Language and Education in Hong Kong and Macao." *Comparative Education*, 40 (2): 215–239.

Brooks, Abigail & Hesse-Biber, Sharlene Nagy. 2007. "An Invitation to Feminist Research." Pp.1–24 in *Feminist Research Practice: A Primer*, edited by Sharlene Nagy Hesse-Biber and Patricia Lina Leavy. Thousand Oaks: Sage Publications.

Buikema, Rosemarie and Iris van der Tuin, eds. 2009. *Doing Gender in Media, Art, and Culture.* New York: Routledge.

Bussemaker, Jet and Rain Voet, eds. 1998. *Gender, Participation and Citizenship in the Netherlands.* Aldershot Hants: Ashgate.

Castles, Stephen and Miller Mark J, eds. 2009. *The Age of Migration: International Population Movements in the Modern World.* 4th edition. London: Palgrave Macmillan.

Chan, Yuk Wah, David Haines and Jonathan H. X. Lee, eds. 2014. *The Age of Asian Migration: Continuity, Diversity and Susceptibility Volume 1.* Newcastle upon Tyne: Cambridge Scholars Publishing.

Chang, Jung. 1991. *Wild Swans: Three Daughters of China.* London: Simon and Schuster.

Chang, Jung. 2013. *Empress Dowager Cixi.* London: Vintage.

Chao, Wan-Jung. 趙婉容 2009. 跨國孟母? 新加坡的中國陪讀媽媽 (*Transnational Mencius's Mother? The China-National "Study Mama" in Singapore.*) Unpublished Master Thesis. Hsinchu, Taiwan: National Tsing-Hua University.

Chen, Hongmou 陳宏謀 *Jiaonu Yigui* 《教女遺規》 [Inherited Guide for Educating Women]. Accessed from: Chinese Text Project: http://ctext.org/wiki.pl?if=en&res=636436.

Cheng, Lucie and Edna Bonacich, eds. 1984. *Labor Immigration under Capitalism: Asian Workers in the United States before World War II.* Berkeley and Los Angeles: University of California Press.

Cheng, Lucie, Suellen Cheng, Judy Chu, Feelie Lee, and Majorie Lee. 1984. *Linking Our Lives: Chinese American Women of Los Angeles.* Los Angeles: East West Discovery Press.

Cheng, Yi-Wen. 2002. "Who Can Get the Job? Unfair Competition in Chinese City Labor Market." [誰來上崗? 中國城市勞動力市場的不平等競爭]. *Taiwan: A Radical Quarterly in Social Studies,* 48: 45–94.

Chodorow, Nancy. 1978. *The Reproduction of Mothering: Psychoanalysis and Sociology of Gender.* Berkeley: University of California Press.

Chou, Wah-Shan. 2001. "Homosexuality and the Cultural Politics of *Tongzhi* in Chinese Societies." *Journal of Homosexuality*, 40(3/4): 27–46.

Chow, Rey. ed. 2000. *Modern Chinese Literary and Cultural Studies in the Age of Theory: Reimagining a Field.* Durham, NC: Duke University Press.

Chow, Yiu Fai, Sandra Zwier, and Liesbet van Zoonen. 2008. "Bananen, Modelminderheid en Integratie: Mediagebruik en Identificaties onder Jonge Chinezen in Nederland (Bananas, model minority and integration: Media use and identifications among young Chinese in the Netherlands)." *Migrantenstudies*, 24(1): 72–85.

Chow, Yiu. F. 2009. "Multicultural Schizophrenia: "You are different, you are Chinese"". *Amsterdam Social Science*, 1(4): 45–52.

Chow, Yiu. F. 2011. "Moving, Sensing Intersectionality: A Case Study of Miss China Europe." *Signs: Journal of Women in Culture and Society*, 36(2): 411–436.

Christiansen, Flemming. 1998. "Chinese Identity in Europe," Pp. 42 – 63 in *The Chinese in Europe*, edited by Gregor Benton and Frank N. Pieke. London: Macmillan.

Chua, Amy. 2011. *Battle Hymn of the Tiger Mother.* London: Bloomsbury.

Chun, Allen. 1996. "Fuck Chineseness: On the Ambiguities of Ethnicity as Culture as Identity." *Boundary 2: An International Journal of Literature and Culture*, 23(2): 111–138.

Chun, Allen. 陳亦麟 _1999. "Jiegou Zhongguoxing: lun zuqunyishi zuowei wenhua zuowei rentong zhi aimei buming" 解構中國性: 論族群意識作為文化作為認同之曖昧不明 _[Fuck Chineseness: On the Ambiguities of Ethnicity as Culture as Identity]. *Taiwan: A Radical Quarterly in Social Studies*, 33: 103-131.

Collins, Patricia H. 1986. "Learning from the Outsider Within: The Sociological Significance of Black Feminist Thought." *Social Problems*, 33(6): 14–32.

Collins, Patricia H. 1987. "The Meaning of Motherhood in Black Culture and Black Mother/Daughter Relationships." *Sage: A Scholarly Journal on Black Women,* 4(2): 4–11.

Collins, Patricia H. 1990. *Black Feminist Thought: Knowledge, Consciousness, and the Politics of Empowerment.* Boston: Unwin Hyman.

Collins, Patricia Hill. 1994. "Shifting the Center: Race, Class, and Feminist Theorizing about Motherhood," Pp. 371–389 in *Representations of Motherhood*, edited by Donna Bassin. Yale: Yale University Press.

Collins, Patricia Hill. 2000. *Black Feminist Thought: Knowledge, Consciousness, and the Politics of Empowerment*. 2nd ed. New York: Routledge.

Crenshaw, Kimberlé. 1989. "Demarginalizing the Intersection of Race and Sex: A Black Feminist Critique of Antidiscrimination Doctrine, Feminist Theory, and Antiracist Politics." *University of Chicago Legal Forum*, 14: 538–554.

Crenshaw, Williams Kimberlé. 1994. "Mapping the Margins: Intersectionality, Identity Politics, and Violence Against Women of Color," Pp. 93–118 in *The Public Nature of Private Violence*, edited by Martha Albertson Fineman and Rixanne Mykitiuk. New York: Routledge.

Croll, Elisabeth. 1977. "A Recent Movement to Redefine the Role and Status of Women." *The China Quarterly*, 71: 591–597.

Croll, Elisabeth. 1978. *Feminism and Socialism in China.* Oxon: Routledge.

Cummins, Jim. 1992. "Language Proficiency, Bilingualism and Academic Achievement." Pp. 16–26 in *The Multicultural Classroom: Readings for Content-area Teachers*, edited by Patricia A. Richard-Amato. USA: Longman.

Davis, Kathy. 2008. "Intersectionality as Buzzword: A Sociology of Science Perspective on What Makes a Feminist Theory Successful." *Feminist Theory*, 9 (1): 67–85.

de Beauvoir, Simone. [1949] 1989. *The Second Sex*, translated by Howard M. Parshley. New York: Vintage Books.

de Leeuw, Marc and van Wichelen, Sonja. 2014. "Institutionalizing the Muslim Other: *Naar Nederland* and the Violence of Culturalism," Pp. 337–354 in *Dutch Racism*, edited by Philomena Essed and Isabel Hoving. Amsterdam: Rodopi.

de Meester, Edith, Mulder Clara H. and Fortuijn Joos Droogleever. 2007. "Time Spent in Paid Work by Women and Men in Urban and Less Urban Contexts in the Netherlands." *Tijdschrift voor Economische en Sociale Geografie*, 98 (5): 585–602.

Deng, Wei-Zhi 邓伟志. _1994. *Jindai Zhongguo Jjiating de Biange* 《近代中国家庭的变革》 _[The Family Transformation in Contemporary China]. Shanghai: Renmin Chubanshe.

DeSouza, Ruth. 2004. "Motherhood, Migration and Methodology: Giving Voice to the "Other." *The Qualitative Report*, 9(3): 463–482.

Dikötter, Frank. 1994. "Racial Identities in China: Context and Meaning." *The China Quarterly*, 138(0): 404–412.

Dikötter, Frank. 2005. "Race in China." Pp. 177–204 in *China Inside Out: Contemporary Chinese Nationalism and Transnationalism*, edited by Pal Nyiri & Joana Breidenbach. Budapest: Central European University Press.

Dinnerstein, Dorothy. 1977. *The Mermaid and the Minotaur: Sexual Arrangement and Human Malaise.* New York: Harper and Row.

Driessen, Geert. 1996. "Minority Language and Culture Teaching in the Netherlands: Policies, Arguments, Evaluation and Prospects." *Compare: A Journal of Comparative Education*, 26(3): 315–333.

duCille, Ann. 1994. "The Occult of True Black Womanhood: Critical Demeanor and Black Feminist Studies." *Signs: Journal of Women in Cultural and Society*, 19: 591–629.

Enloe, Cynthia. 1989. *Bananas, Beaches and Bases: Making Feminist Sense of International Politics*. London: Pandora Press.

Essed, Philomena and David Theo Goldberg, eds. 2002. 2nd edition. *Race Critical Theories: Text and Context.* Oxford: Blackwell.

Essed, Philomena and Isabel Hoving, eds. 2014. *Dutch Racism.* Amsterdam: Rodopi.

Essed, Philomena and Kwame Nimako. 2006. "Designs and (Co) Incidents: Cultures of Scholarship and Public Policy on Immigrants/ Minorities in the Netherlands." *International Journal of Comparative Sociology*, 47 (3-4): 281-312.

Essed, Philomena and Sandra Trienekens. 2008. "'Who Wants to Feel White?' Race, Dutch Culture and Contested Identities." *Ethnic and Racial Studies*, 31 (1): 52–72.

Essed, Philomena. 1986. *The Dutch as an Everyday Problem: Some Notes on the Nature of White Racism.* (Working paper no.3) Amsterdam: Centre for Race and Ethnic Studies, Universiteit van Amsterdam & Vrije Univesiteit.

Essed, Philomena. 1990. *Everyday Racism: Reports from Women of Two Cultures.* Claremont: Hunter House Inc.

Essed, Philomena. 1991. *Understanding Everyday Racism: An Interdisciplinary Theory.* Newbury Park, CA: SAGE.

Essed, Philomena. 1995. "Gender, Migration and Cross-Ethnic Coalition Building." Pp. 48–63 in *Crossfires: Nationalism, Racism and Gender in Europe*, edited by Lutz et al. London: Pluto Press.

Ex, Carine T.G. M. and Jan M. A. M. Jannsees. 2000. "Young Females' Image of Motherhood." *Sex Roles*, 43 (11/12): 865–890.

Fan, Cindy. 2008. *China on the Move: Migration, the State, and the Household.* Oxon: Routledge.

Fan, Lloyd Sheng-Pao. 2007. "My Land, Your Land, but Never China's: An Analysis of Taiwan's Sovereignty and Its Claim to Statehood." *Taiwan International Studies Quarterly*, 6(3): 141–181.

Fielde, Adele F. 1887. *Pagoda Shadows: Studies from Life in China.* London: T. Ogilvie Smith.

Fillmore, Lily Wong. 1991. "When Learning a Second Language Means Losing the First." *Early Childhood Research Quarterly*, 6: 323–346.

Fillmore, Lily Wong. 2000. "Loss of Family Language: Should Educators be Concerned?" *Theory into Practice*, 39 (4): 203–210.

Firestone, Shulamith. 1970. *The Dialectic of Sex: The Case for Feminist Revolution.* New York: Bantam Books.

Flowerdew, John. 1999. "Writing for Scholarly Publication in English: The Case of Hong Kong." *Journal of Second Language Writing*, 8(2): 123–145.

Ford, Thomas H. 2009. "Mary Wollstonecraft and the Motherhood of Feminism." *WSQ: Women's Studies Quarterly*, 37(3&4): 189–205.

FORUM. 2011. *FORUM Factsheet: Chinese in the Netherlands*. Institute for Multicultural Affairs, Utrecht. Online. Available at: http://www.forum.nl/Portals/International/english-pdf/Factsheet-Chinese-in-the-Netherlands.pdf

Francis, Becky; Louise Archer & Ada Mau. 2009. "Language as Capital or language as Identity? Chinese Complementary School Pupils' Perspectives on the Purposes and Benefits of Complementary Schools." *British Educational Research Journal*, 35(4): 519–538.

Freedman, Maurice. 1970. ed. *Family and Kinship in Chinese Society*. Stanford: Stanford University Press.

Friedan, Betty. 1963. *The Feminine Mystique*. New York: Delacorte Press.

Friedman, Susan S. 1995. "Beyond White and Other: Relationality and Narratives of Race in Feminist Discourse." *Signs*: *Journal of Women in Cultural and Society*, 21: 1–49.

Gellner, Ernest. 1995. "Introduction: Nationalism and Xenophobia." Pp. 6–9 in *New Xenophobia in Europe* edited by Bernd Baumgartl and Adrian Favell. London: Kluwer Law International.

Ghorashi, Halleh. 2002. *Ways to Survive, Battles to Win: Iranian Women Exiles in the Netherlands and the United States.* New York: Nova Science.

Gijsberts, Mérove, Willem Huijnk and Ria Vogels, eds. 2011. *Chinese Nederlanders: Van Horeca naar Hogeschool,* Den Haag: Het Sociaal en Cultureel Planbureau. http://www.scp.nl/english/Publications/Summaries_by_year/Summaries_2011/The_Chinese_in_the_Netherlands).

Gilligan, Carol. 1982. *In a Different Voice.* Cambridge, Massachusetts: Harvard University Press.

Golden, Marita. 1983. *Migration of the Heart*. New York: Ballantine.

Grewal, Inderpal and Caren Kaplan, eds. 1994. *Scattered Hegemonies: Postmodernity and Transnational Feminist Practices*. Minneapolis: University of Minnesota Press.

Griffin, Nicholas John. 1973. *The Use of Chinese Labor by the British Army, 1916-1920: The "Raw Importation", its Scope and Problems*. Unpublished Ph.D. thesis. Oklahoma: University of Oklahoma.

Gronold, Daniela, Brigitte Hipfl and Linda Lund Pederson, eds. 2009. *Teaching with the Third Wave.* Utrecht: ATHENA 3 Advanced

Thematic Network in Women's Studies in Europe, University of Utrecht and Center for Fender Studies, Stockholm University.
Gutmann, Ethan. 2014. *The Slaughter: Mass Killings, Organ Harvesting, and China's Secret Solution to Its Dissident Problem*. New York: Prometheus Books.
Hall, Stuart. 2002. "Race, Articulation, and Societies Structured in Dominance." Pp.38 in *Race Critical Theories: Text and Context*, edited by Philomena Essed & David Theo Goldberg. Oxford: Blackwell.
Han, Wen-Jui. 2010. "Bilingualism and Socioemotional Well-being." *Children and Youth Service Review*, 32:720–731.
Hanks, William F. 2005. "Pierre Bourdieu and the Practice of Language." *Annual Review of Anthropology*, 34: 67–83.
Harding, Sandra. 2004. *The Feminist Standpoint Reader: Intellectual and Political Controversies*. New York: Routledge.
Hays, Sharon. 1996. *The Cultural Constructions of Motherhood*. New Haven and London: Yale University Press.
Hesse-Biber, Sharlene Nagy and Patricia Lina Leavy, eds. 2007. *Feminist Research Practice: A Primer*. Thousand Oaks: Sage Publications.
Highbaugh, Irma. 1948. *Family Life in West China*. New York: Agricultural Missions, Inc.
Hill, Shirley A. 2008. "African American Mothers: Victimized, Vilified, and Valorized," Pp.107–121 in *Feminist Mothering*, edited by Andrea O'Reilly. New York: State University of New York Press.
Ho, Calvin. 2010. *Heritage Language Loss in the Chinese Community in Argentina*. Unpublished MA Thesis. United Sates: Swarthmore College.
Hoe, Yow Cheun. 2013. *Guangdong and Chinese Diaspora: The Changing Landscape of Qiaoxiang*. Oxon: Routledge.
hooks, bell. 1982. *Ain't I a Woman: Black Women and Feminism*. London: Pluto Press.
hooks, bell. 1984. *Feminist Theory: From Margin to Center*. New York: South End Press.
hooks, bell. 1989a. "Choosing the Margin as Pace of Radical Openness." *Framework*, 36: 16.
hooks, bell. 1989b. *Talking Back: Thinking Feminist, Thinking Black*. New York: South End Press.
Hossen, Abul. 2012. "Social Isolation and Loneliness among Elderly Immigrants: The Case of South Asian Elderly Living in Canada." *Journal of International Social Issues*, 1(1): 1–10.
Hsia, Hsiao-Chuan. 2000. "Ziben guojihua xia de guojihunyin – yi Taiwan de "waiji xinniang" xianxiang weili" 資本國際化下的國

際婚姻－以台灣的"外籍新娘"現象爲例 [Transnational Marriage and Internationalization of Capital: The Case of the 'Foreign Bride' Phenomenon in Taiwan]. *Taiwan: A Radical Quarterly in Social Studies*, 39:45–92.

Huang, Shu-Yi. 黃淑怡 2008. 臺灣「少子女化問題」之政策建構---女性主義立場的分析 (*A Feminist Standpoint Analysis on Taiwan's Policy Construction of the "Babybust Problem"*), Unpublished Master Thesis. Taipei, Taiwan: Shih Hsin University.

Huang, Yi-Jiuan. 黃儀娟 2010. 跨文化母職倫理與教養態度之質性研究－以移居美國之台裔女性知識份子為例 (*Qualitative Research on Motherhood and Parenting Attitudes When Moving between Cultures: Taking Well-educated Taiwanese American Women as Examples.*) Unpublished Master Thesis. Chiayi, Taiwan: Nan-Hua University.

Huang, Yu and Chin-Chuan Lee. 黃煜、李金銓 2003. "90 Niandai Zhongguo dalu minzuzhuyi de meiti jiangou." 90年代中國大陸民族主義的媒體建構 [Media Construction of Chinese Nationalism in the 1990s]. *Taiwan: A Radical Quarterly in Social Studies*, 50: 49–79.

Institute for Multicultural Affairs. 2011. Forum factsheet "Chinese in the Netherlands " http://www.forum.nl/Portals/International/English-pdf/Factsheet-Chinese-in-the-Netherlands.pdf

Irigaray, Luce. 1977. Translated by Carolyn Burke, 1985. *This Sex Which is Not One.* New York: Cornell University Press.

Ishigawa, Yoshihiro. 1999c " Inu to Chukokujin ha hairubekarazy" (Review the issue of Chinese and Dogs are Forbidden) Pp.75–94 in *Kantaiheiyo no Kokusai Chitsujyo no Mosaku to Nihon: Dai Ichiji Taisengo kara 55nen Taisei Seiritsu*, edited by Ito Yukio and Kawada Minoru. Tokyo: Yamakawa Shuppansha. 「犬と中国人は入るべからず」問題再考」 伊藤之雄、川田稔編『環太平洋の国際秩序の模索と日本』山川出版社.

Jayawardena, Kumari. 1986. *Feminism and Nationalism in the Third World*. London: Zed.

Jen, Gish. 1996. *Mona in the Promised Land*. New York: Alfred A. Knopf.

Johnson, Kay A. 1983. *Women, the Family and Peasant Revolution in China.* Chicago: University of Chicago Press.

Kandiyoti, Deniz. 1991. "Identity and its Discontents: Women and the Nation." *Millennium*, 20(3): 429–444.

Kao, Li-Jen. 高麗珍 2010. *Malaixiya Bincheng difang huarenyimin shehui de xingcheng yu fazhan* 馬來西亞檳城地方華人移民社會的形成與發展 [Formation and Development of Chinese Immigration in Penang

Malaysia]. Unpublished master's thesis. Taipei: National Normal University.
Kao, Xi-Jun. 高希均 1993. "Juren yu Xiaolong de Jiehe-Jingji Zhongguo."「巨人與小龍的結合－經濟中國」 [Combined the Giant with Dragons: Economy China]. *Vision*, January: 24-26.
Kawash, Samira. 2011. "New Directions in Motherhood Studies." *Signs*, 36(4): 969–1003.
Kelly, John D. 1993. "Review: Language and Symbolic Power." *American Journal of Sociology*, 98(5): 1200–201.
Knijn, Trudie. 1994. "Social Dilemmas in Images of Motherhood in the Netherlands." *The European Journal of Women's Studies*, 1: 183–205.
Knijn, Trudie. 2004. "Changes and Risks of Individualization in the Netherlands." *Social Policy & Society*, 3(1): 57–65.
Kofman, Elenore. 1999. "Female 'Birds of Passage' a Decade Later: Gender and Immigration in the European Union." *The International Migration Review*, 33(2): 269–299.
Koh, James Y. and William G. Bell. 1987. "Korean Elders in the United States: Intergenerational Relations and Living Arrangements." *The Gerontologist*, 27: 66–76.
Koh, Jessie B., Yi Shao Kim, and Qi Wang. 2009. "Father, Mother and Me: Parental Value Orientations and Child Self-identity in Asian American Immigrants." *Sex Roles*, 60: 600–610.
Korteweg, Anna C. 2006. "The Construction of Gendered Citizenship at the Welfare Office: An Ethnographic Comparison of Welfare-to-Work Workshops in the United States and the Netherlands." *Social Politics: International Studies in Gender, State and Society*, 13(3): 313–340.
Kowles, Jane Price and Ellen Cole, eds. 1990. *Woman-Defined Motherhood*. New York & London: State Harrington Park Press.
Kupper, Kristen. 2010. *Work-Life Balance: Balancing Work-Life and Operations in the Elderly Care, Home Care, and Maternity Care.* Master thesis. Business Administration, Track Human Resource Management, University of Twente.
Lee, Ben-Hua 李本華 1989. *Nuxing Zhishifenzi yu Taiwan Shehi Fazhan* 《女性知識份子與台灣社會發展》 [Female Intellectuals and Social Development in Taiwan]. Taipei: Linking Publishing.
Lee, Young-Me. 2007. "The Immigration Experience among Elderly Korean Immigrants." *Journal of Psychiatric and Mental Health Nursing*, 14: 403–410.
Leibkind, Karmela, Inga Jasinskaja-Lahti and Erling Solheim. 2004. "Cultural Identity, Perceived Discrimination and Parental Support as

Determinants of Immigrants' School Adjustments: Vietnamese Youth in Finland." *Journal of Adolescent Research*, 19(6): 635–656.

Lentin, Ronit. 2004. "Strangers and Strollers: Feminist Notes on Researching Migrant M/Others." *Women's Studies International Forum*, 27: 301–314.

Leung, Maggi W.H. 2003. "Beyond Chinese, Beyond Food: Unpacking the Regulated Chinese Restaurant Business in Germany." *Entrepreneurship & Regional Development*, 15:103–118.

Li, Goufang. 2006. "Biliteracy and Trilingual Practices in the Home Context: Case Studies of Chinese-Canadian Children." *Journal of Early Childhood Literacy*, 6(3): 355–381.

Li, Mengying. 2005. "The Role of Parents in Chinese Heritage-Language Schools." *Bilingual Research Journal*, 29(1): 197–207.

Li, Minghuan. 1998. "Living Among Three Walls? The Peranakan Chinese in the Netherlands." Pp.167–183 in *The Last Half Century of Chinese Overseas*, edited by Elizabeth Sinn. Hong Kong: Hong Kong University Press.

Li, Minghuan. 1999b. *We Need Two Worlds: Chinese Immigrant Associations in a Western Society*. Amsterdam: Amsterdam University Press.

Li, Minghuan. 2002. "A Group in Transition: Chinese Students and Scholars in the Netherlands." Pp. 173–188 in *Globalizing Chinese Migration: Trends in Europe and Asia*, edited by Pal Nyiri and Igor Saveliev. Aldershot; Burlington VT: Ashgate Publishing Company.

Liamputtong, Pranee. 2010. *Performing Qualitative Cross-Cultural Research.* Cambridge: Cambridge University Press.

Liber, Marylène. 2013. ""When You Look Chinese, You Have to Speak Chinese": Highly Skilled Chinese Migrants in Switzerland and the Promotion of a Shared Language." Pp. 134–159 in *Multiple Identities: Migration, Ethnicity, and Membership*, edited by Paul Spickard. Indiana: Indiana University Press.

Lin, An-Wu. 林安梧 _1994. *Taiwan, Zhongguo Maixiang Shijieshi*《台灣•中國邁向世界史》[Taiwan, China towards the World History]. Taipei: Tonsan Publications.

Link, Perry. 2011. *Liu Xiaobo's Empty Chair: Chronicling the Reform Movement Beijing Fears Most.* New York: The New York Review of Books.

Link, Perry. 2013. *An Anatomy of Chinese: Rhythm, Metaphor, Politics.* Cambridge: Harvard University Press.

Liu, Cha-Hsuan, Aziza Sbiti and Veronique Huijbregts. 2008. S*til Verdriet: Chinese Migranten en Gezondheid*. Rotterdam: MIKADO.

Liu, Cha-Hsuan, David Ingleby and Ludwien Meeuwesen. 2011. "Barriers to Health Care for Chinese in the Netherlands." *International Journal of Family Medicine*, 2011: 1–10.

Liu, Cha-Hsuan, Ludwien Meeuwesen, Floryt van Wesel, and David Ingleby. 2013. "Beliefs about Mental Illness among Chinese in the West", *International Journal of Migration, Health and Social Care*, 9(3): 108 – 121.

Liu, Cha-Hsuan. 2014. *Suffering in Silence: The Adequacy of Dutch Mental Health Care Provision for Ethnic Chinese in the Netherlands.* Unpublished doctorate dissertation. Utrecht: Utrecht University.

Liu, Hong. 2004. "Looking Forward, Looking Back: An Interview with Wang Gung Wu." Pp.13-21 in *Diasporic Chinese Ventures: The Life and Work of Wang Gungwu*, edited by Gregor Benton and Houng Liu. London: Routledge.

Liu, Lydia. 1994. "The Female Body and Nationalist Discourse: The Field of Life and Death Revisited," Pp. 37– 62 in *Scattered Hegemonies: Postmodernity and Transnational Feminist Practices*, edited by Inderpal Grewal and Caren Kaplan. Minneapolis: University of Minnesota Press.

Long, Denggao and Han, Qiming. 2008. "Beyond Culture: Economic Analysis of the Characteristics of Overseas Chinese Business." Pp: 52–65 in *Chinese Entrepreneurship in a Global Era*, edited by Raymond Sin-Kwok Wong. Oxon: Routledge.

Lorde, Audre. 1984. *Sister Outsider: Essays and Speeches by Audre Lorde*. New York: The Crossing Press.

Lu, Yu-Xia 呂玉瑕 1981. "Shehui bianqianzhong Taiwan funu zhi shiyeguan" 社會變遷中台灣婦女之事業觀 [Taiwanese Women's Career Attitude in a Changing Society]. *Bulletin of the Institute of Ethnology Academia Sinica*, 50: 28–62.

Lutz, Helma, Ann Phoenix and Nira Yuval-Davis, eds. 1995. *Crossfires: Nationalism, Racism and Gender in Europe*. London: Pluto Press.

Lutz, Helma. 1997. "The Limits of European-Ness: Immigrant Women in Fortress Europe." *Feminist Review*, 57: 93–111.

Lutz, Helma. 2010. "Gender in the Migratory Process" *Journal of Ethnic and Migration Studies*, 36(10): 1647–663.

Lutz, Wolfgang, Rudolf Richter and Chris Wilson, eds. 2006. *The New Generations of Europeans: Demography and Families in the Enlarged European Union*. London: Bath Press.

Lykke, Nina. 2010. *Feminist Studies: A Guide to Intersectional Theory, Methodology and Writing*. New York: Routledge.

Mak, Geertje. 2000. *Sporen van Verplaatsing: Honderd Jaar Nieuwkomers in Overijssel*. [Traces of Displacement: New Comers in Overrijssel Hundred Years Ago]. Deventer: IJsselacademie.

Man, Guida. 1995. "The Experience of Women in Chinese Immigrant Families: An Inquiry into Institutional and Organization Processes." *Asian and Pacific Migration Journal*, 4 (2/3): 303–326.

Mangelson, Michael E. 1992. "Taiwan Re-Recognized: A Model for Taiwan's Future Global Status." *Brigham Young University Law Review*, 1: 231–251.

McClintock, Anne. 1994. *Imperial Leather: Race, Gender and Sexuality in the Colonial Conquest*. New York: Routledge.

Meeuwse, Karina. 2010. *Oostenwind: Honderd Jaar Chinezen in Nederland*, Karakter Uithoorn: Uitgevers B. V.

Mingshi 《明史》 [The History of Ming].

Mohanty, Chandra. 1991. "Under Western Eyes: Feminist Scholarship and Colonial Discourses" Pp. 333–358 in *Third World Women and the Politics of Feminism*, edited by Chandra T. Mohanty, Ann Russo and Lourdes M. Torres. Bloomington: Indiana University Press.

Moody, Ann. 1968. *Coming Age of Mississippi*. New York: Dell.

Morrison, Toni. 1974. *Sula*. New York: Random House.

Morrison, Toni. 1987. *Beloved*. New York: Random House.

Mott, Frank I. 1972. "Portrait of an American Mill Town, Demographic Response in Mid-19th Century Warren, Rhode Island." *Population Studies,* 26 (3): 83–88.

Mouw, Ted and Yu Xie. 1999. "Bilingualism and the Academic Achievement of First- and Second-Generation Asian Americans: Accommodation with or without Assimilation?" *American Sociological Review,* 64(2): 232–252.

Mui, Ada C. 1996. "Depression among Elderly Chinese Immigrants: An Exploratory Study." *Social Work*, 41: 633–645.

Muskens, George. 1996. "Multiculturalism and Political Integration in the Netherlands: Rotterdam, Enschede." *Innovation: The European Journal of Social Science*, 9(1): 33–49.

Musschenga, Albert W. 1998. "Intrinsic Values as a Reason for the Preservation of Minority Cultures." *Ethical Theory and Moral Practice*, 1: 201–225.

Nawyn, Stephanie J, Linda Gjokaj, Debrenna LaFaAgbényiga and Breanne Grace. 2012. "Linguistic Isolation, Social Capital, and Immigrant Belonging." *Journal of Contemporary Ethnography*, 4(3): 255–282.

Ng, Fae Myenne. 1993. *Bone*. New York: Hyperion Books.

Ning, Yi-Bin. 甯應斌 _2009. "Zhongguoren ruhe zaizuo Zhongguoren." 中國人如何再作中國人 _[How Would Chinese be (Alter-Native) Chinese Again?]. *Taiwan: A Radical Quarterly in Social Studies*, 74: 223-238.

O'Reilly, Andrea. ed. 2008. *Feminist Mothering.* New York: State University of New York Press.

Olsen, Laurie. 2000. "Learning English and Learning America: Immigrants in the Center of a Storm." *Theory into Practice*, 39 (4): 196–202.

Omi, Michael & Winant, Howard. 2002. "Racial Formation." Pp. 123–145 in *Race Critical Theories: Text and Context*, edited by Philomena Essed & David Theo Goldberg. Oxford: Blackwell.

Ong, Aihwa. 1999. *Flexible Citizenship: The Logics of Transnationality.* Durham & London: Duke University Press.

Ong, Aihwa.1996. "Cultural Citizenship as Subject-making: Immigrants Negotiate Racial and Cultural Boundaries in the United States." *Current Anthropology*, 37(5): 737–762.

Pai, Hsiao-Hong. 2008. *Chinese Whispers: The True Story behind Britain's Hidden Army of Labour.* London: Penguin Books.

Pai, Hsiao-Hung. 2013. *Invisible: Britain's Migrant Sex Workers.* London: The Westbourne Press.

Parker, Andrew, Mary Russo, Doris Sommer, and Patricia Yaeger, eds. 1992. *Nationalisms and Sexualities*. New York: Routledge.

Pateman, Carole. 1988. *The Sexual Contract*. Cambridge: Polity Press.

Pegg, Scott. 1998. *International Society and the De Facto State*. Aldershot: Ashgate.

Pessar, Patricia R. and Sarah J Mahler. 2003. "Transnational Migration: Bring Gender In." *International Migration Review,* 37(3): 812–846.

Pfaelzer, Jean. 2007. *Driven Out: The Forgotten War Against Chinese Americans*. New York: Random House.

Pieke, Frank and Gregor Benton. 1998. *The Chinese in Western Europe.* Palgrave Macmillan.

Pieke, Frank N. and Harris, Karen L. 1998. "Integration or Segregation: The Dutch and South African Chinese Compared." Pp. 115–138 in *The Last Half Century of Chinese Overseas*, edited by Elizabeth Sinn. Hong Kong: Hong Kong University Press.

Pieke, Frank. 1992. *Helan Huaren de Shehui Diwei* [Social Status of Dutch Chinese] 荷蘭華人的社會地位, translated by Zhuang Guotu. Taipei: Institute of Modern History, Academic Sinica.

Pieke, Frank. 2004. "Chinese Globalization and Migration to Europe", Paper presented at the Research Seminar, Center for Comparative

Immigration Studies, University of California at San Diego, CA. Online. http://ccis.ucsd.edu/wpcontent/uploads/2012/07/wrkg94.pdf

Pruitt, Ida. 1945. *A Daughter of Han: The Autobiography of a Chinese Working Women.* New Haven: Yale University Press.

Qin, Desiree Baolian. 2006. ""Our Child Doesn't Talk to Us Anymore": Alienation in Immigrant Chinese Families." *Anthropology and Education Quarterly*, 37(2): 162–179.

Rattanisi, Ali. 2007. *Racism: A Very Short Introduction.* Oxford: Oxford University Press.

Redding, Gordon. 1993. *The Spirit of Chinese Capitalism.* New York: de Gruyter.

Rich, Adrienne. 1986. *Of Woman Born: Motherhood as Experience and Institution.* New York: W.W. Norton.

Robinson, Jean C. 1985. "Of Women and Washing Machines: Employment, Housework, and the Reproduction of Motherhood in Socialist China." *The China Quarterly*, 101: 32–57.

Roggeband, Conny and Mieke Verloo. 2007. "Dutch Women are Liberated, Migrant Women are a Problem: The Evolution of Policy Frames on Gender and Migration in the Netherlands." *Social Policy & Administration*, 41(3): 271–288.

Rowe, William T. 1992. "Women and the Family in Mid-Qing Social Thought: The Case of Chen Hongmou." *Late Imperial China,* 13(2): 1–41.

Rubin, Gayle. 1975. "The Traffic in Women: Notes on the 'Political Economy' of Sex." Pp. 157-210 in *Toward an Anthropology of Women*, edited by Reyna Reiter. New York: Monthly Review Press.

Sabatier, Colette and John. W. Berry. 2008. "The Role of Family Acculturation, Parental Style, and Perceived Discrimination in the Adaptation of Second-generation Immigrant Youth in France and Canada." *European Journal of Developmental Psychology*, 5 (2): 159–185.

Said, Edward. 1979. *Orientalism*. New York: Random House.

Said, Edward. 2002. "Imaginative Geography and its Representations: Orientalizing the Oriental." Pp.15–37 in *Race Critical Theories: Text and Context*, edited by Philomena Essed & David Theo Goldberg. Oxford: Blackwell.

Salaff, Janet W. 1976. "The Status of Unmarried Hong Kong Women and the Social Factors Contributing to Their Delayed Marriage." *Population Studies*, 30 (3): 391–412.

Scott, Joan. 1991. "The Evidence of Experience." *Critical Inquiry,* 17 (4): 773–797.

Scott, Joan. 1991. "Women's History." Pp. 42–66 in *New Perspectives on Historical Writing*, edited by Peter Burke. University Park: Pennsylvania State University.

Shue, Vivienne. 1980. *Peasant China in Transition: The Dynamics of Development Toward Socialism, 1949-1956.* Berkeley and Los Angeles: University of California Press.

Silver, Rita Elaine. 2005. "The Discourse of Linguistic Capital: Language and Economic Policy Planning in Singapore." *Language Policy*, 4:47–66.

Sinn, Elizabeth. 2012. *Pacific Crossing: California Fold, Chinese Migration, and the Making of Hong Kong.* Hong Kong: Hong Kong University Press.

Smith, Dorothy E. 1987. *The Everyday World as Problematic: A Feminist Sociology.* Toronto: University of Toronto Press.

Smith, Dorothy. 2004. "Women's Perspective as a Radical Critique of Sociology" Pp. 21–34 in *The Feminist Standpoint Reader: Intellectual and Political Controversies*, edited by Sandra Harding. New York: Routledge.

Snitow, Ann. 1992. "Feminism and Motherhood: An American Reading." *Feminist Review*, 40 (Spring): 32–51.

Sohn, Soomin and Christine Wang. 2006. "Immigrant Parents' Involvement in American Schools: Perspectives from Korean Mothers." *Early Childhood Education Journal*, 34 (2): 125–132.

Sorman, Guy. 2008. *The Empire of Lies: The Truth about China in the Twenty-First Century.* New York: Encounter Books.

Su, Bin and Wei Lin. 蘇冰、魏林 _1993. *Zhongguo Hunyin Shi* 《中國婚姻史》 [The History of the Chinese Marriage]. Taipei : Wenchin Chubanshe.

Su, Chien-Ling 蘇芊玲 _1996. *Buzai Mofàn de Muqin* 《不再模範的母親》 [No Longer a Model Mother]. Taipei: Fembooks Publishing.

Sun, Shun-Chih. 2010. ""Taiwan's Sovereignty" as the Pre-requisite for the Synthesis of Taiwanization and Sinicization." *Taiwan International Studies Quarterly*, 6 (3): 139–159.

Svendsen, Stine H Bang. 2014. "Learning Racism in the Absence of 'Race'." *European Journal of Women's Studies*, 21(1): 9–24.

Talpade, Chandra, Ann Russo Mohanty, and Lourdes M. Torres, eds. 1991. *Third World Women and the Politics of Feminism*. Bloomington: Indiana University Press.

Tan, Amy. 1989 (1998). *Joy Luck Club.* London: Vintage.

Tan, Amy. 1991. *The Kitchen God's Wife.* New York: Ivy Books.

Tan, Amy. 1995. *The Hundred Secret Senses*. New York: G.P. Putman's Sons.

Tan, Eugene Kheng-Boon. 2013. "Sinophone Studies: Rethinking Overseas Chinese Studies and Chinese Diaspora Studies." *Sun Yat-sen Journal of Humanities*, 35: 1–26.

Taylor, Lisa K. 2009. "Of Mother Tongues and Other Tongues: The Stakes of Linguistically Inclusive Pedagogy in Minority Contexts." *The Canadian Modern Language Review*, 65(1): 89–123.

Teiwes, Frederick C. 1974. "Before and After the Cultural Revolution." *The China Quarterly*, 58: 332–348.

Teng, Jinhua Emma. 1996. "The Construction of the "Traditional Chinese Women" in the Western Academy: A Critical Review." *Signs*, 22(1): 115–151.

Tomaselli, Sylvana. ed. 1995. *Mary Wollstonecraft: A Vindication of the Rights of Men and A Vindication of the Rights of Woman and Hints.* Cambridge: Cambridge University Press.

Tu, Wei-Ming. 1991. "Cultural China: The Periphery as Center." *Daedalus*, 120 (2): 1–32.

Tu, Wei-Ming. 1994. ed. *The Living Tree: The Changing Meaning of Being Chinese Today.* Stanford: Stanford University Press.

UN Economic Commission for Europe. 2011. *Economic Commission for Europe Statistical Division, Trends in Europe and North America 2001*. New York: UN Economic Commission for Europe.

Van Dijk, Teun A. 1991. *Racism and the Press.* London: Routledge.

Van Dijk, Teun A. 1993. *Elite Discourse and Racism.* Newbury Park, CA: Sage.

Van Dijk, Teun A. 2002. "Denying Racism: Elite Discourse and Racism." Pp. 307–324 in *Race Critical Theories: Text and Context*, edited by Philomena Essed & David Theo Goldberg. Oxford: Blackwell.

Van Heek, Frederik. 1936. *Chineesche immigranten in Nederland.* Amsterdam: J. Emmering's Uitgevers Mij.

Van Oers, Ricky. 2008. "From Liberal to Restrictive Citizenship Policies: The Case of the Netherlands." *International Journal on Multicultural Societies*, 10 (1): 40–59.

VandenHeuvel, Audrey and Mark Wooden. 1997. "Participation of Non-English-speaking-background Immigrants in Work-related Training." *Ethnic and Racial Studies,* 20 (4): 830–848.

Vasta, Ellie. 2007. "From Ethnic Minorities to Ethnic Majority Policy: Multiculturalism and the Shift to Assimilationism in the Netherlands." *Ethnic and Racial Studies*, 30(5): 713–740.

Von Glahn, R. 1996. *Fountain of Fortune: Money and Monetary Policy in China, 1000–1700.* Berkeley: University of California Press.

Waaldijk, Berteke. 2003. "Subjects and Citizens: Gender and Racial Discrimination in Dutch Colonialism at the End of the 19th Century." Pp. 101–118 in *Racial Discrimination and Ethnicity in European History*, edited by Guðmundur Hálfdanarson. Pisa: Edizioni Plus-Università di Pisa.

Walker, Alice. 1976. *Meridian*. New York: Pocket Books.

Walker, Alice. 1982. *The Color Purple.* San Diego: Harcourt Brace Jovanovich.

Wang, Gungwu. 1988. *Changing Attitudes of Southeast Asian Chinese since World War II.* Hong Kong: Hong Kong University Press.

Wang, Gungwu. 1994. *Zhongguo yu haiwai huaren* [China and Overseas Chinese]. Taiwan: The Commercial Press. 王赓武。《中國與海外華人》。_臺北：臺灣商務出版社。_

Wang, Gungwu. 1998. "Upgrading the Migrant: Neither Huaqiao nor Huaren." Pp. 15–33 in *The Last Half Century of Chinese Overseas*, edited by Elizabeth Sinn. Hong Kong: Hong Kong University Press.

Wang, Show-Hui. 王秀惠 _2001. "Ershi shiji chuye ribenren yimin meiguo dui huaren zhi chongji" 二十世紀初葉日本人移民美國對華人之衝擊 _[Impact on Overseas Chinese of Japanese Emigration to the United States in the Early Twentieth Century]. *Bulletin of Historical Research,* 29: 171–205.

Watkins, Paula, Husna Razee and Juliet Richters. 2012. "'I'm Telling You…The Language Barrier is the Most, the Biggest Challenge': Barriers to Education among Karen Refugee Women in Australia." *Australian Journal of Education*, 56(2): 126–141.

Watson, James Lee. 1977b. "Chinese Emigrant Ties to the Home Community." *New Community,* 5: 343–352.

Wekker, Gloria and Herman Christiaan Wekker. 1992. "'Coming in from the Cold': Linguistic and Socio-cultural Aspects of the Translation of Black English Vernacular Literary Texts into Surinamese Dutch." *Babel*, 37(4): 221–239.

Wekker, Gloria and Lutz, Helma. 2001. "Een hoogvlakte met koude winden. De geschiedenis van het gender- en etniciteitsdenken in Nederland." Pp. 25–49 in *Caleidoscopische Visies: De Zwarte, Migranten en Vluchtelingenvrouwenbeweging in Nederland.* Maayke Botman & Nancy Jouwe & Gloria Wekker. Amsterdam: Koninklijk Instituut voor de Tropen.

Wekker, Gloria. 1995. "'After the Last Sky, Where do the Birds Fly?' What can European Women Learn from Anti-Racist Struggle in the

United States?" Pp. 65–87 in *Crossfires: Nationalism, Racism and Gender in Europe*, edited by Lutz et al. London: Pluto Press.

Wekker, Gloria. 2009. "Another Dream of Common Language: Imaging Black Europe…." Pp. 277-289 in *Black Europe and the African Diaspora*, edited by Darlene Clarke Hine, Trica Danielle Keaton, and Stephen Small. Urbana and Chicago: University of Illinois Press.

Wekker, Gloria. 2009. "Into the Promised Land? The Feminization and Ethnicization of Poverty in the Netherlands." Pp.65–77 in *Teaching Intersectionality: Putting Gender at the Center*, edited by Martha Franken, Alison Woodward, Anna Cabó, and Barbara M. Bagihole. EU: ATHENA 3 Advanced Thematic Network in Women's Studies in Europe, University of Utrecht and Center for Gender Studies, Stockholm University.

Wekker, Gloria. 2015. *White Innocence. Paradoxes of Colonialism and Race.* Durham: Duke University Press.

Wendy Chavkin and JaneMaree Maher, eds. 2010. *The Globalization of Motherhood: Deconstructions and Reconstructions of Biology and Care.* Oxon: Routledge.

Wetzels, Cecile. 2005. "Supply and Price of Childcare and Female Labour Force Participation in the Netherlands." *LABOUR*, 19 (Special Issue): 171–209.

Weusten, Josje. 2011. *De Idylle Voorbij: Verbeelding van Moederschap in Nederlandse Literatuur 1980 tot 2010.* Unpublished Ph.D. Dissertations. Maastricht: Universiteit Maastricht.

Wolf, Margery. 1970. "Child Training and the Chinese Family." Pp. 37–62 in *Family and Kinship in Chinese Society*, edited by Maurice Freeman. Stanford: Stanford University Press.

Wolf, Margery. 1985. *Revolution Postponed: Women in Contemporary China.* London: Methuen & Co. Ltd.

Woolf, Virginia. 1938. *Three Guineas.* London: Penguin.

Xin, Ran. 2002. *The Good Women of China: Hidden Voices*, translated by Esther Tyldesley. London: Vintage.

Xu, Shen 許慎 _100CE. *Shuowen Jiezi* 《說文解字》 [Explaining and Analyzing Characters]. Accessed from: Chinese Text Project: http://ctext.org/library.pl?if=gb&res=6541.

Yang, Martin C. 1945. *A Chinese Village, Taitou, Shantung Province.* New York: Columbia University Press.

Yang, Tsui. 楊翠 2005. "Wenhua Zhongguo • dili Taiwan－Xiaolihong 1970 niandai xiaoshuozhong de xiangtu yujing" 文化中國•地理台灣---蕭麗紅一九七 0 年代小說中的鄉土語境 _[Cultural China,

Geographic Taiwan—"Folk Context" of Hisao Li-Hung's Works in the 1970s.]. *Bulletin of Taiwanese Literature,* 7: 1-42.
Yao, Souchou. 2002. *Confucian Capitalism: Discourse, Practice and the Myth of Chinese Enterprise.* London: Routledge.
Ying, Yu-Wen. 1996. "Immigration Satisfaction of Chinese Americans: An Empirical Examination." *Journal of Community Psychology*, 24: 3–16.
Yu, Depeng. 2002. *Chengxiang Shehui: Cong Geli Zouxiang Kaifang – Zhongguo Huji Zhidu Yu Hujifa Yanjiu* [City and Countryside Societies: From Segregation to Opening – Research on China's Household Registration System and Laws]. Jinan: Shandong People's Press.
Yuval-Davis, Nira. 1980. "The Bearers of the Collective Women and Religious Legislation in Israel." *Feminist Review*, 4: 15–27.
Yuval-Davis, Nira. 1997. *Gender and Nation*. London: SAGE.
Zhang, Guochu. 2003. "Migration of Highly Skilled Chinese to Europe: Trends and Perspective." *International Migration*, 41 (3): 73–97.
Zick, Andreas, Thomas F. Pettigrew and Ulrich Wagne. 2008. "Ethnic Prejudice and Discrimination in Europe." *Journal of Social Issues*, 64 (2): 233–251.